James Joyce

D1610577

James Joyce
A Critical Guide

Lee Spinks

Edinburgh University Press

Edinburgh University Press Ltd
22 George Square, Edinburgh

www.euppublishing.com

Typeset in 10.5/13 Sabon
by Servis Filmsetting Ltd, Stockport, Cheshire, and
printed and bound in Great Britain by
CPI Antony Rowe, Chippenham, Wilts

A CIP record for this book is available from the British Library

ISBN 978 0 7486 3835 2 (hardback)
ISBN 978 0 7486 3836 9 (paperback)

Contents

Acknowledgements

My principal debt is to Claire Colebrook, who read successive drafts of the manuscript, and offered many useful observations and suggestions. When writing the book I was grateful for the convivial intellectual atmosphere fostered both by my colleagues at Edinburgh University and the undergraduate students in my James Joyce class; and for the friendship of Miriam Nabarro, Sue Loukomitis, Richard Willis and Martin Reid. My thanks go to the staff of Edinburgh University Library and the staff of the National Library of Scotland for their professionalism and courtesy; and to the School of Languages, Literature and Culture at Edinburgh University for their generous financial support. I am also particularly grateful to Jackie Jones, Commissioning Editor at Edinburgh University Press, for her exemplary stewardship in finally seeing the book into print. The book is dedicated to Keith Spinks and Jane Colebrook.

Abbreviations and Referencing

Throughout the text, references to Joyce's works are from the following editions:

Poems and Shorter Writings, ed. Richard Ellmann, A. Walton Litz and John Whittier-Ferguson (London: Faber, 2001), abbreviated as *PSW*.

Stephen Hero, rev'd edn (London: Jonathan Cape Ltd, 1956), abbreviated as *SH*.

Dubliners, ed. Jeri Johnson (Oxford: Oxford University Press, 2000), abbreviated as *D*.

A Portrait of the Artist as a Young Man, ed. Jeri Johnson (Oxford: Oxford University Press, 2000), abbreviated as *P*.

Giacomo Joyce (London: Faber, 1983), abbreviated as *GJ*.

Exiles (London: Jonathan Cape, 1972), abbreviated as *E*.

Ulysses, ed. Jeri Johnson (Oxford: Oxford University Press, 1998), abbreviated as *U*.

Finnegans Wake (London: Faber and Faber, 1975), abbreviated as *FW*.

Occasional, Critical and Political Writings, ed. Kevin Barry (Oxford: Oxford University Press, 2000), abbreviated as *OCP*.

Critical Writings of James Joyce, ed. Ellsworth Mason and Richard Ellmann (London: Faber, 1959), abbreviated as *CW*.

Letters of James Joyce, vol. 2, ed. Richard Ellmann (London: Faber and Faber, 1966), abbreviated as *L*.

References to Homer's *The Odyssey* are taken from the translation by Richmond Lattimore: *The Odyssey of Homer* (New York: HarperPerennial, 1991).

The choice of Johnson's edition of *Ulysses* in particular merits a brief discussion. The textual history of *Ulysses* is a matter of considerable controversy. *Ulysses* was originally published by Shakespeare and Company in February 1922. Joyce complained upon the novel's publication that the edition contained a significant quantity of textual errors, and, when Harriet Weaver brought out a second edition for the English market in October 1922, a printed list of 'Errata' was included within its pages. Unfortunately this new edition contained a new set of misprints, and the textual condition of the novel was not markedly improved. The situation was complicated still further when Samuel Roth brought out his pirated and bowdlerised edition of *Ulysses* in America in 1926; although Roth was legally compelled to desist from printing soon afterward, his corrupt version of *Ulysses* became the template for the 1934 Random House edition of the novel and remained the standard American edition until 1961. A 1932 Odyssey Press edition of *Ulysses*, prepared by Joyce's friend Stuart Gilbert, sought to bring a degree of order to a chaotic situation, but was later found to contain a not insignificant number of textual errors of its own.

By the 1960s there were a number of editions of *Ulysses* in circulation, each of which was found to contain a quantity of textual errors. The situation was briefly stabilised in 1961, when Random House brought out its own 'corrected edition', but the status of this new edition was subsequently called into question (Dalton 1972). In 1984 the German textual critic Hans Walter Gabler sought to resolve the various textual issues in dispute by issuing his new 'corrected text' of *Ulysses*. Gabler's edition attempted to overcome the problems engendered by the corrupt 1922 edition by returning to Joyce's original manuscript, complete with all its additions, variants and revisions, and treating it as a continuous manuscript text. Although initially acclaimed, the integrity of Gabler's edition has come under repeated challenge over the last twenty years, and both his practices and conclusions remain a matter of intense scholarly debate.

Gabler's 'corrected text' remains a valuable scholarly resource, and should certainly be consulted for insights into Joyce's compositional practice, but it remains difficult to obtain in Britain. Declan Kiberd's Penguin edition is widely available, but its text reprints the relatively corrupt Bodley Head edition of 1960. The best version of *Ulysses* under these circumstances is Jeri Johnson's Oxford World Classics edition, which contains a useful introductory essay alongside a wealth of bibliographical and critical material. It also includes a succinct and detailed account of *Ulysses*' textual history, expertly rehearsing and summarising many of the issues outlined here (Joyce 1998: xxxviii–lvi).

Chronology

1882   James Augustine Joyce (JJ) born (2 Feb.), eldest surviving son of John Stanislaus Joyce, a collector of rates, and Mary Jane Joyce, in Rathgar, Dublin. Phoenix Park Murders (May).

1886   Gladstone's Home Rule Bill defeated.

1888   JJ enrolled at Clongowes Wood College.

1890   Parnell ousted as leader of Home Rule Party.

1891   JJ removed from Clongowes after John Joyce loses his job as rates collector. Death of Parnell (6 Oct.). JJ writes his first poem 'Et Tu, Healy' in response.

1893   JJ enters Belvedere College after the school fees are waived. Gaelic League founded.

1898   JJ enters Royal University (now University College, Dublin).

1899   JJ attends premiere of Yeats' *The Countess Cathleen*. Later refuses to sign a letter of protest against the play.

1900   JJ presents paper 'Drama and Life' to the university Literary and Historical Society.

1901   JJ publishes his polemical essay 'The Day of the Rabblement'.

1902   JJ leaves university and registers for the Royal University Medical College. Meets Yeats, Lady Gregory and George Moore. Decides to leave medical school and move to Paris to study medicine. Brother George dies (3 May).

1903   JJ abandons medicine and begins to concentrate upon a literary career. Returns to Dublin during his mother's last illness. Mother dies (13 Aug.).

1904   JJ begins to compose the stories that will become *Dubliners*; three are published in the *Irish Homestead*. He writes essay 'A Portrait of the Artist'. Develops manuscript of 'Stephen Hero'. Teaches at Clifton School, Dalkey. First goes out with Nora Barnacle (16 June). JJ and Nora begin their continental exile in

Zurich, where Joyce teaches English at the Berlitz School, before they are relocated to Pola.

1905   JJ and Nora remove to Trieste. Son Giorgio born (27 July). Stanislaus arrives in Trieste. *Dubliners* submitted for publication to, and eventually refused by, Grant Richards. *Chamber Music* refused by several publishers. Sinn Féin formed.

1906   Family move to Rome, where JJ works briefly in a bank. JJ contemplates a short story entitled 'Ulysses'.

1907   JJ lectures in Trieste and publishes political journalism. Elkin Matthews publishes *Chamber Music*. Daughter Lucia born (26 July). Abandons 'Stephen Hero' and begins to rewrite it as *Portrait*. Beginning of JJ's eye-troubles. Riots at Abbey Theatre following J. M. Synge's *The Playboy of the Western World*.

1909   JJ and Giorgio travel to Dublin. JJ attempts to secure contract for *Dubliners* with Maunsel and Co. JJ later returns to Dublin to open the city's first cinema.

1911   Home Rule Bill passed in Commons; defeated in the Lords.

1912   JJ's last trip to Ireland. Maunsel and Co. finally refuse to publish *Dubliners*; in response JJ publishes poetical broadside 'Gas from a Burner'.

1914   JJ sends first chapter of *Portrait* to Ezra Pound; Pound accepts poem ('I Hear an Army') for *Des Imagistes*, and arranges serialisation of *Portrait* in the *Egoist*. Grant Richards finally publishes *Dubliners*. JJ writes *Giacomo Joyce*. Makes notes for *Exiles* and begins *Ulysses*. World War One erupts.

1915   Stanislaus interned in Austrian detention centre for duration of war. Italy enters war; JJ and family leave Trieste for neutral Zurich. *Exiles* completed.

1916   B. W. Huebsch publishes *Dubliners* and *Portrait*. Easter Rising in Dublin.

1917   English edition of *Portrait* published by the Egoist Press. Harriet Shaw Weaver begins her lifetime financial support of JJ. JJ sends first three chapters of *Ulysses* to Pound. JJ undergoes his first eye operation.

1918   *Ulysses* begins serial publication in the *Little Review*. Grant Richards publishes *Exiles*. JJ receives financial support from Mrs Harold McCormick. JJ's theatrical group the English Players perform *The Importance of Being Earnest*. End of World War One.

1919   Numbers of the *Little Review* containing extracts from *Ulysses* destroyed by US postal authorities. Revised versions of *Ulysses* material published in the *Egoist*. *Exiles* performed to poor reviews in Munich. Mrs McCormick ceases financially to support JJ. Irish War of Independence begins.

1920   JJ meets Ezra Pound, T. S. Eliot and Wyndham Lewis. Joyce family remove to Paris. Complaint issued against American serial publication of *Ulysses* in the *Little Review* by the New York Society for the Suppression of Vice.

1921   Publication of *Ulysses* in the *Little Review* ceases after its editors are convicted of publishing obscene material. JJ accepts Sylvia Beach's offer to publish *Ulysses* under the imprimatur of her Parisian bookshop Shakespeare and Company. Valery Larbaud delivers his Paris lecture publicising and celebrating the book. End of Irish War of Independence.

1922   *Ulysses* published by Shakespeare and Company (2 Feb.). Irish Civil War begins.

1923   JJ commences *Work in Progress*. End of Irish Civil War.

1924   French translation of *Portrait* published. Extracts from *Work in Progress* appear in the *transatlantic review*.

1926   Samuel Roth begins to pirate *Ulysses* in his magazine *Two Worlds* in New York. General Strike in Britain.

1927   *Pomes Penyeach* published by Shakespeare and Company. Extracts from *Work in Progress* appear in *transition*.

1928   *Anna Livia Plurabelle* published in New York.

1929   Samuel Beckett et al. publish *Our Exagmination* to explicate *Work in Progress*. French translation of *Ulysses* published. *Tales Told of Shem and Shaun* published in Paris. Samuel Roth's pirated edition of *Ulysses* appears in New York.

1930   Publication of Stuart Gilbert's critical guide *James Joyce's Ulysses*. *Haveth Childers Everywhere* published in Paris and New York.

1931   JJ and Nora marry in London (4 July). John Joyce dies (29 Dec.).

1932   JJ writes 'Ecce Puer' to commemorate his father. JJ's grandson Stephen is born. Lucia suffers her first major breakdown.

1933   US District Court rules that *Ulysses* is not obscene and may be published in the USA.

1934   Random House publishes US edition of *Ulysses*. *The Mime of Mick, Nick and the Maggies* published in The Hague.

1936   Bodley Head publishes *Ulysses* in London. Joyce's *Collected Poems* published in New York.

1937   *Storiella as She is Syung* published in London.

1938 JJ finishes *Finnegans Wake* (13 Nov.).

1939 *Finnegans Wake* published in London and New York. Germany invades Poland, precipitating World War Two. JJ removes family from Paris to St Gérard-le-Puy. Herbert Gorman's biography of JJ published in New York.

1940 German invasion of France. JJ removes family to neutral Switzerland.

1941 JJ dies in Zurich (13 Jan.). Buried in the Fluntern Cemetery, Zurich.

Introduction

This book examines the life, works and critical reputation of James Joyce. The son of a dissolute Dublin election agent and rates collector who rose to become one of the brightest stars of European literary modernism, the composer of exquisite late Edwardian lyrics who subsequently created the radically new narrative styles of *Ulysses* and *Finnegans Wake*, and the writer who exiled himself from his native Ireland in order ceaselessly to remake it in his imagination, Joyce's peripatetic career and complex reinvention of modern Western culture has made him a subject of enduring fascination and established him as perhaps the greatest and most enigmatic literary figure of the twentieth century. Simultaneously a defiantly parochial and fiercely international writer, Joyce's avant-garde artworks helped to create the climate of taste by which they would be judged. His systematic transformation of the nature and scope of the novel and his protracted struggle against the legal censorship and suppression of his work extended the possibilities of modern art and helped to redraw the boundaries between the claims of public morality and the rights of artistic expression for his own and succeeding generations.

Part I of this book offers a concise narrative of Joyce's life and literary career. It charts his inauspicious beginnings amid the disintegrating fortunes of a poor Dublin family, his embryonic artistic development as a poet and novelist, his self-imposed exile from Dublin and reinvention of himself as a modernist artist, the literary and cultural scandal provoked by *Ulysses*, his emergence as one of the key writers of his generation, and his sixteen-year struggle to complete his final prose epic. Part 2 provides a critical commentary upon all of Joyce's prose works and explores the style and significance of his poetry and drama. Part 3 traces a historical overview of the critical reception of Joyce's work, from its earliest twentieth-century reviews to contemporary critical discussion, in order to explore how particular styles of reading and modes of critical practice have influenced our understanding of Joyce.

Chapter 1

Life and Contexts

Introduction

This chapter provides a brief account of Joyce's life and literary career, giving details both of his personal circumstances and the development of his reputation as a writer. It draws substantially on the biographies of Joyce mentioned in the 'Further Reading' section for its account. Readers of Joyce are particularly fortunate in being able to consult Ellmann's now classic *James Joyce* (1983), which offers an extensive and influential reading of his life and work. Because no single account of Joyce's life can claim to offer an absolutely authoritative interpretation of its multitudinous detail, readers in search of supplementary information about particular aspects of his biography should consult the works listed in 'Further Reading.' This section also locates Joyce in cultural, historical and political contexts which are of particular significance to his writing and for the criticism they have generated. For this reason, the narrative of Joyce's life is punctuated by subsections dealing with issues such as the historical and political situation of late nineteenth-century Ireland, Irish political nationalism and the rise of the physical force tradition, the Irish cultural revival, and the literary and cultural 'scandal' of *Ulysses*. The accompanying chronology provides a clear sequence of events for reference purposes.

Childhood

James Aloysius Joyce was born in Rathgar, Dublin on 2 February 1882. He was the eldest son of John Stanislaus Joyce and Mary Jane Murray.

Joyce's father was one of the most important influences upon his son's life. His personality, sayings and dispositions are diffused throughout Joyce's work, whether thinly disguised as Simon Dedalus in *A Portrait of the Artist as a Young Man* and *Ulysses* or as one of the disembodied voices that compose the text of *Finnegans Wake*. Born in Cork in 1849, John Joyce moved to Dublin in his early twenties. He invested £500 that he inherited from his father in a Chapelizod Distillery and was appointed secretary to the company. The business soon collapsed, leaving Joyce's father without his investment, but the influence of a relative secured him a position as secretary to the National Liberal Club in Dublin. His successful electioneering for the Liberal candidate led to his appointment to a permanent government position: he became the Collector General of Rates for Dublin. Now John Joyce was in a financial position to take a wife, and he duly married Mary Jane Murray in May 1880. In retrospect, this period represented the high-water mark of his fortunes. His reckless disposition and financial imprudence led him constantly to live beyond his means; from the age of 42 he subsisted on a combination of low-income jobs, borrowed money and small rents eked out from his inherited properties, while always on the look-out for his creditors. Children arrived in rapid succession (John Joyce fathered ten in all: four boys and six girls); as they grew, so did the family debts. One after another of his properties was mortgaged, and the family settled into a joyless pattern of episodic removal to smaller and ever-poorer homes.

These were the circumstances into which James, the eldest child, was born. In 1888 he followed in his father's footsteps and entered Clongowes Wood College. Clongowes provided him with a rigorous Jesuitical education and he benefited considerably from the intellectual order and clarity of its teaching. It was here that Joyce gained his first grounding in Latin, theology and the classics. It was also at Clongowes that he first demonstrated his independent nature. Harshly punished by the prefect of studies for attending class with broken glasses (they had been broken by a fellow pupil), Joyce summoned the courage to complain of his treatment to the rector (Gorman 1941: 34). A version of this episode subsequently occupies a pivotal position in Stephen Dedalus' education in *Portrait* (P: 42). Joyce's schooling at Clongowes ended abruptly in 1891 with the collapse of his father's fortunes. In this year John Joyce was pensioned off from his position in the Rates Office and the family began its relentless slide down the social scale. John Joyce found intermittent work as an advertising canvasser and as a solicitor's calligrapher, but sustained employment was now beyond him, and by 1894 he had sold off the last of his remaining properties. However, following a brief spell with the Christian Brothers School, James was able in 1893 to continue his Jesuitical education at Belvedere College after the school fees were generously waived to permit his admittance. Joyce's admission to his new school was the happy outcome of a chance encounter between his father and Father John Conmee, prefect of studies at Belvedere and former rector of Clongowes; Conmee was moved to make arrangements for the boy in recognition of his precocious academic ability. Joyce repaid Conmee's kindness with a period of diligent academic study, winning scholarly prizes for his Intermediate Examinations in 1894 and 1895.

The six years Joyce spent at Belvedere were notable for several striking developments in his personality and attitudes. It was during this period that the 14-year-old Joyce was accosted by a prostitute and embarked upon his sexual life; the illicit character of this encounter was perhaps responsible for defining the nature of the sexual act in his mind as an ambiguous mixture of furtiveness, fascination and shame. This experience acquired additional resonance for Joyce because it coincided with the loss of his religious belief. His maturing intelligence had sharpened itself by playfully satirising the more sophistical tenets of Catholic orthodoxy; the combination of his sexual awakening and his emotional recoil from the rhetorical ferocity of Jesuitical sermonising against the physical appetites recast his view of religion as an indispensable tool of moral and social repression. The role in his imaginative life once played by Catholicism was now taken over by a new divinity: art. He began a series of prose sketches entitled *Silhouettes* which sought to disclose sudden moments of illumination or crisis within the turmoil of impoverished Dublin life, and composed *Moods*, a collection of poems that rehearsed a litany of outworn Romantic phrases and dispositions (Ellmann 1983: 50). More significantly, it was at Belvedere that Joyce made his first acquaintance with the work of the late nineteenth-century Norwegian playwright Henrik Ibsen. The ironic detachment of Ibsen's mode of dramatic presentation, his undeviating attention to the truth of human nature beyond the frameworks of religious and moral law, and his attempt to create mythical structures to accommodate modern experience supplied Joyce with the rudiments of an aesthetic credo that would become central to each of his published works.

The University Years: 1898–1902

In 1898 at the age of 16 Joyce began to read for a Bachelor of Arts degree at University College, Dublin. Over the next four years he took a desultory interest in a broad spectrum of subjects including Latin, French, English, Italian, Mathematics, Natural Philosophy and Logic. More important than Joyce's tenuous commitment to formal academic study was the systematic course of reading upon which he now embarked. Joyce's literary reading was both eclectic in its range and defiantly modern in its taste: it embraced figures such as the medieval poet Dante Aligheri; the contemporary Italian poet, novelist and dramatist Gabriele D'Annunzio; the stylistic radicalism of the novelist Gustave Flaubert; the French symbolist poets; the scandalous naturalism of Emile Zola; and the plays of Ibsen and his successor Gerhart Hauptmann. At the same time, he sedulously developed his interest in aesthetic theory and philosophy: the work of Aristotle, Thomas Aquinas and Giordano Bruno now began to exert a profound influence upon his imagination. Joyce's reading of Aristotle reconfigured the Greek's idea of tragic emotion (including the cathartic effects of pity and terror) to emphasise the achieved stasis and autonomy of the work of art. Building upon the Aristotelian notion of catharsis, Joyce proposed a theory of aesthetic or 'dramatic emotion' as the arrest of a sensibility before a powerful experience or feeling. In this static moment of aesthetic apprehension, the particular elements that constitute an experience are intuited in an ideal and timeless synthesis. Stephen Dedalus expatiates upon this new understanding of tragic and aesthetic emotion at some length in his conversations with his companions Cranly and Lynch in the final part of *Portrait*.

From Aquinas Joyce also derived the notion of the impersonality and autonomy of the work of art as well as a distinction between the aesthetic apprehension of the beautiful and the presentation of moral ideas. An artwork, Aquinas believed, is an object that expresses its own structural laws and internal relations, not the subjective personality of the artist who creates it. The role of the artist consists in the perfection of aesthetic form; the exterior ends to which an artwork may be put are a lesser and secondary matter. Stephen's now famous aesthetic speculation about the nature and role of the author-God reproduces this Thomistic belief in the autonomy and impersonality of art (*P*: 181). The influence upon Joyce of the sixteenth-century philosopher and heretic Giordarno Bruno was more oblique, but he was stirred by Bruno's refutation of any ontological distinction between God and the universe he created and his insistence upon the original unity of cosmological being. For Bruno the universe is infinite and contains an infinite number of worlds. If God is omnipotent he must be able to think an infinity of thoughts, including the thoughts that each of us is thinking; because Bruno admits no distinction between thinking and being, this thought is actualised in an infinite number of worlds. The primordial unity of being is an expression of this divine nature; existence is produced by the infinite repetition of difference. Aspects of Bruno's philosophy are evident in *Finnegans Wake* where the book of the world is a cyclical narrative that takes the repetition of difference as its structural principle. Each reading of this potentially endless text creates new interpretations from the proliferating contexts produced by previous readings; to 'end' a reading of the novel is to be propelled back to the beginning to see the world anew in the act of its infinite unfolding.

Two articles Joyce wrote while at university provide clues to his emerging attitude to art and cultural politics. The first, dating from January 1900, was entitled 'Drama and Life' and was presented as a paper to University College's Literary and Historical Society. It was conceived as a response to the furore surrounding the first performance of W. B. Yeats' play *The Countess Cathleen* at the Irish Literary Theatre (later to become the Abbey Theatre) in May 1899. Yeats' play provoked fierce criticism in some quarters for its allegedly sordid and 'unpatriotic' theme – the selling to the Devil of the soul of Mother Ireland (Countess Cathleen) in order that she might provide for her starving population – and its representation of the Irish peasantry as a primitive and backward people. A group of University College students framed a letter of protest to a local newspaper, condemning Yeats for his portrayal of immoral and unpatriotic sentiments. Joyce proudly refused to sign this letter and then wrote 'Drama and Life' to summarise his view of the issues involved. The paper began by advancing two general propositions: drama is the most elevated of all the arts because it represents the underlying forces and conflicts of human society; but the most universally venerated form of this art, classical Greek drama, is now exhausted and unable adequately to represent the conditions and struggles of modern existence. Modern drama may be distinguished from its classical counterpart, Joyce continues, by its rejection of a necessary connection between ethics and aesthetics. The point of art is not merely to elevate or amuse; it is to present the chaos and drama of real life on the stage (*OCP*: 26). Genuine art is indifferent to morality, patriotism or idealism; it is only true to itself when it deals with the truth of human life (*OCP*: 28). This is the fundamental law against which Yeats' play should be judged, and it is this law that is realised most profoundly of all for Joyce in Ibsen's drama and the novels of Zola and Flaubert.

To Joyce's dismay, the reaction of the Irish Literary Theatre to the criticism of *The Countess Cathleen* was to revert to more traditional and recognisably 'Irish' subjects. He responded to this development in October 1901 in another article entitled 'The Day of the Rabblement'. Joyce began with an epigrammatic statement of intent: 'No man, said the Nolan [Giordano Bruno], can be a lover of the true or the good unless he abhors the multitude; and the artist, though he may employ the crowd, is very careful to isolate himself' (*OCP*: 50). The true artist separates himself from the multitude because the popular taste of the 'rabblement' is always in thrall to outworn conventions and a specious and unreflective moralism. This is the lesson Ibsen taught a half century ago, Joyce argued, and this is the lesson contemporary Irish writing continues steadfastly to ignore. The legitimate heirs of Ibsen's new aesthetic dispensation, Joyce maintained, are to be discovered, once again, in modern novelists such as Flaubert and D'Annunzio. They alone have recognised that only by developing a style and sensibility purposely at variance with the platitudes and self-deception of the people is it possible to create art of lasting value. It was this iconoclastic dictum, and this singular conception of the artist's vocation and role, that Joyce was to develop over the next forty years.

Joyce's university years were also notable for the beginnings of his literary apprenticeship and the establishment of a number of friendships that later formed the background for some of his novelistic characters. In 1900 he wrote a play heavily influenced by Ibsen entitled *A Brilliant Career*, and a verse drama, *Dream Stuff*, only fragments of which still survive. He submitted the former to the critic William Archer for assessment; Archer acknowledged the manuscript's literary quality but shrewdly judged that Joyce's talents were not primarily dramatic in nature. Undeterred, Joyce translated two of Hauptmann's plays in the summer of 1901 and submitted them to the Irish Literary Theatre; it was partly his disappointment at their rejection that led him to compose 'The Day of the Rabblement'. Meanwhile Joyce's youthful enthusiasm for the poetry of W. B. Yeats manifested itself in a slim volume of lyrics which he also sent for review to the long-suffering Archer, tactfully who advised him that there was 'as yet more temperament than anything else in your work' (Ellmann 1983: 83). Joyce's embryonic artistic development did not, of course, take place in a vacuum. His social circle at this time was composed of a close-knit but vibrant series of friendships with a group of men whose lively interest in literature, politics and Irish culture provoked him into debate and led him to articulate and refine his own ideas and opinions. Three members of this group were of particular importance: George Clancy, Francis Skeffington and John Francis Byrne. Clancy, who appears disguised as Davin in *Portrait*, was a nationalist and a devotee of Gaelic sport and culture; he even prevailed upon Joyce to take Irish lessons for a short period. Skeffington, later reborn in *Portrait* as McCann, had a formidable reputation as an intellect and wit; his passion for vegetarianism, pacifism and rights for women became the satirical object of Joyce's amused scepticism. Perhaps Joyce's closest early friendship, though, was with Byrne, immortalised as Cranly in *Portrait*; Byrne's intelligence and quiet self-confidence made him the perfect receptacle for Joyce's youthful plans and confidences.

A shadow was cast over Joyce's final months at University College when his brother George died of typhoid fever in March 1902. Joyce already felt that he had exhausted everything university could offer him; he left University College with a pass degree three months later. Graduation left him at a cross-road, with neither a position nor funds; his father suggested that he take a job at the local Guinness brewery, a bluntly pragmatic piece of advice Joyce later lampooned in *Finnegans Wake*. He declined this suggestion and registered with Byrne for a place at Dublin's University Medical School. Although he did not yet know it, his life in Ireland was already drawing to a close.

Historical and Political Contexts

The Ireland into which Joyce was born still bore the scars of the political tumult that had threatened to tear the country apart during the nineteenth century. This political crisis began with widespread anti-Catholic discrimination by the British state and its Protestant representative class (composed of legislators, landlords and the judiciary); deepened inexorably following the devastation inflicted upon the peasantry by the Great Famine of 1846–50; and eventually found expression in the series of nationalist movements calling for independence from the British state that helped to shape the political climate of Joyce's first forty years. These movements ultimately gave rise to two of the defining episodes of modern Irish political history: the 1916 Easter Rising and the Irish Civil War of 1922–3.

Nationalism and the Political Effects of the Irish Famine

Irish opposition to British colonial rule intensified throughout the nineteenth century. It received much of its initial impetus from the political campaigns of the Catholic leader Daniel O'Connell. In the 1820s O'Connell formed the Catholic Association to argue for the rights of Irish Catholics; his campaign had a profound impact upon the political climate and resulted in the passing of the 1829 Catholic Emancipation Bill, which made it possible for Catholics to sit in Parliament at Westminster and to hold public offices. O'Connell subsequently created the Repeal Association in 1840 in order to revoke the 1800 Act of Union between Britain and Ireland which had dissolved the Irish parliament and entrenched anti-Catholic discrimination at a legal and political level. This new campaign made a number of minor gains for Irish Catholics, including among its achievements a new Poor Law and a limited degree of municipal reform, but it failed to secure its principal aims: a repeal of the Act of Union and a substantial improvement in the social condition of the Irish peasantry. However, the Repeal Association quickly found a new source of support in the 'Young Ireland' movement. This grouping, which contained both Catholics and Protestants (men such as Charles Gavan Duffy, Thomas Davis and William Smith O'Brien), published a newspaper entitled *The Nation* advocating repeal of the Act of Union and the rebirth of the idea of the Irish nation. The Young Irelanders represented this new nation in cultural, as well as political, terms as a secular and pluralist community which drew equally upon both Catholic and Protestant traditions. For this vision to take root, they believed, it was crucial to reinvent the historical image of an independent Ireland. They therefore published 'The Library of Ireland,' a series of popular histories that projected images of heroic Irish resistance to British imperialism and vague premonitions of an independent Irish Republic.

A rift with O'Connell in the mid-1840s left the movement temporarily becalmed, but it flared into life once more in reaction to the catastrophe of the Famine. The Irish Famine was a humanitarian disaster that strained to breaking point the relations between the British state and its Irish subjects. The origin of the Famine lay in the blight of the staple potato crop. Without the potato crop the Irish peasantry had nothing to eat and nothing to sell. Bereft of receipts for their produce, hundreds of thousands of starving peasants found themselves unable to pay rent on their tenant properties and were evicted by their British and Protestant landlords. This massive displaced population was confronted with a choice between three nightmare scenarios: starvation in the countryside, forced confinement in disease-ridden workhouses or enforced migration on 'coffin ships' to the United States of America. The famine left over one million dead; the combined effects of famine, disease and emigration reduced the Irish population from eight to five millions in less than a decade. The failure of the British state to ameliorate Irish despair – indeed, its perceived complicity in exacerbating the Famine's worst consequences by elevating the idea of self-help above state assistance – had a powerful catalytic effect upon the revival of Irish political nationalism over the next seventy years.

In the pages of *The Nation* and *The United Irishman* Young Irelanders savaged the incompetent and self-interested British response and renewed their call for an Irish parliament to deal with Irish internal affairs. The British government countered this resistance by suspending the Habeas Corpus Act, which meant that inmates need no longer appear before a court for judgement on whether or not they had been lawfully imprisoned; and by passing the Coercions Bill and the Treason/Felony Act in order to limit freedom of assembly and circumscribe freedom of the press. Against this background of political repression, and inspired in part by the French Revolution of 1848, a faction of Young Irelanders made the fateful transition to armed insurrection. They organised a violent revolt against the Crown in County Tipperary, but this uprising was quickly contained by British forces; a number of Young Ireland leaders were transported to Australia, while a few more escaped to America. Although a failure in political terms, the 1848 Young Ireland revolt set the stage for the two dominant nineteenth-century Irish nationalist campaigns: Home Rule and the Fenian movement.

A crucial issue in nineteenth-century Irish politics was the control and ownership of land. Large swathes of rural Ireland were owned by absentee British landlords who employed agents to ensure the maximum return for their holdings. This system had two pernicious consequences: land rents were set at almost twice the level of mainland Britain, and the division of holdings into the largest possible number of rentable units limited the productive capacity of the land. Both of these factors contributed to the ravages of the Famine. Landlords' agents also worked closely with the Royal Irish Constabulary to enforce immediate eviction of tenants temporarily unable to pay their rent. The injustice of the *rentier* system and evidence of widespread collusion between landlords and state representatives produced massive resentment among the rural poor. Their dissent became politically explosive when a combination of circumstances (the destruction of crops by incessant rainfall, the return of potato blight between 1877 and 1879 and the depression of produce prices following the mass importation of cheap meat and corn from the new American markets) led to another famine in 1879. In the same year, Michael Davitt created the Land League to agitate for reform of the rent system and progress toward tenant ownership. Later in 1879 Davitt helped form the National Land League to spearhead the drive for reform under the leadership of Charles Stuart Parnell.

The figure of Parnell brought together land reform and the political movement towards Home Rule which sought to free Ireland from direct rule from Westminster and give the Irish a larger stake in the management of their own affairs. The campaign for Home Rule had been augmented by Isaac Butt's foundation of the Home Rule Association in

1870. Butt sought limited home rule: a Dublin parliament responsible for domestic affairs, with Irish Members of Parliament continuing to sit at Westminster. The Home Rule Association was quickly replaced by the more politically outspoken Home Rule League which, in the General Election of 1874, elected fifty-nine MPs committed to Home Rule for Ireland. After Butt's death in 1879 the Irish parliamentary party elected Parnell as its leader. Parnell's strategy was to combine moderate and militant Irish nationalists in a joint campaign for land reform and political independence. On the former issue, he argued for the social ostracism of anyone purchasing the land of an evicted tenant: his successful campaign against a Captain Boycott in Mayo in 1880 introduced the verb 'to boycott' into the English language. Parnell's aggressive assault upon the limited provisions contained within Prime Minister William Gladstone's 1881 Land Act led to his imprisonment in Kilmainham Jail and the suppression of the National Land League. He was released after less than a year and continued his Home Rule campaign. His position was seriously compromised by the 'Phoenix Park Murders' of 6 May 1882 in which Lord Frederick Cavendish, British Secretary for Ireland and his Undersecretary, Thomas Henry Burke, were assassinated in a Dublin park by a group named 'The Invincibles' dedicated to the forcible expulsion of the British imperial presence in Ireland. Parnell's political enemies alleged his complicity in the plot; although he was eventually exonerated by a parliamentary commission in 1890, his political career was severely retarded in the interim. In 1886 Prime Minister Gladstone presented his first Home Rule Bill to Parliament. The Bill was doomed from the outset, a consequence of both its impractical political vision of limited Home Rule with an Irish parliament stripped of fiscal and security powers, and the resistance of the Conservative opposition and a substantial section of the ruling British Liberal Party, which saw its potential success as a reward for insurrectionary violence and the political dissidence of the National Land League. The issue split the Liberals and Gladstone's government fell. In 1889 one of Parnell's parliamentary colleagues, Captain O'Shea, named Parnell as the correspondent in a divorce suit brought against his wife Katherine ('Kitty'). The suit was granted and although Parnell subsequently married Kitty, he was hounded out of office by a combination of the Roman Catholic hierarchy and English parliamentary opinion. Parnell never recovered his influence with Irish nationalists and died, a broken man, in October 1891.

The Great Famine and the failure of the 1848 rebellion were also the foundational causes of the other significant Irish nationalist tradition: the Fenian movement. Fenianism was distinguished by its belief in the necessity of physical force to free Ireland of British rule. The movement's initial impulse came from two survivors of the Young Ireland revolt, James Stephens and John O'Mahoney. In 1858 Stephens established the Irish Republican Brotherhood in Dublin and O'Mahoney inaugurated the Fenian Brotherhood in America. The IRB gradually began to develop a strategy of guerrilla warfare in Ireland and mainland Britain. The aftermath of an attack on Chester Castle in north-west England led to the execution of three Fenians in Manchester in 1867: they became known as the 'Manchester Martyrs'. Meanwhile the aforementioned Phoenix Park Murders demonstrated the Fenians' occasional capacity to strike at the heart of the British establishment. But the movement still lacked an effective political organisation and strategy. This began to be supplied in the 1890s by Arthur Griffith. Griffith rejected the continuing political compromise enacted by the Irish parliamentary party at Westminster, but also believed that the adoption of political violence was a hopeless and counter-productive tactic. He argued instead for the withdrawal of Irish representatives from Westminster and the constitution of an Irish assembly which might have equal weight with the British parliament under the auspices of the Crown. In 1899 he set up a newspaper entitled the *United Irishman* to proselytise for this position. The programme also became the central platform of the political party Sinn Féin ('Ourselves Alone') that Griffith helped to create in 1905.

The Easter Rising and the Irish Civil War

The two defining Irish political events of Joyce's lifetime were the 1916 Easter Rising and the Irish Civil War. The Easter Rising represented the confluence of a number of forces committed to securing Irish independence by force. Three forces were particularly significant: the IRB, the Irish Volunteers (an 'army' of about 2,000 armed and trained men set up in opposition to the Ulster Volunteer Force, a British sponsored group which sought to prevent home rule), and the Irish Citizen Army (a socialist movement headed by James Connolly to defend workers from oppression by strike-breaking employers and the police). These forces were brought into temporary and fateful alignment by a sudden transformation of historical circumstances: the outbreak of World War One in 1914. The Great War stretched the British state, and its military in particular, to the limit, and appeared to provide the perfect opportunity for an Irish rebellion. The IRB set up a military council to plan the rising and to provide a focal point for the various revolutionary groups. Among the leaders of the uprising were Pádraig Pearse, James Connolly, Thomas

MacDonagh, Joseph Plunkett and Eamon de Valera. The rising was planned for Easter 1916. Despite the loss of a large shipment of guns and continuing uncertainty about the timing and scope of the assault, the council leaders decided to adhere to their original schedule. On Easter Monday 1916 the revolutionaries seized the General Post Office in Dublin. The Irish tricolour was raised above the GPO and Pearse delivered a 'Proclamation of the Irish Republic' to the watching Dubliners. However, as soon as the British Army recovered their poise and regrouped, their superiority in arms and numbers proved irresistible. After four days of savage fighting, the GPO was stormed and the rebel leaders arrested. Fifteen rebels were executed, including Pearse and MacDonagh, while de Valera was given a life sentence which was overturned a year later following the exertion of pressure by American-Irish sympathisers. The Easter Rising was undoubtedly a political failure, but it has retained a lasting importance to the Irish republican imagination as a symbol of blood sacrifice and heroic resistance to imperial authority.

These events set the stage for the Irish War of Independence and the Irish Civil War. A majority of the Irish MPs elected to the British parliament in the election of 1918 were members of Sinn Féin. Rejecting British imperial control of Irish affairs, these Sinn Féin representatives refused to take their seats at Westminster, choosing instead to set up an alternative (and, in the eyes of the British authorities, illegal) parliament in Dublin called the Dial Eireann. The Dial immediately announced Irish independence and the Irish Republican Army began to wage a military war upon the British administration governing Ireland. This conflict became known variously as the Anglo-Irish war and the Irish War of Independence. It lasted from January 1919 until December 1921, when the British government and representatives of the Dial signed the Anglo-Irish Agreement. Among the main clauses of the agreement were the withdrawal of British troops from Ireland, the partition of Ireland into the Irish Free State and Northern Ireland (although the British king continued to be represented within the Free State's governmental machinery), and the institution of an oath of allegiance to be sworn by Irish elected representatives to the Free State itself.

The Anglo-Irish treaty was ratified in January 1922, formally creating the Irish Free State, but a conflict quickly ensued between its supporters and opponents. Opposition to the agreement was fomented particularly by the partition of Ireland and the Oath of Allegiance, which was widely interpreted as an act of involuntary submission to the British king. De Valera, who had been elected President of the Irish Republic by the Dial in 1919, resigned his office and led Sinn Féin into armed conflict with the

British and Free State establishment. This anti-treaty faction briefly threatened the judicial and political apparatus in Dublin, but was soon forced back into the countryside where it conducted a guerrilla campaign that culminated in the assassination of the pro-treaty republican Michael Collins in August 1922. However, the pro-treaty forces gradually gained the military ascendancy in the Civil War and de Valera called a ceasefire in May 1923. He was imprisoned for a year following the cessation of hostilities, but returned to politics to create a new party, Fianna Fáil, in 1926. Fianna Fáil's electoral victory in 1932 restored de Valera to the Irish presidency and he remained in office throughout the last nine years of Joyce's life.

Literary and Cultural Contexts

Two developments in particular furnish the immediate cultural backdrop to Joyce's artistic career: the Irish literary and cultural revival of the 1880s and 1890s and the broader stylistic experimentation of European literary modernism. The first two decades of Joyce's life were synonymous with what has come to be known as the 'Celtic Revival'. This revival took several forms. One dominant strand, developing out of the recrudescence of Irish nationalism following the 'Young Ireland' movement, and associated with figures such as Douglas Hyde and Charles Gavan Duffy, sought to create an image of Irish identity unconstrained by the cultural forms and stereotypes imposed upon it by the British imperial inheritance. In 1893 Hyde established the Gaelic League in order to reassert the dignity of Irish language and literature and encourage its teaching in schools and colleges, and to popularise specifically Irish cultural practices such as dance, music and games. This project drew support from those nationalists who wished to de-anglicise Irish culture; Hyde's famous 1892 lecture 'On the Necessity for De-Anglicising the Irish People' expresses one of the league's primary political preoccupations. Other contemporary developments, like the Celtic Literary Society and the Gaelic Athletic Association, broadened and deepened this revivalist impulse. From the 1880s onwards Irish identity was reconceived by the revival in fairly specific terms as rural, anti-imperialist, Celtic, anti-metropolitan and Catholic. Accompanying this shift was a renewed attention to Irish cultural history, a flurry of interest in the development of the Celtic 'race', and a newly self-confident assumption of the essential nobility of the Irish people.

The one element of revivalist thought that resonates within Joyce's work is its resolutely anti-colonial emphasis. Joyce was unswerving in his denunciation of the misery and deprivation inflicted upon Ireland by imperial British policy: each of his novels, and a good deal of the political journalism he composed during his stay in Trieste registers the imprint of this attitude. However, in other respects Joyce was severely critical of what he took to be the antiquated and conservative cultural politics of revivalism, with its cast of pious and beneficent rural types and its infantile mythic reconfiguration of the Irish character. He reserved particular scorn for the authoritarianism and inflexibility of certain nationalist political positions and satirised them throughout his corpus, most notably in the 'Cyclops' episode of *Ulysses*. A closer parallel to Joyce's own experience is to be found in the Irish literary (rather than merely 'Celtic') revival of fin-de-siècle Ireland. What makes the writers of the Irish Literary Revival significant to a reading of Joyce is that, like him, they enjoyed an imaginatively vital, but also culturally ambivalent relationship to Irish history and traditions. Figures like W. B. Yeats, John Millington Synge, Lady Augusta Gregory and Oscar Wilde were either Protestants whose birth and education forced them to inhabit an ambivalent position both within and outside an Irish cultural sphere determined largely by its opposition to British imperialism, or a Catholic whose rejection of Irish social and moral conservatism led him to explore versions of 'Irishness' from a position of cultural exile. The literary strategies and techniques these writers developed to express their particular perspectives upon modern Irish culture offer some intriguing similarities with aspects of Joyce's own writing practice.

These techniques and strategies are clearly evident in the work of Yeats, Synge and Wilde. Up to the publication of *In the Seven Woods* (1904), Yeats' poetry was remarkable both for its reconfiguration of mythic archetypes and its insistent doubleness of perspective. Unable because of his religion and social background to identify himself too closely with the Irish historical narrative of anti-colonialism, Yeats turned instead to a mythic reinvention of place. His mythic transformation of the Gaelic bardic tradition of *dinnsheanchas*, or poems that detail the knowledge of the lore of a place, represented Ireland as a cultural space bearing the scars of its colonial occupation while remaining unassimilable in its radical difference and singularity to any version of the past that imperial history might offer. A similar impulse lay behind the stylistic experimentation of Syngean drama. In his effort to represent an order of Irish experience irreducible to the linguistic and cultural codes of metropolitan English, the Irish playwright John Millington Synge renounced naturalism and realism in favour of a vibrant new form of folk-speech. His literary remodelling of the dialect of the islands of Aran off the west coast of Ireland created a synthetic literary idiom known as 'Hiberno-English' that sought to evoke the traces of a past world while gesturing by its stylistic novelty to a mode of sensibility yet to come into being. In this sense Synge's visionary re-creation of the Irish past provides a compelling analogue to Joyce's revolutionary rewriting of Homeric epic in *Ulysses* and his development of a syncretic mythic language in *Finnegans Wake*. For all its vicissitudes, meanwhile, the example of Wilde offered Joyce a tantalising glimpse of the creative possibilities afforded by exile. While Wilde's flamboyant and theatrical mode of self-fashioning was inimical to Joyce's temperament, his insistence that what we call 'identity' was an ongoing dialogue between a multiple series of selves lies at the core of Joyce's work. For Joyce, as for Wilde, 'Irishness' could only be experienced as an imaginative event from a location beyond its borders and mores. In other words, the international perspective was necessary for a national vision to be born.

Joyce was also influenced by the revolutionary shifts in style and sensibility that came to be grouped beneath the generic label of 'literary modernism'. Two writers who came to prominence in the second half of the nineteenth century had a particular impact upon the formation of his style and world view: Gustave Flaubert and Henrik Ibsen. Flaubert's influence may be detected in Joyce's use of free indirect style: a mode of narrative presentation that employs the formal structure of third-person narrative prose while retaining the characteristic inflections of a first-person voice. This narrative technique, which enabled Joyce to switch swiftly and almost imperceptibly between different and often incommensurable points of view, was one of the devices he employed to create a crucial ironic distance between the impersonal authorial voice and the perceptions of his characters. Its effect was that the reader was no longer absolutely sure which perspective was being endorsed or satirised at any point of the text, and was no longer able to rely upon a single interpretative context (the author's implied beliefs and values) to establish the meaning of particular actions or statements. From Ibsen, Joyce took the conviction of an attitude as well as elements of a style. Ibsen's drama reconfirmed Joyce in his belief that the paralysis of modern life arose from its adherence to a set of repressive social and moral conventions. The force of life, Ibsen insisted, should not be subordinated to timeless religious and moral laws; the power and value of genuinely modern art was to discover the fundamental truths of human nature without recourse to any imposed law or value. These human truths were universal and potentially democratic: they exist to be discovered in the life of the ordinary citizen, whose mode of being is itself an epic subject worthy of an epic treatment. Ibsen's influence upon Joyce is evident in his play *Exiles*, but it also extends to the thematic preoccupations and dramatic narrative style of *Portrait* and *Ulysses*.

A First Version of Exile

Joyce received his degree of Bachelor of Arts in October 1902. He had already made the acquaintance of several of the leading figures of literary Dublin, who had been both impressed and disarmed by his intellectual candour and forthright opinions. His first port of call was George Russell, a minor figure of the literary revival known for his generosity to young writers. Joyce read Russell a selection of his lyric poetry while implying, with characteristic disdain for public opinion, his indifference to any critical response Russell might deliver (Gorman 1941: 74). Russell was sufficiently impressed by the promise of Joyce's work that he undertook to offer him advice and encouragement and to write in praise of his talents to Lady Gregory and W. B. Yeats. Russell's advocacy prepared the way for the first meeting between Joyce and Yeats, two men destined to take their place among the greatest figures in twentieth-century literature, a meeting that Joyce approached in typically iconoclastic fashion. Despite his admiration for Yeats' poetry, and notwithstanding the gulf separating a writer of national renown from a young apprentice, Joyce persisted in offering astringent criticism of the older man's work. According to Yeats' amused recollection, Joyce concluded his analysis by asking him his age. Upon receiving the answer, he sighed heavily and replied, 'I thought as much. I have met you too late. You are too old' (Ellmann 1954: 88).

Joyce's attitude to his circumstances at this time, as his encounter with Yeats suggests, was one of restlessness and frustration. He found Dublin society parochial and constricting and the literary revival nostalgic and backward-looking, while his way forward seemed uncertain and obscure. To begin to sound the depths of his literary abilities, he decided, he needed to free himself from these encumbrances and conduct his own experiment in living and thinking. It was with these ideals in mind that Joyce left Dublin for Paris in the autumn of 1902 to undertake the first brief stage of his literary exile. His ostensible reason for removing to Paris was to enter medical school, but this ambition quickly dissipated when he discovered that college fees had to be paid immediately and in cash. He was not, in any case, serious about becoming a doctor; the 20-year-old who arrived in the French capital with slender means and a slim collection of poems in manuscript was determined to transform himself into a writer. Paris was not yet the vibrant centre of international modernism it was soon to become, but it was a place where the effects of Zola's 'immoralist' fiction and the influence of the French symbolist poets could still be felt and where excitingly 'modern' ideas about art and culture were being strenuously debated. Most importantly for Joyce, life in Paris provided him with the opportunity to transcend the limitations of provincial Irish society and to begin to fashion himself as an artist.

Joyce took extravagant delight in exploring his new city, wandering extensively along its boulevards and byways, and experiencing first-hand one of the great themes of twentieth-century literature: the imaginative drama of the cultural outsider adrift in the modern metropolis. His temperamental inclination, though, was always to impose form and structure upon the variousness of new experience, and so he quickly gave himself over to a systematic programme of reading and critical reflection. He devoted most of 1903 to an attempt to define an aesthetic that might underpin the mode of literature he wanted to develop. This aesthetic was rigorously classical in temper, drawing primarily upon Aristotle and Aquinas, although it also revealed the influence of Flaubert. The results of Joyce's deliberations appear in his Paris notebooks as a series of terse, condensed paragraphs in which he explored a series of propositions elucidating the proper function of art. He derived a number of aesthetic axioms from these examinations which were to make a lasting impression upon his subsequent narrative work. The end of all art, Joyce declares, is the apprehension of the beautiful, which manifests itself in the state of stasis or arrest wrought upon us by pity and terror in tragedy or joy in comedy. The aim of comic art is to provoke that sense of joy engendered by the possession of some good; tragedy, by contrast, imparts the aspects of sorrow that always accompany the loss of a good or virtue. Because possession of a quality or feeling is a higher mode of being than the sense of deprivation, it follows that comedy is the superior mode of the two. In more general terms, the ultimate end and justification of art can only be apprehended in aesthetic, rather than moral or political terms. 'Art,' Joyce concluded, in words that he would later put into the mouth of Stephen Dedalus, 'is the human disposition of sensible or intelligible material for an aesthetic end' (CW: 145).

Joyce did not conceive of this rigorous aesthetic formulation as a substitute for the art of composition; on the contrary, the refinement of ideas concerning the presentation of experience was always, for him, the prologue to creative expression. The necessary connection between aesthetic theory and practice is nowhere more evident than in *Portrait*, where Joyce's scrupulous categorisation of aesthetic terms forms the basis for

Stephen Dedalus' exposition of the artwork in his conversations with Lynch. The privilege that Joyce accorded the achievement of stasis in aesthetic apprehension – the moment in which perception is cleansed of improper emotion to reveal the fundamental character of an experience – also began to shape the style of his prose. Apart from a handful of lyrics, the primary literary outcome of Joyce's first Parisian sojourn was a small collection of prose passages that sought to disclose, from the flurry of random impressions, the particular quality of an insight, mood or apprehension that formed the substantive core of an experience and gave it its significance. He collected these prose fragments under the title *Epiphanies*. As Joyce was to suggest in *Stephen Hero*, the term 'epiphany' was abstracted here from its religious context and reconfigured in aesthetic rather than spiritual terms. It no longer signified the revelation of divinity but rather the abrupt revelation of the 'whatness' of a thing in which 'the soul of the commonest object, the structure of which is so adjusted, seems to us radiant' (*SH*: 218). This style of epiphanic disclosure, and the subtle interrogation of consciousness and perception it made possible, subsequently became crucial to Joyce's narrative technique in *Portrait* and *Ulysses*.

Joyce's eighteen-month stay in France gave him the time and space to refine his aesthetic ideas and prolong his experimentation with narrative form. It was also the scene of a fortuitous and portentous discovery: on a trip to Tours he chanced upon a copy of Édouard Dujardin's 1888 novel *Les Lauriers sont coupés* (*The Bay Trees are Cut*) which introduced him to the technique of 'interior monologue' that he would take to new heights in *Ulysses*. However, Joyce's time in France was not without difficulty: occasional journalism and sporadic language-teaching often proved insufficient to sustain his basic needs, and his sojourn in Paris was punctuated by letters home so harrowing in their detail that even his father felt compelled to remit money to him. It was, however, a telegram, not a letter, that brought Joyce's Parisian adventure to a close. During Easter 1903 he received the laconic and devastating message 'Mother Dying Come Home Father'. His first attempt at literary exile was at an end.

A Year of Living Dangerously: 1903–4

Joyce returned to a home overshadowed by the imminent death of his mother. Mary Jane Joyce lay upstairs dying a slow and protracted death from cancer of the liver; her eldest son attended her as best he could, his mind overwhelmed by a riot of contradictory emotions. His mother's letters had helped sustain him during those first difficult months in Paris, and the pair had once more drawn close. At the same time, her emotional support and approbation had given him the confidence to renounce the bonds of filial loyalty and take his first steps toward artistic and moral independence. Distraught as he was at his mother's terminal condition, Joyce could not but feel that that his return to Dublin threatened the fragile freedom he had fought so hard to establish. This volatile combination of loyalty and iconoclasm exploded when Joyce's mother, in spiritual agony because of her son's impiety, begged him to make his confession and take communion (Ellmann 1983: 129). Everything in Joyce's nature rebelled at this attempted imposition: he refused his mother's tearful entreaties and set his face against the moral self-betrayal they betokened. Despite the breach his refusal caused between son and dying mother, Joyce recognised at once that 'there was only one device to obey. *Non serviam*' (Gorman 1941: 110). When Mary Jane Joyce died on 13 August 1903, Joyce's grief was genuine and profound; but his mother's death severed the last vital attachment he felt to the family home. Now the promise and the challenge of the future lay all before him. It would, however, take more than a year for his odyssey to begin.

Although the year 1903–4 was to be one of the most significant of Joyce's life, its momentous character was not immediately apparent. Joyce spent the months after his mother's death in a bout of sustained and melancholy dissolution. Now a young man of 21, he began to drink regularly and to excess; accompanied often by a group of drunken medical students, he also began to frequent the brothels of Dublin's notorious night-town district (Gorman 1941: 111). These evenings were spent in the reckless pursuit of pleasure for its own sake, but they eventually provided much of the material for the nightmarish 'Circe' episode of *Ulysses*. At this time Joyce was also much in the company of Oliver Gogarty, a Trinity College medical student who had already established a formidable reputation as a wit, aesthete and composer of bawdy songs. Gogarty's unhappy sense of Joyce's intellectual superiority and Joyce's need to emphasise this fact at every opportunity made for a tense and brittle friendship; Joyce seemed constantly to expect betrayal at Gogarty's hands and detected traces of it in their least exchange. He later captured aspects of Gogarty's wit and self-interestedness in the character of Buck Mulligan in *Ulysses*. That Joyce befriended Gogarty at all suggests that neither his dissolute evenings nor the long afternoons he spent reading in the National Library of Dublin could satisfy his need for imaginative release. Joyce quickly discerned that Gogarty's companionship was also inadequate to this need, and he began to turn his thoughts back towards the business of writing. This process was hastened in January

1904 when he heard that a new literary journal called *Dana* was looking for submissions. Sensing an opportunity, he quickly composed a short autobiographical story which, at his brother Stanislaus' suggestion, he called 'A Portrait of the Artist' (Ellmann 1983: 144). In this short narrative fragment Joyce suddenly began to fashion a style that combined subtle modulations of narrative perspective with a renewed attention to the interior drama of consciousness. By using free indirect style to imbue the narrative with traces of his protagonist's sensibility and point of view, he began to grope his way towards the technical innovations of *A Portrait of the Artist as a Young Man*. These innovations were rather too much for the editors of *Dana* to countenance, and Joyce's story was politely, but firmly, rejected. He was not to be so easily dissuaded. He had now developed a narrative style that enabled him to lay hold upon, without expressing an overt attitude towards, his literary subject (Kenner 1987: 50). Meanwhile his own experiences would provide the grand theme for this new style to interrogate: the conflict between the needs of the rebellious artist, committed to the moral freedom of body and mind, and the authoritarian proscriptions of Church, home and family. Stanislaus' diary entry for 2 February 1904, his brother's twenty-second birthday, records the swift maturation of these themes in Joyce's mind:

> Jim is beginning his novel, as he usually begins things, half in anger, to show that in writing about himself he has a subject of more interest than their [the editors of *Dana*] aimless discussion. I suggested the title of the paper 'A Portrait of the Artist', and this evening, sitting in the kitchen, Jim told me his idea for the novel. It is to be almost autobiographical, and naturally as it comes from Jim, satirical. He is putting a large number of his acquaintances into it, and those Jesuits whom he has known. I don't think they will like themselves in it. He has not decided on a title, and again, I made most of the suggestions. Finally a title of mine was accepted: 'Stephen Hero', from Jim's own name in the book 'Stephen Dedalus'. (Stanislaus Joyce 1971: 12)

Here, sketched out in miniature, was the origin of 'Stephen Hero', the story which Joyce would develop, slowly and painstakingly over the next decade, into *A Portrait of the Artist as a Young Man*, his first published novel. He had already finished the first section of the novel by early February, its theme and style coming together quickly in his mind:

> To suggest the Christian and pagan elements in his mind, even to the point of absurdity, Joyce called himself Stephen Daedalus (then to make it a little less improbable, Stephen Dedalus) after Christianity's first martyr and paganism's greatest inventor. Stephen would be a saint of literature, and like Dedalus would invent wings to soar beyond his compatriots, and a labyrinth, a mysterious art based on great cunning. (Ellmann 1983: 148)

Nora

It would, however, be many years before Joyce could earn a living by writing; he had now to turn his mind to the mundane business of finding paid employment. He found it in the early spring of 1904 when he was appointed to a teaching position at the Clifton School in Dalkey. Teaching bored Joyce, although he appears to have been popular enough with his students, but he later drew upon the experience, and in particular upon the markedly pro-British sympathies of its Ulster-Scot headmaster Francis Irwin, for the 'Nestor' section of *Ulysses*. It was at this time that Joyce's emotional life underwent a profound and decisive transformation when he met Nora Barnacle, the woman who was to become his wife and the mainstay of the last forty years of his life. Joyce first encountered Nora while strolling down Nassau Street in Dublin on 10 June 1904. He was immediately attracted to this tall, vivacious and curiously self-possessed young woman; upon engaging her in casual conversation he was further taken by her direct and unaffected manner. He quickly discovered that she hailed from Galway, had arrived in Dublin six months earlier, and was currently employed as a chambermaid at Finn's Hotel in the city. The pair arranged to meet on 14 June but to Joyce's consternation Nora failed to keep the appointment. In response, he sent her a brief anguished note and a new appointment was agreed. The two finally met on 16 June a day Joyce would later consecrate in *Ulysses* as the date for his epic narrative of domestic estrangement and final reconciliation.

The relationship progressed quickly over the next few months; by the end of the summer Joyce was sending Nora passionate love-letters proclaiming the depth and urgency of his feelings for her. It was, in some ways, a curious match; Nora was, in comparison to Joyce, uneducated and unlettered: she was neither bookish nor reflective in nature, scornful of intellectual posturing and 'deep' conversation, and easily bored by the world of art and writing. Joyce later commented sardonically to his friend Frank Budgen upon her utter imperviousness to his work and reputation: 'You know, you can see I am some sort of personality. I have an effect of some kind on people who come near me and who are my friends. But my wife's personality is absolutely proof against any influence of mine' (Ellmann 1983: 434). The incongruity of her position as the consort of one of the great avant-garde modern writers did not escape Nora; as she later remarked to Maria Jolas: 'You can't imagine what it was like for me to be thrown into the life of this man' (Ellmann 1983: 159). Nora's lack of cultural sophistication was of little moment to someone of Joyce's supreme intellectual self-confidence; he glimpsed in her other virtues that far outweighed her indifference to his own preoccupations. Thus Nora was spirited, independent and self-contained; she had a sharp practical intelligence and a streetwise sensibility; she was steadfastly loyal and – a real virtue in Joyce's eyes – prepared to place his interests before her own; while her seemingly imperturbable demeanour concealed the same extravagantly passionate nature Joyce recognised in himself. He would eventually celebrate many of Nora's qualities, and poke fun at her instinctive anti-intellectualism, in the character of Molly Bloom; more constant than Molly, if no less aware of her husband's limitations, Nora would become the one indispensable and unchanging feature of Joyce's restless cosmopolitan existence.

Their relationship was not, however, without its vicissitudes. While living back at home Joyce had taken up drinking; to Nora's disquiet, his fondness for alcohol led to several embarrassing social scenes. One particular episode had portentous implications: drunk upon St Stephen's Green, Joyce importuned a woman and was beaten by her companion; he was, if hearsay is to be credited, supported and taken home by a Mr Alfred H. Hunter, a man believed to be a Jew and the husband of a faithless wife. Here in microcosm was a prototype of Leopold Bloom: Joyce's original short-story version of 'Ulysses' had a Mr Hunter as its protagonist. Joyce's sporadically drunken and vagabond lifestyle at this time had one other significant literary consequence. Locked out one night from the home of his Aunt Josephine Murray, with whom he had taken up temporary residence, Joyce found refuge with Oliver St John Gogarty at the Martello Tower at Sandycove. Joyce remained a few days with Gogarty and another guest Samuel Chenevix Trench, a member of an old Anglo-Irish family; one night Trench, dreaming that a blank panther was poised to attack him, fired gunshots near Joyce's sleeping head, thereby precipitating his departure. For Joyce, already smarting from the rumour that Gogarty had suggested his stubborn refusal to take communion and make his confession had hastened his mother's death, the incident was one more sign of the impossibility of life in Dublin. He underlined the significance of this moment of rupture by recreating it as the opening scene of *Ulysses*.

The intense three-month relationship between Joyce and Nora reached its climax in September 1904 when he asked her to leave Ireland and elope with him. Joyce had managed to secure a position teaching English at the Berlitz school in Zurich (although he was almost immediately relocated to Trieste in Italy); the salary promised to provide a sufficient, if modest, income for the young couple. Despite the brevity of their relationship and her ignorance of foreign languages, Nora spiritedly accepted his proposal; the pair arrived in Paris on 10 October to begin their great continental adventure. A pattern quickly established itself that persisted throughout their years in Trieste, Zurich and Paris: Joyce's spendthrift and bibulous habits repeatedly brought the domestic economy to the point of collapse; Nora's practicality (coupled with his brother Stanislaus' stoic generosity) then redeemed the family from the brink of ruin. At times Nora despaired of her husband's drinking; in 1918 she famously threatened to destroy the manuscript of *Ulysses* unless he moderated his consumption. Her absolute emotional support for Joyce did not temper her distrust of his celebrity and the broader intellectual world: she refused to read *Ulysses*, believing it to be salacious and distasteful; upon hearing that the psychoanalyst Carl Jung had eulogised the 'psychological peaches' that the novel contained, she offered the devastating riposte upon her husband 'He knows nothing at all about women' (Ellmann 1983: 629). Nora remained the constant presence during Joyce's decades of self-imposed exile from Ireland; she bore him a son, Giorgio, in 1905 and a daughter, Lucia, in 1907.

A Dubliner in Europe

From Paris the pair travelled quickly on to Zurich, where Joyce planned to assume his promised position at Berlitz. To his consternation, no position was available for him; fortunately a vacancy was discovered in Trieste, an Italian city that formed a reluctant part of the Austro-Hungarian Empire, to which the couple now removed, only for Joyce to find himself once more surplus to requirements. Eventually Joyce was relocated to Pola, a city 150 miles south of Trieste, where he finally took up his teaching position. Teaching once again bored Joyce, but it was sufficiently intellectually untaxing to allow him creative energy for the major works upon which he was soon to embark. In Pola Joyce initially continued to work upon the manuscript of *Stephen Hero*, but his dissatisfaction with the style of the novel led the project to stall. Before leaving for Zurich, Joyce had also submitted a collection of lyrics entitled *Chamber Music* to the poet and critic Arthur Symons, in the hope that Symons might find them a publisher. Symons sent the manuscript on in turn to the publisher Grant Richards, whose name would be linked with Joyce's own for the next decade. Richards answered Joyce equivocally, a tone Joyce would come to recognise and deprecate, but declined to publish the poems.

In 1905 Joyce and Nora were forced to leave Pola. The Austrian authorities discovered a spy ring that included an Italian national; in reprisal they summarily expelled all aliens from the city. In truth Joyce was happy to leave a city he found limited; this feeling of relief was compounded when he secured a position at the Berlitz school in Trieste. The great port of Trieste, with its vibrant mix of Italians, Hungarians, Austrians and Greeks, and its lively political culture (inspired in part by socialist and Irredentist or anti-imperialist opposition to Austro-Hungarian rule) was more agreeable to his temperament; here was a cosmopolitan city with a vivid array of social and cultural differences for Joyce to explore. For a time he struggled on with *Stephen Hero*, but then quickly redirected his attention to a collection of short stories he would come to call *Dubliners*. The inspiration for these stories had initially come from George Russell, who, having read with interest the incomplete manuscript of *Stephen Hero*, asked Joyce in the summer of 1904 to contribute a story to the *Irish Homestead* newspaper. Joyce responded by composing 'The Sisters', a boldly experimental piece whose wholly equivocal mode of narratorial indirection promised, he later realised, to solve the technical difficulties posed by *Stephen Hero*. Now in Trieste Joyce began to plan a cycle of stories that would expose and illuminate what he saw as the moral and spiritual paralysis of modern Irish culture. The stories were written with extraordinary speed, in a sustained creative burst lasting from about May to October 1905. Upon their completion, he sent the manuscript off to Grant Richards, who initially accepted them for publication; however, the refusal of Richard's printer in early 1906 to typeset the stories on the grounds of their alleged objectionable and indecent content brought the project to a standstill. This would remain the situation for eight long years, despite a lengthy correspondence between the two principal parties and Joyce's steadfast insistence upon the morality and propriety of his work.

The double disappointment of failing to secure the publication of *Chamber Music* and *Dubliners* had a profound effect upon Joyce: it reinforced his refusal to compromise with external pressures and bred in him an even more resolute independence of outlook. Yet the artist cannot live by art alone: Joyce's modest resources were stretched to their limits by the birth of his son Giorgio in July 1905. His initial solution to his predicament was to invite his brother Stanislaus to join the Triestine household (and share its myriad expenses), which Stanislaus duly did in October. Soon, however, Joyce's boredom at Berlitz and his frustration at the retardation of his literary hopes provoked a more radical thought: if he was to be forced to submit himself to drudgery, why not earn more money for his troubles? With this thought in mind, he applied for, and secured, a job at the bank of Nast-Kolb and Schumacker in Rome in May 1906. Removed to Rome with his family, Joyce worked steadily, if dispassionately, at his clerical duties, took on a few English language students to supplement his income, and continued to press Richards unsuccessfully to bring *Dubliners* into print. But for all the interest and diversion that Rome created, Joyce's situation was still parlous: living increasingly beyond his means in a foreign capital with a young child to support and two books no closer to publication.

An unexpected shaft of light appeared in the form of the imminent publication of *Chamber Music*. Arthur Symons, to whose assistance Joyce had turned following Richards' rejection of the poems, managed to place the volume with the publisher Elkin Matthews. Events moved swiftly from this point and *Chamber Music*, the first of Joyce's books to appear, was published in April 1907. Although Joyce now affected to dislike the poems, their appearance encouraged him greatly and he returned to composition with renewed energy. He spent his last few months in Rome slowly rehearsing the details of 'The Dead', a story that would eventually conclude *Dubliners* by bring the collection's style and critical dissection of contemporary Dublin to its apotheosis. Equally significantly, Joyce began to toy with an idea for a short story entitled 'Ulysses' exploring the life of a cuckolded Dublin Jew named Hunter. This story, abandoned after a few months, would ultimately require a revolution in style to bring to fruition; this revolution would take Joyce sixteen years to accomplish. The appearance of *Chamber Music* briefly confirmed Joyce in his perception of himself as an artist, but the monotony of clerical life depressed his spirits. He took a sporadic interest in Italian anti-imperialist politics, attending sessions of the socialist congress in Rome and identifying himself with the radical anti-parliamentary politics of the Italian philosopher and socialist Antonio Labriola. For once, though, events in Ireland appeared more urgent than elsewhere; Joyce's interest was caught in particular by the emergence in 1905 of Sinn Féin under the leadership of Arthur Griffith and the prospect it seemed to extend for Irish economic and cultural independence. Joyce's own position, expounded in a crucial letter to Stanislaus of 6 November 1906, combined a socialist and nationalist politics qualified only by an innate distrust of Celtic revivalism: he might, he rather sniffily remarked, consider himself a nationalist if it were not for the continual insistence on the language question. In the meantime he was content to consider himself to be a self-conscious, and no doubt ultimately repudiated, cultural and political exile. Ireland, however, remained a long way away.

Nearer to home, Joyce felt impelled to choose between a numbing clerical routine that sapped his imaginative energy and the search for a style
of life that made it possible to write. The decision was abruptly made: in
February 1907 Joyce submitted his notice to his employers and the family
returned to Trieste and Stanislaus.

Towards a *Portrait of the Artist*: 1907–14

Back in Trieste, Joyce settled quickly into a renewed round of teaching
supplemented by occasional journalism for the newspaper *Il Piccolo
Della* to which he contributed a series of articles on the subject of Ireland
and Empire. This routine was momentarily disturbed by the birth of his
daughter Lucia in July 1907, but still permitted him sufficient leisure to
rethink the style and structure of *Stephen Hero*. Joyce now conceived of
the book as the gradual development of an aesthetic sensibility throughout five long sections; this structure eventually formed the basis of
Portrait. He had still not accomplished the stylistic breakthroughs that
would bring his new novel into focus and the manuscript was once more
set aside. Joyce was temporarily brought low that July by an attack of
rheumatic fever, which was the first of a series of breakdowns in his
health; an outbreak of iritis the following year anticipated the severe eye
trouble that would afflict and often incapacitate him for the rest of his
life. Despite these difficulties and the depression of his spirits caused by
the continuing lack of progress concerning *Dubliners*, Joyce found the
energy to travel with Giorgio to Dublin in 1909, his first return for five
years. The visit had one happy consequence: Joyce was able to restore
cordial relations with a father still resentful of his abrupt elopement in
1904. His spirits were further uplifted when he secured an agreement
with the Dublin publishers Maunsel and Co. to bring out *Dubliners*.
Accompanied by Giorgio and his younger sister Eva, Joyce returned to
Trieste in good heart; barely a month later he was back again in Dublin.
Eva's astonishment that Dublin did not have a single one of Trieste's
myriad cinemas caught her brother's imagination: he determined to find
a business syndicate to back his plans to bring modern cinema to the
benighted Irish (and himself a handsome profit in the process). Joyce
eventually found the necessary backing from a group who had successfully pioneered cinemas in Trieste and the Cinematograph Volta in
Bucharest. Fired with enthusiasm, and the prospect of 10 per cent of the
profits, he obtained a hall and a licence for a Cinematograph Volta in
Dublin; the cinema opened in December 1909 to mild local interest, but
dwindling returns and poor management forced its closure a few months

later without Joyce receiving any of his anticipated remuneration. More bad news awaited him. Concerned about their potential legal liability for printing objectionable material, Maunsel and Co. backtracked upon their plan to publish *Dubliners*. Joyce's exasperated negotiation with the firm lasted a further fruitless two years, a period of emotional strain that greatly impaired his powers of composition. At one point close to despair, Joyce threw a manuscript section of *Portrait* into the fire; only the prompt intercession of his sister Eileen rescued it from incineration. His mood turning from despair to fury, Joyce composed an involved history of his alleged mistreatment at the hands of Richards and Maunsel and Co. and sent it to the Irish press; it made its idiosyncratic appearance in the pages of *Sinn Féin* in September 1911.

Joyce was once more back in Dublin in the summer of 1912. Nora's week-long absence from Trieste while visiting her relatives in Galway had whipped him into a jealous fury; after three or four days of increasingly lurid foreboding of her faithlessness, he could bear the separation no longer and followed her to Ireland. While in Dublin, Joyce made one last desperate effort to propel Maunsel and Co. into publishing *Dubliners*. He agreed reluctantly to delete 'An Encounter', a story about a schoolboy's ambiguous meeting with a pederast, and to indemnify the publisher against the cost of the first edition if it were to be seized by the police. George Roberts, Maunsel and Co.'s cautious managing director, now for-mulated a new set of complaints against the book: he demanded that Joyce change the first paragraph of 'Grace', three paragraphs in 'Ivy Day', sections of 'The Boarding House', and every proper name the stories con-tained (Ellmann 1983: 334). Upon receipt of Joyce's angry refusal to meet these conditions, Roberts suggested he buy the typesheets of *Dubliners* for £50 and have the book printed himself. Joyce agreed to this scheme, but Roberts' printer intervened, refusing to hand over typesheets containing material so defamatory to Ireland. The entire sorry business came to a conclusion on 11 September 1912 when the printer summarily destroyed the typesheets before Joyce could reclaim them. Desolate and furious, Joyce left Ireland that same night, never to return. He occupied his journey back to Trieste in composing 'The Holy Office', a scabrous poetic satire upon Irish hypocrisy and Ireland's censorious printers. From this time on, he would revisit Ireland only in his imagination.

Both Joyce's spirits and his finances improved a little in 1913 when he was appointed to a teaching position at a Triestine high school, the Scuola Superiore di Commercio Revoltella. His teaching duties were not onerous, and he continued to supplement his income by taking on private students. One of these students, who has been tentatively identified as

Amalia Popper, was to play a small but significant part in Joyce's life. Joyce conceived a passion for this young woman and began to meet her outside classes; a year later, in the summer of 1914, he would write a history of his infatuation under the self-deprecatory title *Giacomo Joyce*. The 'affair', such as it was, seems to have consisted mainly of furtive meetings and bouts of intense conversation; it petered out gently a year after it began. Joyce's biographer Richard Ellmann speculates that Amalia Popper's 'Southern European looks' may well have given him another model for Molly Bloom in *Ulysses*; the fact that she was the daughter of a Jewish businessman whose first name was Leopoldo only makes the identification more tempting (Ellmann 1983: 342). What is certain is that Joyce's relationship with this young woman, consummated or otherwise, reawakened him to imaginative life after the depressive effects of his recent disappointments. Spurred on by romantic infatuation, whilst vulnerable to the ennui that such attachment so often provokes, Joyce composed a number of new poems, some of which made their appearance a decade later in *Pomes Penyeach*. The same intense feelings also led him in *Giacomo Joyce* to mine a vein of self-conscious and hyperbolic lyricism that would come later to characterise some of Stephen Dedalus' more precocious effusions in *Portrait*:

> My voice, dying in the echoes of its words, dies like the wisdom-wearied voice of the Eternal calling on Abraham through echoing hills. She leans back against the pillowed wall: odalisque-featured in the luxurious obscurity. Her eyes have drunk my thoughts: and into the moist yielding welcoming darkness of her womanhood my soul, itself dissolving, has streamed and poured and flooded a liquid and abundant seed . . . Take her now who will! (*GJ*: 14)

In retrospect, Joyce needed the boost to his spirits that *Giacomo Joyce* supplied. Both Martin Secker and Elkin Matthews rejected *Dubliners* in quick succession in 1913, leaving his literary career as uncertain as before.

Breakthrough

If 1914 was to prove perhaps the most significant year of Joyce's life (1904 and 1922 are the other principal contenders), two letters that he received at the end of 1913 marked a decisive shift in his fortunes. The first was from Grant Richards, asking to consider *Dubliners* one more time; the second was from Ezra Pound, the American poet, critic and cultural *provocateur*, asking if Joyce had any work he might submit to a new literary magazine called the *Egoist*. Before Joyce could reply to the second letter, Pound wrote again praising Joyce's poem 'I Hear an Army' and asking to include it in his anthology *Des Imagistes*. Joyce happily accepted the invitation, and quickly dispatched to Pound the first part of *Portrait*. Pound was immediately impressed by the quality and originality of Joyce's prose and commended it to the *Egoist*; the magazine began to serialise the novel in February 1914. The sudden appearance of *Portrait* in print recalled Joyce to the fact that he had yet to complete the novel; he spent the next six months sedulously writing and revising its second and third sections. The serialisation of *Portrait* in the *Egoist* considerably sharpened Joyce's profile within British literary culture and made the publication of *Dubliners* a more attractive commercial proposition. Suitably emboldened, Joyce wrote to Richards on 19 January 1914 informing him of his novel's imminent serialisation and requesting a definite decision concerning his stories. Ten days later Richards finally agreed to publish *Dubliners*, bringing down the curtain on an almost decade-long dispute. Less than five months later, on 15 June, *Dubliners* finally appeared, to polite if somewhat indifferent reviews, but absolutely no legal objection. Meanwhile the outbreak of World War One in the summer and autumn of the year (Austria declared war on Serbia on 28 July 1914; Britain entered the conflict two months later) proved in one way rather fortuitous for Joyce: the serialisation of *Portrait* was abruptly suspended, giving him time to complete the novel's last two parts. *Portrait* was eventually completed in the first months of 1915, by which time Joyce was already at work upon *Ulysses* and beginning to write *Exiles*.

Joyce appeared supremely unconcerned by the advent of war; his indifference continued even after Italy entered the conflict in May 1915. His curious indifference to national and international political turmoil would later characterise his response to the Easter Rising of 1916 in Dublin; he sympathised up to a point with the rebels' resistance to the coercions of the British state, but felt resignedly that the entire enterprise was doomed from the beginning. This iconoclastic attitude notwithstanding, his life was to be disturbed by the war in several ways. Heedless of the change in domestic political circumstances wrought by the conflict, Stanislaus persisted in his irredentist politics; in January 1915 his outbursts against the constricting influence of the papacy and the Austro-Hungarian Empire led to his arrest and internment in an Austrian detention camp for the duration of the war. Meanwhile Italy's participation in the conflict necessarily made the Austro-Hungarian authorities wary of Trieste's considerable Italian population; fearing the onset of repressive military measures against foreigners, Joyce decided to move his family from Trieste to neutral Zurich in June. He had by this time virtually completed *Exiles* and was already proceeding smoothly with *Ulysses*: he had the first two episodes of the novel in draft by the beginning of June. Joyce was encouraged at this time to receive a letter from the American publisher B. W. Huebsch signalling an interest in bringing out an American edition of *Dubliners*. Huebsch lacked the requisite funds to commit himself to an edition at the present time, but he did manage to persuade his friend H. L. Mencken to accept 'A Little Cloud' and 'The Boarding House' for publication in the May 1915 edition of the small, but influential American magazine *Smart Set*.

Zurich

The Zurich within which Joyce now took his place was a European capital already alive to the stirrings of international modernism. It was here, in venues such as the Café Voltaire, that new movements like surrealism and Dadaism first began to find their voice. Joyce settled in his usual way by offering English lessons and touring the bars and cafés, but unknown to him his circumstances were about to take a favourable turn. Alerted to the fact of Joyce's hurried relocation, W. B. Yeats managed to secure him a grant of £75 from the Royal Literary Fund in July 1915. Not to be outdone, a year later Ezra Pound agitated for and obtained an award of £100 for Joyce from the Civil List. These generous bequests sustained him through a year beset with problems. News that the printers of the *Egoist* had raised objections over the content of *Portrait* provided Joyce with an unwelcome reminder of his difficulties with *Dubliners*; his anxieties increased when Grant Richards, Martin Secker and Duckworths turned down the manuscript in quick succession. At this time Joyce was also trying to find a theatre willing to put on *Exiles*; he sent it hopefully to the Abbey Theatre, but Yeats regretfully declined it towards the end of the year. Joyce's spirits dipped perceptibly, but Pound and Harriet Weaver, the editor of the *Egoist* who would play a prominent supporting role in Joyce's life over the next twenty-five years, undertook to find him a publisher for his work. Their quest took them to America; eventually Harriet Weaver informed Joyce that B. W. Huebsch was prepared to bring out an American edition of *Portrait*. The news was, in fact, even better than they imagined, for in December 1916 Huebsch published both *Dubliners* and *Portrait* in New York within weeks of one another. *Portrait*, in particular, garnered some favourable American reviews; encouraged by this, Harriet Weaver brought out an

English edition of the novel in February 1917. Her initial print run of 750 copies sold out completely in less than six months.

Disaster struck Joyce in early 1917 when his eyes were afflicted by a severe attack of glaucoma and synechia, two conditions that could lead to complete blindness. He was confined to his apartment for most of the spring; his condition made writing almost impossible. This outbreak was the prelude to another severe attack in August which necessitated an operation that permanently reduced the vision in his right eye. But Joyce was then rescued by the uncanny good fortune that always seemed to present itself when he had reached his lowest ebb. An anonymous benefactor made him a gift of £200 in four instalments, and in August he received word that Richards had finally agreed to publish *Exiles*. The first bequest was supplemented a year later by another anonymous bestowal of the not inconsiderable sum of about 1,000 Swiss francs (roughly £40) a month; this arrangement came into effect in March 1918 and continued for some eighteen months. Curious as to the identity of his mysterious supporter, Joyce eventually established his second patron to be Mrs Harold McCormick, a thespian and reputedly one of the richest women in Zurich (Ellmann 1983: 412). These two awards enabled him to devote himself full time to composition; by early 1918 he had revised the first three episodes of *Ulysses* to the point where they were ready to be published. Joyce dispatched these episodes to Pound, who judged them excellent, and advised him to send them to Margaret Anderson and Jane Heap's *Little Review*, a small avant-garde American magazine. Publication of *Ulysses* in serial form officially began in the *Little Review* in March 1918.

An unforeseen consequence of Joyce's unexpected financial good fortune was a bizarre legal entanglement that ultimately received bleakly comic expression in *Ulysses*. Temporarily awash with funds, Joyce agreed to enter into partnership with one of his café-friends, Claude Sykes, in order to produce a number of plays in English for the Zurich stage. They gave their company the grandiloquent name of 'The English Players': Sykes was to function as producer and director, while Joyce, unbelievably enough, was accorded the role of business manager. After a brief struggle Joyce received official approval for the players from the British Consul-General A. Percy Bennett – Bennett, it appears, was disgruntled with Joyce for failing to offer wartime service – and the company prepared an inaugural production of *The Importance of Being Earnest* (Ellmann 1983: 423). The company's fortunes worsened dramatically when Joyce nominated Henry Carr, a minor consular official, for the part of Algernon. Although the production passed off well enough in April 1918, Carr became incensed when he received only ten francs payment for his prominent role, and angrily demanded remuneration for the clothes he had bought to dress his character. Never a diplomat, Joyce then threw petrol onto the flames by not merely refusing Carr's request but demanding money from him for the sale of tickets. At this point Carr snapped, calling Joyce a swindler, and allegedly threatening him with violence. His pride affronted, Joyce tried first to have Carr dismissed from the consular service; and failing in this objective, he instituted legal proceedings against him for libel and money owed for tickets. The legal suits dragged on for almost a year: Joyce won the second, with an award of sixty francs; he eventually lost the libel case, but managed, by pleading poverty, to escape with paying only fifty francs in damages. He would, however, take his revenge in literary form in the 'Circe' episode of *Ulysses*, where Bennett and Carr are depicted as the two drunken and loutish British soldiers who assault Stephen Dedalus in the street.

It was also in 1918 that Joyce first made the acquaintance of the English painter Frank Budgen. Budgen was to become perhaps Joyce's closest friend during the second half of his life: in Zurich the two met regularly to drink and discuss writing, art and the various affairs of the day. It was to Budgen that Joyce gave his most detailed explanation of the literary style and Homeric framework of *Ulysses*; Budgen's subsequent account of these conversations, *James Joyce and the Making of Ulysses*, provides the most intimate and detailed record of the novel's composition. In May Joyce's attention was momentarily distracted from *Ulysses* by the happy news of the publication of *Exiles*: the play was brought out simultaneously by Huebsch in the United States and Grant Richards in England. *Exiles* later received its first performance in Munich in August 1919 where it played to small audiences and disappointing reviews. Meanwhile Joyce pressed on remorselessly with *Ulysses*, writing as frequently and for as long as his iritis permitted. He progressed at a steady pace, completing upon average an episode every two to three months from March 1918 to October 1921 when the novel was finally completed. He continued to publish episodes in the *Little Review*, although he soon longed for an agreement to publish the novel in its entirety. He was encouraged in this hope by favourable references to the extant parts by T. S. Eliot and Ezra Pound (although Pound's nervousness about Joyce's cloacal preoccupation offered a grim portent of the legal difficulties Joyce was soon to encounter); however, Harriet Weaver's attempt to persuade Leonard and Virginia Woolf to publish *Ulysses* at their new Hogarth Press met with little success.

In the summer of 1919 Joyce took the decision to leave Zurich. He had a number of reasons for wishing to depart: he had already lived in the city for four years, both food and accommodation were expensive, and the climate appeared to have had a deleterious effect upon his health. His relationship with Mrs McCormick had also suddenly worsened; a keen devotee of the new psychoanalytical method, she appears to have been piqued by Joyce's refusal to consult her acquaintance C. G. Jung, and soon after ceased to remit him funds. The confluence of these factors lent Joyce's memories of Trieste a golden sheen; in October he returned his family to the city they had left so precipitately in the middle of war. The loss of Mrs McCormick's patronage left him more financially constrained, although his situation had been considerably ameliorated before leaving Zurich by the receipt of another mysterious anonymous bequest. A solicitor's telegram informed Joyce that an unnamed client wished to settle £5,000 pounds upon him; it was to be several months before he discovered that the benefactor was his friend and supporter Harriet Weaver. Money, however, had the unfortunate habit of running through Joyce's fingers; to assure himself of the semblance of a steady income, he returned to his former teaching position at the Scuola Superiore di Commercio Revoltella. He was by now hard at work upon the 'Nausicaa' and 'Oxen of the Sun' episodes of *Ulysses*. For the character of Gerty McDowell he drew upon his memories of a young Swiss woman. While still in Zurich at the end of 1918, Joyce had embarked upon a brief relationship with Marthe Fleischmann, whose dreamy romantic affectation and cultivated self-regard awoke his comic instincts even as he strove vainly to seduce her. The furtive 'affair' was often conducted through letters; Marthe's role in this illicit and incongruous correspondence may well also have inspired the character of Martha Clifford in *Ulysses*. The composition of 'Oxen in the Sun', in particular, considerably drained Joyce's creative resources; he also missed his expansive and thought-provoking conversations with Budgen; while his relations with Stanislaus, understandably unsettled by the sudden return of his effortlessly superior older brother, were strained. An unexpected invitation from Pound to visit him in the warmer clime of Sirmione, by Lake Garda, lightened his mood; Joyce fulfilled this engagement in August 1920, thereby occasioning the first meeting of these two great modernist pioneers. In Sirmione, Pound counselled Joyce to consider leaving Trieste and joining him in Paris. He would then be living in one of the most cosmopolitan and dynamic cultural centres in the world; and in Paris he could try to arrange French editions of his fiction. Joyce took Pound's advice to heart and, a month later, the Joyce family rejoined Pound in the

French capital. He had now arrived in the city in which he would complete one masterpiece, write another, and live out all but one of the remaining years of his life.

Paris

After Trieste, Joyce found Paris initially to be a disorientating whirl of sensation. With a son of 15 and a daughter of 13 also feeling the effect of the displacement, he felt the need to settle quickly. Fortunately for Joyce, Pound had already begun to put his considerable energy to work on his behalf by arranging for Madame Ludmilla Bloch-Savitsky to translate *Portrait* into French. Such was Pound's power of persuasion that the translation was begun without an agreement to publish the novel in place; a contract was subsequently signed with Édition de la Sirène in August 1921, although the book would not appear for another three years. Joyce soon settled sufficiently to turn his attention back to *Ulysses*; the composition of the long episode 'Circe' occupied him for the entire second half of 1920. Not long after he had recommenced the novel, a meeting of considerable import took place. While attending a literary soirée in July, Joyce was approached by an American woman, Sylvia Beach, who had the year previously opened a bookshop called Shakespeare and Company in the city. Joyce warmed to Beach's intelligent sympathy for his work and visited her bookshop the following day. Although neither could know it at the time, the subsequent publication of *Ulysses* had its roots in this encounter. Acclimatising himself to Paris afforded Joyce yet another opportunity to live beyond his means; his financial situation was salvaged once more by the remarkable and long-suffering Harriet Weaver, who sent him the munificent sum of £2,000 to underwrite the completion of his novel. Notwithstanding the fact that he had not yet completed *Ulysses*, interest in Joyce grew quickly, encouraged assiduously by Pound; visitors were keen to catch a glimpse of the enigmatic Irishman in their midst. One famous visit to Joyce in August 1920 by T. S. Eliot and Wyndham Lewis was not a success; the combination of the reserved American, the irascible Canadian and the elaborately formal Dubliner proved agreeable to none of their tastes. Lewis subsequently contributed a sardonic account of the meeting in his memoir *Blasting and Bombardiering* (Lewis 1937: 74–6).

Despite agonising bouts of iritis in May and July 1921, Joyce pressed on with the last three episodes of *Ulysses*. His renewed urgency did not compromise his fastidious attention to even the smallest detail; letters continued to be sent to relatives and friends requesting clarification on every aspect of Dublin geography, history and architecture. One such letter to his aunt Josephine Murray asking for information subsequently utilised in 'Eumaeus' gives a flavour of the whole by making explicit the connection between the height of a Dublin railing and the wording of a paragraph (Joyce L: 175). After the catechistic complexity of 'Ithaca', the associative drift of Molly's night-thoughts in 'Penelope' came easily to Joyce; and he finally completed *Ulysses* on 29 October 1921. He had now produced his masterpiece; but the battle to see it into print had only just begun.

The Scandal of *Ulysses*

The difficulties Joyce experienced getting *Dubliners* published were to be reproduced on a larger scale with *Ulysses*. Joyce's second novel is now regarded as a modernist classic, but the history of its publication was characterised by frequent legal skirmishes concerning censorship and the right to free expression. Instalments of *Ulysses* continued to appear in the *Little Review* throughout 1918 and 1919 despite the intensifying interest of the American postal authorities, who maintained a vigilant stand against the transmission of obscene and legally questionable material. With two-thirds of the novel in manuscript, Joyce was looking by the middle of 1919 to secure a more regular source of publication. He was therefore encouraged by the interest of Harriet Weaver, who was keen to publish the manuscript in book form. In a development that must have recalled to Joyce dark memories of his dispute with Grant Richards, Harriet Weaver was soon to withdraw her interest after a succession of printers refused to set the typescript of the novel. In these unnerving circumstances Joyce decided to seek an American publisher, although the decision of the United States Post Office to seize and burn four issues of the *Little Review* containing the *Ulysses* extracts was a bleak portent of the troubles ahead. Joyce offered the manuscript to B. W. Huebsch, the company that had published the American editions of all his previous work, but Huebsch was unwilling to commit itself to an immediate decision. This circumspection proved warranted when, in September 1920, a formal complaint against the *Little Review* was lodged by the New York Society for the Suppression of Vice.

The legal prosecution of *Ulysses* came to an American court in February 1921. The principal cause of complaint was the *Little Review*'s publication of the 'Nausicaa' section with its disclosure of Gerty MacDowell's undergarments and Bloom's onanistic response. The case was defended unenthusiastically by the New York lawyer John Quinn, who had earlier warned the magazine editors that publication was liable to lead to legal action. The court proceedings were not without their comic aspects, which were generally inspired by the ingenuity of Quinn's defence. If Joyce's work was as incomprehensible as most pejorative critics claimed, Quinn wondered, how could it be said to outrage public decency? Moreover, if discussion of *Ulysses* led to the kind of violent denunciation of its contents typified by the prosecution, how could the novel be deemed to have a corrupting effect upon public morals? Despite Quinn's fleet footwork, the judges found the editors guilty of publishing obscene material and fined each of them the token sum of fifty dollars.

The chief consequence of this judicial reverse was to make publication of *Ulysses* even more legally perilous and commercially unattractive. Huebsch accordingly declined to publish the novel without substantial deletions, all of which Joyce refused to contemplate. Into the breach stepped Joyce's Parisian acquaintance Sylvia Beach, who proposed to bring out a copy of the novel under the imprint of Shakespeare and Company. Her proposition was supported by the intervention of Harriet Weaver, who undertook to publish an English edition of *Ulysses* under the imprimatur of the Egoist Press, while giving Joyce another £200 as an advance on future royalties. Joyce gratefully accepted both contracts and *Ulysses* was eventually published in Paris to coincide with Joyce's fortieth birthday on 2 February 1922.

The publication of *Ulysses* did not put an end to the controversies surrounding the novel. In the second half of 1922 American censorship authorities confiscated and destroyed 500 copies of the Egoist edition, while a similar quantity were seized by English customs authorities at Folkestone. The novel was subsequently banned in Britain. Indeed, during the first few years of the appearance of *Ulysses* the novel was concurrently suppressed in Britain and America, two territories within which it might otherwise have enjoyed an early and widespread readership. *Ulysses* did acquire some initial champions – important early critical support appeared in the form of T. S. Eliot's review 'Ulysses, Order and Myth' in *The Dial* of 1923 and Stuart Gilbert's 1930 study *James Joyce's Ulysses* which drew on discussions with Joyce to explicate the novel's underlying design – but its public profile remained that of an obscure and proscribed book. This situation was complicated further in 1926 when news reached Joyce from America that Samuel Roth, proprietor of the magazine *Two Worlds* in which Joyce had previously placed extracts from *Work in Progress* (the working title of *Finnegans Wake*), was publishing pirated instalments of *Ulysses*. Because the copyright of *Ulysses* was not protected by American law, Roth proceeded to publish an amended version of the Telemachiad (the first three episodes of the novel) without seeking Joyce's approval or remitting any payment to him. Joyce responded by organising an international protest against Roth's piratical practices. The letter of protest condemning Roth eventually attracted 167 signatures, including those of Albert Einstein, Ernest Hemingway, T. S. Eliot and Benedetto Croce. Roth was ultimately compelled to cease publication by a judgement of the Supreme Court in October 1928. Meanwhile the breadth and quality of the international support for *Ulysses* propelled the debate surrounding the novel beyond vague rumours about its 'scandalous' contents and refocused attention upon its status as an innovative and challenging work of art.

The Road to *Finnegans Wake*

The composition of *Finnegans Wake* occupied Joyce for sixteen of his last eighteen years. He began his enigmatically entitled *Work in Progress* in Paris in March 1923; the title was supplied by Ford Madox Ford, who published the first extract of the novel in his *transatlantic review* in January 1924. Joyce worked initially with great speed and energy; although the four main sections of the completed novel were not to be completed until November 1938 he had finished much of Parts 1 and 2 by 1926. However, a number of factors seriously retarded his progress. The deterioration of his eyesight now gravely limited the time he could spend at his desk; he had had to endure eight eye operations by the end of 1925. The descent of his daughter Lucia into schizophrenia in the mid-1920s also proved a source of considerable emotional anxiety. Perhaps most damagingly of all, the published extracts of his manuscript met with a barrage of critical rejection and ridicule. To take one example, the 'Anna Livia Plurabelle' section that concludes the first narrative movement, now considered one of Joyce's most brilliantly sustained passages of lyrical prose and which became the subject of his famous 1932 recording, was greeted with incomprehension when first published in the French Magazine *Le Navire d'Argent* in October 1925. Elsewhere English printers simply refused to typeset it for the *Calendar of Modern Letters*. Closer to home, Stanislaus condemned the entire project as a tiresome bore, never to change his opinion ('I for one would not read more than a paragraph of it, if I did not know you,' he wrote to his brother in August 1924), and Ezra Pound, hitherto Joyce's stalwart champion, refused to accept extracts of *Work in Progress* for *The Egoist* (*L*: 103). In the late summer of 1926 the New York *Dial*, to which Joyce had submitted for consideration some passages from the second narrative movement, first hesitated over publishing the material, then called for deletions, before eventually rejecting the manuscript. Chastened by this reverse, Joyce ceded a little ground to his critics by sending his now famous letter to Harriet Weaver of 15 November 1926, which contained a brief interpretative key to the opening pages of the novel. He was, however, further deflated by a letter from Pound the same month, with its peremptory judgement upon the extant sections: 'Nothing so far as I can make out, nothing short of divine vision or a new cure for the clapp can possibly be worth all the circumambient peripherization' (L: 145).

Joyce's labours upon *Work in Progress* received a significant boost when he met Eugene Jolas at the end of 1926. A self-consciously avant-garde writer and thinker, Jolas was seeking to effect nothing less than a revolution in language and sensibility. With his wife Maria, he founded the surrealist and avant-garde Parisian magazine *transition*, which they described somewhat grandiloquently as 'An International Quarterly for Creative Expression'. Jolas was captivated by *Work in Progress*, judging it to be one of the great modern breakthroughs in technique for which he had been searching; he arranged to publish extracts from it serially in *transition* from April 1927. Such support may, in the short term, have done Joyce's cause more harm than good because his work was published alongside Eugene Jolas' provocative manifesto 'The Revolution of the Word' which, with its exultation of the unfettered freedom of the creative artist and its disdain for the 'plain reader', helped to fashion an image of Joyce as a maverick and self-indulgent obscurantist. His isolation was further compounded by the scathing assault on his work perpetrated by Wyndham Lewis in his *Time and Western Man*. So disillusioned had Joyce become by 1927 that, in one of the most astonishing episodes of modern literary history, he considered handing the entire project over to his acolyte, the poet James Stephens, for completion.

The generally adverse criticism of *Work in Progress* by his friends and family had a profound effect upon Joyce. His first reaction, apart from dismay, was to take one step backwards in order to keep moving forwards. Perhaps to demonstrate that he was still capable of composing in a less boldly experimental style, Joyce showed his friends the slim collection of poetry he had completed since the publication of *Chamber Music*. Upon receiving a broadly appreciative response – Pound dissented on the grounds of the poetry's archaism and languidly Edwardian sensibility – he decided to have the poems published under the jocular title *Pomes Penyeach*. The volume was published by Shakespeare and Company in July 1927; it appeared to an almost universal critical silence. Keen, meanwhile, to display the sheer stylistic variety of *Work in Progress*, Joyce arranged for the independent publication of the lyrical and melodious 'Anna Livia Plurabelle' section, which was brought out in a small edition by Crosby Gaige in New York in October 1928. If this move was intended to placate his critics, it paid no immediate dividend: the book quickly met with a hostile review in T. S. Eliot's *Criterion* magazine.

However, Joyce's friends and supporters rallied to his side by publishing a collection of critical essays defending and explicating *Work in Progress* entitled *Our Exagmination Round his Factification for Incamination of Work in Progress* (Joyce himself provided the slyly ironic title) in May 1929. The volume contained an essay by a young Irishman named Samuel Beckett, who would go on to become Joyce's friend and amanuensis; many years later Beckett would receive the Nobel Prize for Literature. That Joyce still felt the need to defend, or at the very least draw attention to, his work was also suggested by the assistance he gave to Stuart Gilbert in completing his introductory guide *James Joyce's Ulysses* in 1930. Not content with helping to explain his work, Joyce also felt the need to explain his life. In 1930 he began to search for a biographer worthy of this momentous subject. He believed that he had discovered such an individual in Hebert Gorman, to whom 'he made it clear that he was to be treated as a saint with an unusually protracted martyrdom' (Ellmann 1983: 631). Gorman's biographical labours would take almost a decade to complete, due in no small measure to Joyce's continual interference and demand for revisions; the book would not appear until 1941, the year of Joyce's death. While setting in train a narrative account of his life, Joyce also took steps to legalise his relationship with Nora; the pair were married on 4 July 1931, while on a visit to London.

Joyce was struck a severe blow by the death of his father on 29 November 1931. The pair had often quarrelled, and had not met for many years; nevertheless Joyce's fiction resonated to the sound of his father's sayings, and the two had grown close through correspondence. So distraught was Joyce at his father's death that he felt he could no longer continue with *Work in Progress*; the feeling eventually passed, but his spirits remained depressed for several months. A brief respite arrived three months later when Giorgio and his wife Helen presented him with a grandson, Stephen, who would become one of the delights of his last decade. To eulogise his father and mark the birth of his grandson Joyce composed 'Ecce Puer', which, in the delicate counterpoint of its final stanza, looks out tentatively upon the future while continuing to mourn the past. His unhappiness was compounded by Lucia's eventual collapse into profound mental illness; despite Joyce's, and particularly Nora's, best efforts to accommodate her abrupt shifts of mood and increasingly bizarre behaviour within the family home, she was about to begin her itinerant progress through a series of mental institutions. His daughter's perilous situation compromised to some degree the pleasure Joyce felt when B. W. Huebsch secured the pre-publication rights for *Finnegans Wake* at the end of 1931 and Random House bought the American rights for *Ulysses* in February 1932. However, these two agreements signalled an upswing in Joyce's literary fortunes which continued with the appearance of a new edition of *Ulysses* by the happily named Odyssey Press later the same year incorporating new proofs corrected by Stuart Gilbert. Joyce had long sought an English edition of *Ulysses*; after a number of false starts precipitated by fears of legal prosecution, his wish was granted in January 1934 when John Lane agreed to publish the novel. In keeping with the history of *Ulysses*, there were still obstacles to be negotiated along the way: a printer's rebellion suspended publication in the summer of 1934; and it would be two more years before the novel was published in England.

During the long and difficult genesis of *Finnegans Wake*, Joyce was sustained, as ever, by Nora, and also by Paul Leon, a young Russian émigré he met in the early 1930s, who had a stabilising influence upon several aspects of the writer's life. Functioning both as Joyce's secretary and companion, Leon organised his correspondence, assisted with the French translation of 'Anna Livia Plurabelle', negotiated on Joyce's behalf for the English edition of *Ulysses*, and even, at once point, helped to decorate his flat. At this time Joyce was also frequently in the company of Samuel Beckett, to whom he sometimes dictated portions of *Work in Progress* in his Parisian flat. Beckett had earlier been the luckless subject of Lucia's romantic attention, and his relations with Joyce had cooled after his rejection of her; by the mid-1930s they had been restored sufficiently for Beckett to provide a fascinating insight into one feature of Joyce's compositional method:

> Once or twice [Joyce] dictated a bit of *Finnegans Wake* to Beckett, though dictation did not work very well for him; in the middle of one such session there was a knock at the door which Beckett did not hear. Joyce said, 'Come in,' and Beckett wrote it down. Afterwards he read back what he had written and Joyce said, 'What's that Come in'? 'Yes, you said that,' said Beckett. Joyce thought for a moment, then said 'Let it stand.' He was quite willing to accept coincidence as his collaborator. Beckett was fascinated and thwarted by Joyce's singular method. (Ellmann 1983: 649)

A renewed bout of concentrated literary activity from the beginning of 1937 drove *Work in Progress* towards its conclusion. Occasionally Joyce thought of making a trip back to Ireland, but the plans never advanced beyond conjecture. As European politics lurched towards catastrophe, he often affected in conversation a studied indifference to political matters: had he not, in any case, exposed the horror of racism and extreme nationalism once and for all in *Ulysses*? Whatever the face he turned to public affairs, Joyce's sympathies were aroused by the plight of European Jewry and he intervened through contacts to help a number of his Jewish acquaintances secure safe passage to America and Ireland. He was also greatly troubled by the situation of Lucia, who was currently incarcerated in a Parisian sanatorium; his fears for her safety were temporarily assuaged by news of plans to evacuate patients from the city if the imminent threat of German invasion were realised. It was in these momentous and trying circumstances that *Work in Progress* was finished. By the autumn of 1938, Joyce was left with only the last pages of the novel to finish; he composed the marvellous climax of Anna Livia Plurabelle's final monologue in less than a week. *Finnegans Wake* was eventually completed on 13 November 1938. Superstitious as ever, Joyce was desperate to have the book published on his birthday three months later; he spent the intervening period in a blizzard of revisions and proof-reading. In one sense his wish was realised: an advance copy of the novel was dispatched to him by Faber and Faber on 30 January 1939; his fifty-seventh birthday on 2 February could now be turned into a triumphant celebration. Three months later, after a sixteen-year gestation, *Finnegans Wake* was officially launched upon an unsuspecting world.

Last Days

Finnegans Wake was published simultaneously in London and New York on 4 May 1939. The reviews it attracted were, in the main, either bemused or hostile; Joyce was gratified by the sympathetic account of the novel offered by Harry Levin, but resigned himself to the fact that the novel was likely to remain at odds with critical opinion for some time to come. But by this time Joyce had more than unsympathetic critical reviews to occupy his attention. The rapid military advance of Nazism cast a huge shadow over continental Europe; within a year France would succumb to German occupation. Joyce realised that life in Paris was rapidly becoming untenable; but Lucia's parlous mental state made it difficult for the family to leave the city. Eventually Joyce was able to move the family south to Saint-Gerard-Le-Pay over Christmas 1939; even though the German Army briefly occupied the town in June 1940 the family was left unharmed. Following an exhausting quest for exit visas and permission to leave the country – Joyce refused upon principle to apply for an Irish passport that would enable him to leave France as a citizen of a neutral country – the entire Joyce family was allowed to depart for Zurich in neutral Switzerland in December 1940. Joyce's respite was, though, destined to be brief. On 9 January 1941 he was rushed to hospital suffering from a perforated duodenal ulcer; he died from complications following surgery four days later. He was buried the next day in the Fluntern cemetery; loyal to the last, Nora spared him the indignity of a religious service.

Further Reading

Despite being subjected to Joyce's close critical supervision, and constrained by the fact that the volume concludes in the middle of 1939, some eighteen months before Joyce's death, Herbert Gorman's early biography (Gorman 1941) still repays attention. It is lucidly written, tightly organised and provides a wealth of information concerning Joyce's imaginative development and his years in Trieste and Paris. Both Stanislaus Joyce's *Complete Dublin Diary* (Stanislaus Joyce 1971) and his unfinished memoir *My Brother's Keeper* (Stanislaus Joyce 1958) afford fascinating glimpses of Joyce's early home life and university years. Although both books reverberate occasionally to the sound of domestic points being scored, Stanislaus is a generally very sympathetic reader of his brother's character: the anecdotal evidence he supplies of Joyce's opinions, tastes and prejudices offers valuable contexts for the interpretation of his early work; and the diary, in particular, remains the best first-hand account of the genesis of *Stephen Hero*. Frank Budgen provides a captivating portrait of Joyce at work upon *Ulysses* in Trieste (Budgen 1934); his record of their conversations yields indispensable insights into Joyce's attitude to Homeric myth and his manipulation of style, character and plot. Joyce's letters to Sylvia Beach (Banta and Silverman 1987) yield valuable insights into the publication of *Ulysses*; these insights are amplified by Sylvia Beach's own recollections of this momentous episode in literary modernist history (Beach 1959). Ultimately, though, Ellmann (1983) represents the pinnacle of biographical work upon Joyce: comprehensive in its grasp of the social and historical circumstances of Joyce's era, astute in its literary and cultural judgements, dispassionate although warm in its assessment of Joyce's character, the product of refined intelligence and wide learning, it has been judged by many critics to be the greatest literary biography of the last century. Although subsequent critics have called into question aspects of Ellmann's reading of Joyce's politics (Nolan 1995), his study should still constitute the first port of call for the reader keen to discover more about Joyce's life and times. Such is the book's authority and richness of detail that its biographical judgements are unlikely ever to be seriously challenged.

Chapter 2
Work

Introduction

This chapter provides a descriptive account of, and critical commentary upon, the body of Joyce's work. Although space and consideration is given to representative work from each of the volumes Joyce published during his lifetime, the discussion pays particular attention to the four prose works upon which Joyce's literary reputation rests. While conforming throughout to the chronological order of Joyce's publications, this section nonetheless seeks to establish a number of thematic and stylistic connections between his works. Because any overview of Joyce's literary production must take account of the difficulties he faced actually seeing his work into print, brief attention is given to his struggle against the censorious pressure of publisher and printer: these issues are amplified in the discussions of Joyce's biography and critical reputation in Parts 1 and 3. The generally perceived 'difficulty' of Joyce's mature prose work has always been a complicating factor in its critical reception; in an effort to ease comprehension, the discussion of *Ulysses* and *Finnegans Wake* is divided into discrete sections corresponding to particular episodes or narrative movements of the works concerned. This arrangement of textual materials also assists the identification of a cluster of common novelistic themes that will become the explicit concern of Part 3.

Chamber Music (1907)

Although Joyce's international reputation was made as a novelist, his name first appeared to the public in the guise of a poet. His first published work was *Chamber Music*, a slim collection of lyric verse. It contained thirty-six poems individually identified by roman numerals in a verse sequence exploring the progress of a doomed love affair which, in their musicality and simplicity of organisation, harked back to the songs of the Elizabethan lyricists, Shakespeare and Shakespeare's contemporary, the composer John Dowland. Joyce's second volume of poetry, *Pomes Penyeach*, was published in 1927 during the composition of *Finnegans Wake*. These poems display a much freer and more expressionistic use of rhythm and imagery and convey a sharper and more ironic perspective upon private experience. The two volumes were brought together in Joyce's *Collected Poems* of 1936, to which Joyce added one of his most famous lyrics 'Ecce Puer'.

It is often forgotten that Joyce's poetry was included in the inaugural 1914 imagist anthology *Des Imagistes*. The strengths and weaknesses of his work come into relief when considered in the context of the imagist movement with which his work was directly contemporary. Imagist poetics sought to recover the precision and power of the image from its subordination to outmoded poetic language. Demanding the direct presentation of the image within a rhythm organic to the mode of sensibility it discloses, imagist writers rejected archaic diction, needless abstraction, false sonority, sentimentality, didacticism and narrative periphrasis. These hard-won lessons constitute the exacting standard against which the lyrics from *Chamber Music* may be judged. Here is poem II:

> The twilight turns from amethyst
> To deep and deeper blue,
> The lamp fills with a pale green glow
> The trees of the avenue.
>
> The old piano plays an air,
> Sedate and slow and gay;
> She bends upon the yellow keys,
> Her head inclines this way.
>
> Shy thoughts and grave wide eyes and hands
> That wander as they list –
> The twilight turns to darker blue
> With lights of amethyst. (*PSW*: 14)

Here simplicity of diction combines with sparseness of phrase to present the unadorned image; subtle modulation of rhythm (the unobtrusive expansiveness of 'Sedate and slow and gay') isolates and emphasises qualities of mood and atmosphere. The lyric's verbal economy reduces the landscape to a few resonant images; the unforced relationship between these images transforms a poetic landscape into a climate of feeling. Yet here, as elsewhere in *Chamber Music*, the formal strengths of the poem are undermined by weaknesses of conception and execution. Joyce's lapse into archaism of diction ('that wander as they list') betrays the slightly second-hand quality of the verse; its emotional poise is cheaply won because it is already familiar from the depiction of a thousand romantic attitudes: the world dissolving in fading evening light, the tinkling of a distant piano, the inclining head of the beloved bent in care or reverie. The mannered poverty of this type of attitudinising sentiment is on display throughout the sequence; it manifests itself in poem III where a forlorn lover is apotheosised as 'O lonely watcher of the skies' and the 'sighs / Of harps' entreat 'Love' to 'unclose' (does Joyce mean 'open'?) the 'pale gates of sunrise' (*PSW*: 15). Too often in *Chamber Music* clarity of poetic perspective disintegrates beneath the weight of a poeticising diction: 'And the night wind answering in antiphon / Till night is overgone?' (*PSW*: 15). Inevitably, the repetition of an exhausted poetic language leads occasionally to bathos: 'His song is softer than the dew / And he is come to visit you' (*PSW*: 16). Joyce's tonal and technical difficulties arise in part because he is attempting to reanimate dead material; the opening of poem IX '(Winds of May, that Dance on the Sea') could have been borrowed from any one of Yeats' 'Celtic Twilight' poems (*PSW*: 21). His larger problem is that he never appears certain if the effect intended by these lyrics is pathos or pastiche. Perhaps this ambivalence is what Joyce meant to suggest when he told Herbert Gorman that 'I wrote *Chamber Music* as a protest against myself' (Ellmann 1983: 149). Judged from the perspective of Joyce's entire career, however, the value of *Chamber Music* becomes clear. Here, for the first time, Joyce begins to inhabit a mode of speech without committing himself fully to the worldview it implies; this interplay between pathos and pastiche, and the ironic exactitudes it makes possible, later underpins the stylistic breakthrough of *Dubliners*. By the time Joyce wrote *Portrait*, his technical mastery of an ironically qualified lyricism enabled him to compose pastiche which was, from the point of view of Stephen Dedalus, the very measure of emotional sincerity:

> Are you not weary of ardent ways,
> Lure of the fallen seraphim?
> Tell no more of enchanted days.
> Your eyes have set man's heart ablaze
> And you have had your will of him.
> Are you not weary of ardent ways? (*P*: 188)

Further Reading

Joyce's poetry is generally considered to be a minor aspect of his overall artistic achievement; consequently it has received little exclusive critical attention. Kenner (1987; first published 1955) has a higher estimation of Joyce's poetry than most other critics; he contributes a chapter on *Chamber Music* expounding upon its ironic elegance and its indebtedness to the lyric modulations of Paul Verlaine and Ben Jonson. Parrinder (1984) is less effusive about the volume's merits, but usefully draws attention to its characteristic and unsettling combination of simplicity and obliquity. Grose (1975) offers a much harsher estimation of Joyce's verse in claiming that by our taste today, in the post-Pound-and-Eliot era, these poems are 'exercises in factitious emotion-mongering' (Grose 1975: 46). While acknowledging the limitations of many of Joyce's lyrics, Warner (1982) makes a convincing case for the artfulness of Joyce's reconfiguration of Renaissance, metaphysical and pre-Raphaelite images and illusions.

Dubliners (1914)

Dubliners was Joyce's first published prose work. It is tempting to discern an immense significance in the coincidence of the publication of this collection of enigmatic, elliptical and startlingly 'modern' stories with the momentous beginnings of World War One, which seemed to mark a permanent rupture between the 'old' world of stolid Edwardian social hierarchies and a nameless 'new' world still waiting to be born. Such a temptation should, however, be resisted. For while *Dubliners* originally appeared in 1914, the stories were composed a decade earlier (between 1904 and 1905) and offered to the publisher Grant Richards in December 1905. The story of Joyce's struggle to get his writing into print (and the compromises he was compelled to accept by a publisher fearful of transgressing the law concerning the printing of objectionable material) reveal in microcosm the life-long difficulty he was to experience retaining control over his work and setting it before his readers in its unexpurgated form. He initially submitted twelve stories to Richards who, after some deliberation, signed a contract to publish them in March 1906. A month before, Joyce submitted a new story 'Two Gallants', which the printer refused to typeset on the grounds of its immorality: under English law the printer was as legally culpable as the publisher for the appearance of objectionable material. In response to Joyce's protestations, Richards discovered more objectionable material in other stories (such as the reference to 'a man with two establishments to keep up' in 'Counterparts' and the use of 'bloody' in 'Grace'). When Joyce pointed out the absurdity of outlawing these details while accepting the entirety of 'An Encounter' (which presented a boy's encounter with a lecherous old man as its central incident), Richards also demanded the excision of this story. This dispute over the propriety of *Dubliners* continued for the next eight years, during which time Joyce submitted the manuscript unsuccessfully to other publishers and composed a public letter complaining of his treatment at Richards' hands. Eventually he agreed to amend phrases and scenes in individual stories, and Richards finally published *Dubliners* in 1914. The volume had by now expanded to comprise fifteen stories following the inclusion of 'Two Gallants', 'A Little Cloud' and Joyce's first masterpiece 'The Dead'.

Joyce's extended correspondence with Richards concerning *Dubliners* is remarkable for the series of aesthetic judgements by which he sought to explain the thematic character and stylistic innovation of the stories. His introductory letter to Richards represented the collection in the following terms:

> I do not think that any writer has yet presented Dublin to the world. It has been a capital of Europe for thousands of years, it is supposed to be the second city of the British Empire and it is nearly three times as big as Venice. Moreover, on account of many circumstances which I cannot detail here, the expression 'Dubliner' seems to me to have some meaning and I doubt whether the same can be said for such words as 'Londoner' and 'Parisian' both of which have been used by writers as titles. From time to time I see in publishers' lists announcements of books on Irish subjects, so that I think people might be willing to pay for the special odour of corruption which, I hope, floats over my stories. (*L*: 122–3)

Joyce's reference to an 'odour of corruption' which 'floats' over his stories prefigures the style of narratorial indirection and ironic equivocation that characterises the entire collection. Writing a year later in protest at Richards' intention to 'deform' his work, Joyce offered a more general statement about his aesthetic aim and technique:

> My intention was to write a chapter of the moral history of my country and I chose Dublin for the scene because that city seemed to me the centre of paralysis. I have tried to present it to the indifferent public under four of its aspects: childhood, adolescence, maturity and public life. The stories are arranged in this order. I have written it for the most part in a style of scrupulous meanness and with the conviction that he is a very bold man who dares to alter in the presentment, still more to deform, whatever he has seen and heard. (*L*: 134)

The relationship between this 'scrupulous meanness' of style and the 'paralysis' of modern Irish culture is crucial to Joyce's purpose in *Dubliners*. The first indication of its significance appears in 'The Sisters', the opening tale of the collection, which Joyce grouped alongside 'An

Encounter' and 'Araby' under the thematic heading 'Childhood'. 'The Sisters' takes paralysis as its central theme: it recounts the paralysis and death of the priest, Father Flynn, and the effect this episode has upon the sensibility of Joyce's young male narrator. That the exact nature of this effect is difficult to determine is one consequence of the 'meanness' of Joyce's narrative, which scrupulously restricts itself to the limited point of view of the boy himself. 'The Sisters' is narrated from the perspective of a childish consciousness capable of registering the force, but unable fully to determine the significance, of the events it encounters. In consequence, Joyce's reader is also compelled to inhabit an uneasy position between knowledge and significance, unable precisely to establish which details are crucial and which incidental to the meaning of a scene, and unsure how far the narrator should be trusted in the emphasis he confers upon particular events. The ambiguously rendered relationship between event and significance is evident from the story's opening paragraph:

> There was no hope for him this time: it was the third stroke. Night after night I had passed the house (it was vacation time) and studied the lighted square of window: and night after night I had found it lighted in the same way, faintly and evenly. If he was dead, I thought, I would see the reflection of candles on the darkened blind for I knew that two candles must be set at the head of a corpse. He had often said to me: *I am not long for this world*, and I had thought his words idle. Now I knew that they were true. Every night as I gazed up at the window I said softly to myself the word *paralysis*. It had always sounded strangely in my ears, like the word *gnomon* in the Euclid and the word *simony* in the Catechism. But now it sounded to me like the word of some maleficent and sinful being. It filled me with fear, and yet I longed to be nearer to it and to look upon its deadly work. (*D*: 3)

The boy's narrative tone oscillates between an arch and exaggerated poise (evident in the studied exactitude of those adjectives 'lightly' and 'evenly') and the representation of details that portend an undisclosed, because unknown, meaning. This tension between representation and revelation emerges because the narrator's precocious articulacy enables him to find words for a form of experience that he is not yet able to comprehend. He has read words like 'simony' and 'maleficent' in books and heard them intoned in the religious service, but he remains unsure how they relate to the world of actions and motivations. As a term to describe the buying and selling of religious preferments, 'simony' hints darkly at Flynn's rumoured violation of priestly ethics; this hint is ignored by the narrator for whom the word has meaning only within the liturgical context of the Catechism. The boy's sensibility lies suspended between the rich interior world of verbal self-consciousness and the enigmatic outer world of social and moral conventions. The word 'paralysis' sounds 'strangely' in his ears because it momentarily awakens him to the fraught relationship between word and world as it drifts beyond its immediate referent (Father Flynn's deathly condition) to embrace both his own response to this event and the inability of his adult company to explain the mystery of Flynn's last days. This pervasive sense of paralysis extends itself to the reader, who remains unsure what relationship might be established between words like 'paralysis', 'gnomon' and 'simony' within a narrative that appears either unwilling or unable to make an explicit connection between them.

Each stage of 'The Sisters' complicates the relationship between language and the world it purports to describe. Father Flynn, the narrator's uncle remarks, had a 'great wish' for the boy, although the nature of this wish is never revealed. The word hints at the mysterious nature of religious vocation, but this benevolent implication is quickly undermined by Old Cotter's subsequent insistence that he wouldn't like children of his 'to have too much to say to a man like that', which appears to detect a sinister and predatory undercurrent to Flynn's attention (D: 4). Nothing is ever securely known here because nothing is ever unequivocally stated: the adult world is characterised for the boy by ellipsis and evasion whilst the proper moral context for actions and attitudes is left vague and undetermined. 'When children see things like that,' Cotter remarks of Flynn's behaviour with typical pronominal inexactitude, 'you know, it has an effect . . .' (D: 4). The absence of a narrative perspective that might supply a link between these scattered phrases and order them into knowledge places the reader in the same position as the narrator: we struggle, like him, to 'extract meaning' from Cotter's 'unfinished sentences'. At the same time, the value of Joyce's technique of restricted and qualified narrative point of view for a story about a child's induction into the mysterious realm of adulthood gradually reveals itself. For the narrator is presented with a series of perturbing questions about the character of religious faith and the moral ambiguity of human experience that propel him to the limit of childish innocence, but which cannot be resolved from within this perspective. The boy's unsettling sense of being marooned upon the indistinct landscape between innocence and experience manifests itself in his dream that Flynn's restless spirit has something to confess to him from its unquiet grave:

> In the dark of my room I imagined that I saw again the heavy grey face of the paralytic. I drew the blanket over my head and tried to think of Christmas. But the grey face still followed me. It murmured; and I understood that it desired to confess something. I felt my soul receding into some pleasant and vicious region; and there again I found it waiting for me. It

> began to confess to me in a murmuring voice and I wondered why it smiled
> continually and why the lips were so moist with spittle. But then I remem-
> bered that it had died of paralysis and I felt that I too was smiling feebly as
> if to absolve the simoniac of his sin. (*D*: 4)

In this dream an oblique entreaty from the mysterious adult world of sin
and transgression insinuates itself into a childish mode of fantasy and
escape. Despite withdrawing into his imagination and fantasising about
Christmas, the boy is temporarily drawn to the image of the paralysed
priest; for a second he embodies the role of confessor and tastes its
sublime power; and the relationship between the poles of innocence and
experience is subtly, but irreversibly, disturbed. The region into which his
soul recedes is no longer absolutely defined by the rigid binary opposi-
tions of religious instruction; the private adult world of the confessional
is both 'pleasant' *and* 'vicious', as befits a culture in which the enforce-
ment of spiritual authority is both a means of self-transcendence and a
mode of social control.

At the heart of the story lies Father Flynn's enigmatic religious epiphany.
Crushed by the weight of his spiritual duties, the priest unaccountably
breaks a chalice, and is then discovered one night alone in the confessional:

> And what do you think but there he was, sitting up by himself in the dark
> in his confession-box, wide-awake and laughing-like softly to himself?
> She stopped suddenly as if to listen. I too listened; but there was no sound
> in the house: and I knew the old priest was lying still in his coffin as we had
> seen him, solemn and truculent in death, an idle chalice on his breast.
> Eliza resumed:
> – Wide-awake and laughing to himself . . . So then, of course, when they
> saw that, that made them think that there was something gone wrong with
> him. (*D*: 10)

This moment represents the sudden intrusion of the supernatural into
mundane life. Flynn, his sisters lament, had always been 'too scrupulous'
in his religious observances; this scrupulosity afforded him an insight into
the supernatural order of such shattering force that it cannot be
recounted in human terms. But that which transcends the human, Joyce
ironically implies, eventually diminishes the human: unnerved and enfee-
bled by his revelation, Flynn abjures the spiritual labour of faith and falls
back upon the procedures and protocols of religious doctrine. Avid for
initiation into a secret realm of knowledge and truth, the boy listens
attentively to Flynn's stories about the catacombs and the ceremonies of
the Mass. He is awe-struck by the sacred weight of priestly duty and the
secrecy of the confessional, and wonders how anyone has the courage to
undertake them. Renouncing these questions in mirthless laughter, the

old man deflects the boy's gaze away from the mystery of faith towards the corpus of ecclesiastical law and scriptural doxa that translate the supernatural into merely historical knowledge. Now the noviciate is forced to patter through the responses of the Mass 'which he had made me learn by heart' and regaled with the liturgical works of the Church Fathers, who 'had written books as thick as the Post Office Directory and as closely printed as the law notices in the newspaper, elucidating all these intricate questions' (D: 5). Life is subordinated to the paralysis of repetition and stock response as the boy is given over to a religious machine designed to produce obedient souls.

'The Sisters' explores the idea of paralysis in several of its aspects. If Flynn's physical decrepitude also symbolises a paralysis of attitude, his sisters' stultified response to his decline is rooted in a paralysis of language. One of the fundamental aesthetic principles of *Dubliners* is that the limits of a character's world-view are defined by the limits of their language. A way of speaking about the world, Joyce implies, is identical to a way of seeing the world. One reason the sisters spend their lives suspended in a fog of vagary and superstition is that they inhabit a discourse that slides over the surface of details without attempting to grasp their specificity or individual significance. Lamenting her brother's death, Eliza declares: 'God knows we done all we could, as poor as we are – we wouldn't see him want anything while he was in it.' Here the vagueness of the pronoun renders it unclear whether 'it' refers to a physical, moral or spiritual condition. The fate of Flynn's soul is similarly treated: 'He was no great trouble to us,' Eliza recalls, 'Still, I know he's gone and all to that . . .' (D: 8). Language is paralysed in statements like these by being forced to work at a crucial distance from self-consciousness. How, for example, is Eliza's gnomic assertion that the broken chalice 'contained nothing' to be understood when the object is invested with both physical and symbolic properties? Unlike the sisters, the boy remains semi-attuned to the semantic mystery of language: his eye fastens greedily upon the 'vague name of *Drapery*' and the odd locution '*Umbrellas Re-Covered*' (D: 5). Yet paralysis continually threatens. The boy's last memory of Eliza quietly transforms a broken into an 'idle' chalice (D: 10). But his narrative slides unreflectively past the suggestive implications of this transposition and language forecloses upon perception once again.

'An Encounter' presents a darker vision of the relationship between innocence and experience. The boyhood of Joe Dillon and his gang is spent in boisterous imitation of episodes from Wild West comics which offered 'doors of escape' from the dull routine of school. Within this blithe realm of boyish camaraderie the entreaties of the adult world are, however, slowly beginning to be felt: the narrator prefers detective stories to Wild West adventures because their pages were sometimes illuminated by 'unkempt fierce and beautiful girls' (*D*: 11). The boys desire 'real adventures' which can only be found 'abroad' in the enticing world of adulthood. They play truant for a day, relishing their freedom from the influence of school and home, and prepare to live out their outlaw fantasies in new and uncharted spaces.

The boys' desultory and increasingly aimless wandering culminates in their encounter with a predatory older man. At this point the narrative structure of the story precisely counterpoints two forms of desire: the narrator's desire for an escape into the mysterious world of men intersects with a man's desire for entry into the uncomprehending world of children. The character of the stranger underlines a crucial aspect of the theme of paralysis: the subjection of a life to an endless cycle of repetitive gestures. The man sidles up to the boys and insinuates himself into their conversation, asking them about their favourite books, their 'little' sweethearts and the soft bodies of girls:

> He began to speak to us about girls, saying what nice soft hair they had and how soft their hands were and how all girls were not so good as they seemed to be if only one knew. There was nothing he liked, he said, so much as looking at a nice young girl, at her nice white hands and her beautiful soft hair. (*D*: 16)

Here a deliberately restricted style of speech discloses a deliberately restricted style of being. The stranger's predatory intentions are revealed both in his opportunistic confusion of innocence with experience and his artful reproduction of the artless, repetitive and unsophisticated rhythms of childish speech. The images and emphases of his discourse come full circle: it begins with the 'nice soft hair' and 'soft' hands of girls, repeats the first adjective in its invocation of their 'nice white hands', and closes with its opening image of 'beautiful soft hair'. Like the ceaseless repetition of the pornographic image, his speech is unable to develop beyond a fixation or fetish as it cleaves to the contours of the exposed and vulnerable body. The cumulative force of these repeated images affords the narrator a glimpse of the self-enclosed circuit of one kind of adult desire:

> He gave me the impression that he was repeating something which he had leaned by heart or that, magnetized by some words of his own speech, his mind was slowly circling round and round in the same orbit . . . He began to speak on the subject of chastising boys. His mind, as if magnetized again by his speech, seemed to circle slowly round and round its new centre. (*D*: 16–17)

The boy's narrative mimics the stranger's narcissistic self-involvement, revolving slowly around its new axis: 'magnetised by some words', 'slowly circling round', 'seemed to circle slowly round', 'as if magnetised by his speech'. Narcissistic self-regard becomes the fulcrum of the plot as well as the rhetorical structure: the man retreats momentarily to a nearby field to masturbate while the boys look warily on. Because Joyce ties narrative representation so closely to the perspective of the perceiving subject, the story only hints at the nature of this sexual act; adult sexuality is, after all, at the limit of what a child feels able to repeat or understand. Joyce offers only Mahoney's elliptical observation: 'I say . . . He's a queer old Josser!' (D: 16). Joyce's coded revelation was not only projected to the very edge of the childish imagination; its implications initially escaped both Grant Richards and his censorious printer. 'An Encounter' occupies this ambiguous position between experience and the barely comprehending gaze: the effect of this occluded point of view appears in the narrator's necessarily vague description of the stranger's 'strangely liberal' attitude, where 'licentious' might have been a more appropriate adjective (D: 16). Such acts of misrecognition foreshadow the story's ultimate irony. As the man's sexually charged rhetoric soars to its climactic pitch, he dwells upon the pleasure of whipping a young boy 'as if he were unfolding some elaborate mystery' (D: 17). With their haunting allusion to the fate of Father Flynn in 'The Sisters', the pseudo-spiritual overtones of 'elaborate mystery' appear wholly misconceived in the context of this nightmarish descent into depravity and self-obsession. Upon reflection, however, the phrase is entirely appropriate in its emphasis: the boys are having an important and elaborate mystery unfolded to them: the mystery of the violence and opportunism of the adult world. Joyce compounds this irony with a sharper one by suggesting that such calculated disregard for the interests of others may find its origins in the 'innocent' world of childhood. This bleak intimation of the limits of childhood is reflected in the narrator's actions at the end of the story: to make good his escape from the stranger he is prepared to make strategic use of Mahoney, although he has always rather despised him. Even the common bonds of boyhood, Joyce suggests, contain shadowy aspects of the world that will overtake them.

The theme of the alluring, but ultimately disillusioning encounter with the world of sensuous experience recurs in 'Araby'. Joyce enlarges upon this theme by introducing a concern new to *Dubliners*: the antithetical relationship between the promise of romance and the inflexible law of social propriety. Here we discover one of the prime causes of the 'paralysis' of Irish life: the subordination of individuals to a general sense of social 'decency' and 'proper' behaviour. Joyce chooses not to explore this theme at the level of politics or ideology; instead he focuses upon the power of bourgeois morality to make the individual internalise its values and regulate his or her behaviour in accordance with conservative social mores. Eventually, he suggests, we internalise these values to the point where we either conform unreflectively to a general moral law or experience guilt and shame at transgressing its boundaries. The story begins with a pervasive sense of the constriction of the individual within an environment too rigid for self-expression:

> North Richmond Street, being blind, was a quiet street except at the hour when the Christian Brothers' School set the boys free. An uninhabited house of two storeys stood at the blind end, detached from its neighbours in a square ground. The other houses of the street, conscious of decent lives lived within them, gazed at one another with brown imperturbable faces. (*D*: 19)

This paragraph affords an excellent example of the unsettling effect of Joycean irony. Irony is generated here by the subtle displacement of a human perspective by two institutions – the school and the home – that come to determine its values and speak for its interests. On the surface, these sentences appear merely to represent the façade of a grim and unremarkable urban environment. But Joyce's rhetoric gradually fuses the external appearance of this cityscape with the repressive and conservative world-view of its inhabitants. The prose flickers constantly between a human and inhuman perspective: the streets are 'blind', which renders them indistinguishable from their denizens, while the houses, rather than their tenants, are 'conscious' of the 'decent' life they embody while they gaze at one another with imperturbable faces.

The enervated tone of Joyce's mean little sentences, with their emphasis upon the uninspiring detachment and mutual watchfulness of suburban existence, contributes to the boyish narrator's sense that life is always being lived elsewhere. 'Araby' begins in an atmosphere of waste and desuetude: the former tenant of the house, a priest, has died in the house's back drawing-room; musty air hangs throughout its rooms. The narrator attempts to escape from his stultifying domestic environment by making a premature leap into the realm of romance; he imagines himself hopelessly in love with the idealised figure of Mangan's sister whose very name 'was like a summons to all my foolish blood' (*D*: 20). The arrival in town of the bazaar Araby provides a visible symbol for his romantic attitude: he vows to attend it and return with a gift for the girl as a token of his adoration. However, the boy's situation does not admit so easily of romance and transfiguration. His uncle returns home hours late after an evening's drinking and the boy is forced to set off for the bazaar in darkness. By the time he arrives, Araby is virtually deserted and most of its stalls are closed. The magic of its name has dissipated to be replaced by the clink of coins and the banal gossip of stallholders. The boy has penetrated the inner sanctum of exotic and forbidden pleasure, but he has arrived too late, and the experience is useless. The echoing vault of the hall only amplifies his sense of presumption and wastefulness. 'Gazing up into the darkness,' he concludes, 'I saw myself as a creature driven and derided by vanity; and my eyes burned with anguish and anger' (D: 24).

Everything conspires to frustrate the boy's romantic longing: his uncle's drunken negligence, his aunt's timid moralism, which expresses itself in the hope that the bazaar was 'not some Freemason affair', his dispiriting poverty, and his impulsive promise to Mangan's sister (D: 21). But romantic desire is also frustrated by romantic rhetoric. In 'Araby' Joyce devises for his narrator a 'romantic' style that teeters upon the edge of self-parody and suspends his existence hopelessly between fantasy and reality. His adolescent infatuation with Mangan's sister recklessly transforms the mundane world into a sacred realm: carrying his aunt's parcels through the market he 'imagined that I bore my chalice safely through a throng of foes' (D: 20). The boy's self-image oscillates absurdly between the two roles of priest of love and romantic hero: his 'eyes were often full of tears' in his 'confused adoration' of Mangan's sister and 'at times a flood from my heart seemed to pour itself out into my bosom'. Within this self-deluding fantasy world, authentic feeling becomes indistinguishable from literary stereotype: the boy's most profound feelings are represented in a dead language culled from popular romance and sentimental novels. Eventually he begins to inhabit a linguistic reality entirely at odds with the drabness of his domestic conditions. 'The syllables of the word *Araby*,' he explains, 'were called to me through the silence in which my soul luxuriated and cast an Eastern enchantment over me' (D: 21). Yet this 'enchantment' represents a paralysing self-bewilderment, not a liberating romantic escape. The 'follies' that obstruct the narrator of Joyce's ironically understated cautionary tale are not just the drudgery of daily chores and domestic prohibitions; they appear decked out in the fantastic garb of a dream of self-transcendence that a bazaar could never hope to realise.

Adolescence

Joyce grouped 'Eveline' along with 'After The Race', 'Two Gallants' and 'The Boarding House' under the heading 'Adolescence'. 'Eveline' is a classic examination of paralysis: it is a story about no longer feeling at home in an environment, but being unable to exchange one's situation for something liberating and new. Its central character (rather than protagonist) Eveline Hill lives an ambiguous existence suspended between identities and roles. Compelled by her brutal widowed father to act as a surrogate mother for her siblings, Eveline's inexperience and fearfulness keep her at a nervous distance from the adult world. The presiding mood of her days combines passive watchfulness, enervation and a nameless sense of threat:

> She sat at the window watching the evening invade the avenue. Her head was leaned against the window curtains and in her nostrils was the odour of dusty cretonne. She was tired. (D: 25)

Eveline watches life pass her by as she sits alone in a house full of dust. The sole active principle in these lines is not Eveline herself but the evening that gradually 'invades' the avenue. The pervasive impression in the story of Eveline's vulnerability to external forces that invade her space and press upon her consciousness is reinforced by the image of her father 'hunting' his children out of the neighbouring field with his blackthorn stick. Even now, at 19, she 'sometimes felt herself in danger of her father's violence' (D: 26).

Into this timorous existence arrives the prospect of a new beginning. Eveline has fallen in love with Frank, a sailor, who has promised her a new life in Buenos Aires. She feels herself to be upon the brink of a radical rupture with her present circumstances: 'She was about to explore another life with Frank.' Yet the feeling persists from the outset that 'Frank' represents the heady prospect of change to a person constitutionally unable to embrace it. Joyce indicates the struggle within Eveline between inert passivity and emotional abandon by dividing his narrative mode between devitalised retrospection and the imperative tone of romantic yearning. He stays close to Eveline's angle of vision: her artless assertion that 'Frank was very kind, manly, open-hearted' suggests a naïve faith in appearances; but these appearances are themselves the commonplace currency of romantic fiction (D: 26–7). What Joyce reveals in Eveline's attachment to Frank is a curiously impersonal form of desire; the words she employs to represent her relationship with him operate at such a level of generality that they could be used to describe any romantic liaison whatsoever. Her statements merely present a stereotypical vision of the ideal male companion. Like many a romantic leading-man, Frank has a bronzed face and a chivalric spirit; he was 'awfully fond of music and sang a little' (D: 27). Joyce's ironic perspective plays off romantic fantasy against mundane reality by creating narrative expectations that are doomed to remain unfulfilled. 'Then they had come to know each other' the narrative optimistically relates, but Frank sees nothing of Eveline's passivity and timidity (D: 27). Wrapping her up in romantic fantasies he takes her to see *The Bohemian Girl*, but the experience leaves her feeling 'pleasantly confused' (D: 32). The disquieting impression that Frank's nature is somewhat more banal than Eveline's idealisation of him suggests is augmented by his cliché-ridden banter: he had 'fallen on his feet' in Buenos Aries and then returned 'to the old country' for a holiday.

Ultimately the question of what Frank's genuine qualities are ceases to be of real significance. He stands in for a profound absence in Eveline's life by personifying a dream of self-invention that she will never have the strength to realise. But the dream, to her, is everything. The distance between her increasingly fervid fantasies and the realities of her emotional situation are registered in the abrupt switch of tone and mood in the tale's final few paragraphs. The scene switches suddenly to the North Wall of Dublin Harbour at the climactic moment of the lovers' elopement, but Eveline's mind is already elsewhere. Her terror of the unknown holds the world at one remove; she 'knew that [Frank] was speaking to her,' but he cannot penetrate the carapace of her self-enclosure (D: 28). The repressive mechanism of religious morality and paternal prohibition roots her to the spot; the prospect of 'escape' is transformed into sacrilege as she stares at the 'black mass' of the waiting boat and moves her lips in 'silent fervent prayer'. Eveline has internalised the repressive codes of her culture to the degree that life is unthinkable without them; paradoxically the prospect of a romantic new life in Argentina represents to her a terrifying death of the self: 'All the seas of the world tumbled about her heart. He was drawing her into them: he would drown her.' Joyce's pitiless gaze reserves an unflinching judgement for such failure of nerve. Eveline is finally glimpsed trapped at the harbour-barrier 'like a helpless animal', incapable of volition or a flicker of human vitality (D: 29).

'After The Race' was one of Joyce's least favourite stories, and the reason for this judgement quickly becomes clear. The problem with the story is that it dispenses with the mode of ironic equivocation and narrative indirection that characterises the rest of *Dubliners*; consequently it becomes too monotonous in tone and heavy-handed in its allegorical purpose. The subject of the story is the impoverishment of the Irish spirit following the accommodations it is forced to make to European culture and American capital. Joyce eventually came to feel that his depiction of Dublin here was too harsh and ungenerous. The city is represented as a 'channel of poverty and inaction' that forms the devitalised backdrop to continental European glamour and expansiveness (D: 30). Through this drab territory 'the Continent sped its wealth and industry'. The motor-race through Dublin symbolises the smooth triumph of unfettered capital across a landscape with which it has no real relationship. The French team, headed by Charles Segouin, are 'virtual victors' and the darlings of the crowd; but their triumph represents a cultural, rather than economic ascendancy: the real money and influence is to be found on the yacht of Farley, the American, to which all the contestants retire at the story's conclusion, and where the lone Irishman Jimmy Doyle will gamble away the inheritance he meant to invest in his future. To be successful in this glittering new world it is necessary to situate oneself in the vicinity of money; Doyle is delighted upon race-day because he 'has been seen by many of his friends that day in the company of these Continentals' (D: 31). In a similar spirit Doyle's father 'modified his views early' to ensure his political opinions presented no barrier to his financial progress (D: 30). All that was once solid now melts into the air: value in this brash modern world is determined by the ceaseless fluctuation of the stock market and the random dispensations of the roulette wheel. Joyce reflects this mutation in modern values by representing human responses and motivations as the *effect* of the inhuman force of money and machines. This inversion is evident during the course of the motor-race: 'The journey laid a magical finger on the genuine pulse of life and gallantly the machinery of human nerves strove to answer the bounding courses of the swift blue animal' (D: 32). Now the 'bounding courses' of machines lend vitality to the surrounding world while the silently watching crowd 'pay homage to the snorting motor'. The sheer mobility and allure of modern capital receives its emblem in the form of Farley's yacht, which represents a floating island of luxury and wealth temporarily anchored off the coast of Ireland. Here the assembled company toast 'Ireland, England, France, Hungary, the United States of America' and settle down to a hand of cards (D: 34). In the 'great game' that ensues, four imperial powers contend for prestige and predominance. As the sole representative of a non-imperial nation, Doyle lacks the resources to compete; he will 'lose, of course' and be relegated to the sidelines. Thus the epiphanic morning sunlight breaks in upon another indebted Irishman, cut adrift from his homeland and 'glad of the dark stupor that would cover up his folly' (D: 35).

So much of the world of 'Two Gallants' is disclosed by the style of its opening paragraph:

> The grey warm evening of August had descended upon the city and a mild warm air, a memory of summer, circulated in the streets. The streets, shuttered for the repose of Sunday, swarmed with a gaily coloured crowd. Like

illumined pearls the lamps shone from the summits of their tall poles upon the living texture below which, changing shape and hue unceasingly, sent up into the warm grey evening air an unchanging unceasing murmur. (*D*: 36)

The ambivalent and paradoxical movement of these sentences ushers in a world dominated by dissimulation and false appearances. Crowds swarm with abundant life yet the streets remain in repose. The enlivening warm air of August dispenses only a 'memory of summer'. The profile of the 'living texture' of the people changes 'unceasingly' but the murmur it produces is 'unchanging'. The shimmering surface of the narrative language has the appearance of respectability and good breeding ('Like illumined pearls'), but none of its statements may be taken at face value. In this regard Joyce's rhetoric anticipates the character of Corely, one of the two 'gallants' of the title, whose disposition simulates a romantic attitude in order to separate unsuspecting women from their savings.

In the milieu of Corely and Lenehan linguistic evasiveness is the precondition for moral elasticity. Speech never comes close to representing its proper object for fear of revealing a character's concealed motivations. The curious vacancy of their discourse is glimpsed early in Lenehan's strained attempt at wit: 'That takes the solitary, unique, and, if I may so call it, *recherche* biscuit!' The implied subject of the story is male prostitution: Corely consorts with various women to procure cash and gifts, while Lenehan appears to live precariously off these dubious transactions. Certainly Lenehan had 'walked the streets long enough' waiting to 'come across some good simple-minded girl with a little of the ready' (*D*: 42–3). But the mercenary nature of their business is never explicitly revealed to the reader because the characters never acknowledge it explicitly to themselves. Instead Joyce's prose mimics the pair's euphemistic self-representations which transform economic dependence into gentlemanly indolence and 'energetic gallantries'. This sense of the deliberate qualification of a character's point of view opens it up to ironic reappraisal: the more we learn about Corely's style of life, the more the expression that he was presently 'about town' acquires a sordid undertone. Lenehan, meanwhile, even crosses the street 'obliquely' (*D*: 41). At the same time, the discrepancy between rhetoric and reality is continually exploited by the two gallants who employ the language of sexual conquest to obscure their real mercenary interests. This kind of double-talk is endemic to their corrupt social world: 'Are you trying to get inside me?' Corely asks Lenehan at one point concerning an issue of financial advantage (*D*: 40). Both men utilise the tactical idiom of the 'gay Lothario' to discuss filching money from credulous women. 'But tell me,'

Lenehan enquires of Corely's forthcoming tryst with a prospective victim, 'are you sure you can bring it off all right? You know it's a ticklish job. They're damn close on that point' (D: 39). The impression that this exchange refers to sexual rather than financial opportunism is reinforced by Lenehan's plaintive challenge to Corely upon his return from his evening engagement: 'Did it come off? . . . Did you try her?' (D: 44–5). But the only value these gallants are capable of perceiving is base coin. Joyce exposes their enthralment to the god of money by an ironic swerve into the language of false enlightenment and pseudo-religion as the triumphant Corely extends 'a hand towards the light' and reveals to his newly admiring 'disciple' the gold coin he has won by his spurious promises (D: 45).

The displacement of pecuniary ambition into the language of romantic expectation is also the central theme of 'The Boarding House'. Mrs Mooney runs a boarding house for a floating population of tourists, music-hall artists and city clerks from whose ranks she hopes to solicit a husband for her daughter Polly. Her underlying motivation is established at the outset with ironical economy: 'All the resident young men spoke of her as *The Madam*' (D: 46). Mrs Mooney's covert pursuit of her material objective divorces appearance from reality; the boarding house is a place in which frankness seems to be the presiding tone ('*I'm a . . . naughty girl. You needn't sham: You know I am*' sings Polly to the residents of the drawing-room), but where vulnerable bachelors will be seduced and outmanoeuvred (D: 46). Polly is happily complicit in this quest for a suitable husband; she maintains throughout a studied pose of 'wise innocence' (D: 48). Her mother's policy is to give her daughter the 'run of the young men'; but despite being taken with Polly's flirtatious charms, none of the residents 'meant business' (D: 47). This last phrase, which conveniently elides an erotic and a contractual implication, presents little ambiguity to Mrs Mooney who 'dealt with moral problems as a cleaver dealt with meat'. She had 'made up her mind' that Bob Doran's casual dalliance with Polly committed him to marrying the girl and plays expertly upon his lack of moral nerve to close the deal.

The main body of 'The Boarding House' details Doran's nerveless capitulation to the forces arrayed against him. Joyce's skilful admixture of economic and moral vocabularies enables him to expose the self-deception of both principal characters who assume an air of injured innocence to disguise their calculation of their own best interests. Thus Mrs Mooney insists upon a moral distinction where none actually exists between marriage and a cash payment for her daughter's 'reparation'; but marriage, in this type of transaction, is already an economic commodity

(D: 49). Doran, for his part, cannot bear to be thought a seducer despite his conviction of his own innocence, and therefore wearily embraces the rhetoric of moral obligation:

> He echoed her phrase, applying it to himself: *What am I to do?* The instinct of the celibate warned him to hold back. But the sin was there; even his sense of honour told him that reparation must be made for such a sin. (D: 62)

What is distinctive about Joyce's cunning exercise in moral dissimulation is the way it plays off Doran's sense of impending exposure and social ruination against our awareness that he is merely the inevitable victim of a sordid domestic scam. Because Doran is a 'serious young man' Mrs Mooney always 'felt sure she would win'; one's investment in a good moral image is, after all, a serious business (D: 49). The ironic perception of a continuous, rather than merely antagonistic, relation between the interests of the main players is vividly disclosed in the final scene of the story, where we pass from Doran's agonised self-reflection to Polly's evening station at her bedroom mirror. Retouching her profile in the looking glass, she adjusts her private image for public consumption just as her new fiancée had done a few hopeless moments before.

Maturity

'A Little Cloud' is the first of four stories (the others are 'Counterparts', 'Clay' and 'A Painful Case') exploring the virtues of 'Maturity', although here the transition from 'Adolescence' is doubtfully managed. Its narrative is a small masterpiece of ironic equivocation. The opening paragraph in which the would-be writer Little Chandler broods upon the qualities of his returning friend Gallaher sets the general tone:

> Eight years before he had seen his friend off at the North Wall and wished him godspeed. Gallaher had got on. You could tell that at once by his travelled air, his well-cut tweed suit and fearless accent. Few fellows had talents like his and fewer still could remain unspoiled by such success. Gallaher's heart was in the right place and he had deserved to win. It was something to have a friend like that. (D: 53)

Each of these establishing sentences gently suspends the claims of its predecessor. The evidence that Gallaher has 'got on' lies in superficial externalities: a 'travelled air', a suit, a 'fearless accent'. Is it, one wonders, a matter for reproach or celebration that 'few fellows had talents like his', and was Gallaher himself one of the 'fewer still' who had remained 'unspoiled' by such a gift? What, moreover, had Gallaher 'deserved to win'? It was 'something', indeed, to have a friend like Gallaher: but was it a *good* thing?

The subject of 'A Little Cloud' is the way in which emotional constriction encourages us to live our lives through others no matter how dubious an example those others may be. Chandler's workaday existence is overshadowed by images of sluggishness and premature senescence: sunset shrouds the park he gazes upon from his office window while old men drowse on benches; altogether he feels the futility of struggling against incipient middle age. On his way to meet Gallaher he feels no connection with the city through which he moves; the 'mansions in which the old nobility of Dublin had roystered' are 'spectral' now and '[n]o memory of the past' touches him (*D*: 54). Yet a few hours in Gallaher's company are enough to forget a lifetime of lassitude; simply thinking about his friendship with the successful London journalist lets him feel 'superior to the people he passed' (*D*: 55). The glimpse of his own image in the mirror of Gallaher's success confirms Chandler in the self-justifying fiction his mediocrity demands: to achieve anything of note one has to abandon benighted Dublin and take one's chances in the wider world. A romantic vision of literary exile momentarily bolsters him, but it is immediately apparent that he is incapable of creative invention: 'Could he write something original? He was not sure what idea he wished to express but the thought that a poetic moment had touched him took life within him like an infant hope.' As Joyce deflects Chandler's reverie towards cliché his imaginative poverty becomes devastatingly clear: perhaps 'English critics' would recognise him as one of the 'Celtic school' by dint of the 'melancholy tone' of his poetry; but should the hint not be taken 'allusions' might also be provided. All things considered, it was a pity his name was not more 'Irish looking' (*D*: 55–6).

Far from offering an escape from stupefying self-enclosure, Chandler's encounter with Gallaher at Corless's confronts him with his inverse image: impotent sensitivity collides with empty expansiveness. Gallaher's bar-room patter is a litany of clichés: the banality of his observation 'Everything in Paris is gay' is rivalled only by the sentiment that 'There is no woman like the Parisienne' (*D*: 58). As Gallaher 'proceeded to sketch for his friend some pictures of the corruption which was rife abroad', Joyce's understated irony infiltrates each of his phrases (*D*: 59). Its presence reveals itself in the portentous self-regard of Gallaher's 'calm historian' tones – he 'seemed inclined' to award the palm for corruption to Berlin – which exist at a considerable stylistic distance from what one imagines his journalistic prose to be. Gallaher is certainly capable of offering a cool ironic appraisal of Chandler's immersion in 'the joys of connubial bliss', but exactly the same ironic perspective envelops his own actions and attitudes (D: 59). This ironic point of view makes itself felt in the implicit tension between the two adjectives Chandler uses to celebrate his friend's 'vagrant and triumphant life' (D: 61). Joyce's broader satirical point that imitative thinking and linguistic cliché have the potential to mutate into vicious cultural prejudice is embodied in Gallaher's repellent observations concerning a new class of 'rich Germans and Jews, rotten with money' (D: 62). Too blinded by the image of his own inadequacy to make this connection for himself, Chandler returns home to enact a savage parody of Gallaher's credo of 'living bravely' by issuing vehement and futile reproofs to a terrified child (D: 63).

'Counterparts' is a thematic companion to 'A Little Cloud'; it also explores the idea of a life compelled by a mediating force or structure to live at a paralysing distance from its own vital interests. But whereas Little Chandler is prevented from expressing his artistic inclinations by his own emotional timidity, Farrington's humanity is steadily repressed by the bureaucratic machine of the modern workplace. Farrington's position as an office copy-clerk exemplifies the automaticity of his working environment; exiled from spontaneous human interaction he spends his days mechanically copying other people's words. The voice of his employer Mr Alleyne descends to him through a speaking-tube; this depersonalised routine of call-and-response reduces Farrington to a mere functionary within a faceless and impersonal system. However, the systemic determination of working relations devitalises everyone within it; when Farrington actually encounters his employer in a professional situation all he sees before him is a 'manikin' (D: 69). Alleyne too has been reduced to the mechanical role he performs; and this reduction of life to a fixed form is captured at the level of the image. Reacting furiously to Farrington's insolent rejoinder, Alleyne 'shook his fist in the man's face till it seemed to vibrate like the hub of some electric machine' (D: 70). This lifeless rhythm of machinic repetition and reflexive response is reproduced in Farrington's pub-rituals; his social life is structured around the same predetermined system of exchanges that have come to define the hell of his working day. Returning home he repeats the tyranny of petty domination visited upon him in the office by beating his own child. Only now does his body experience 'free play' by enforcing humiliating discipline upon a creature one further level down the social scale (D: 75). In the story's darkest irony, his son's desperate pleading, 'I'll say a *Hail Mary* for you, pa, if you don't beat me,' offers no escape from the world of emotional paralysis and social repression it attempts to transcend; the rote repetition of prayer is simply one more way in which the individual cedes autonomy to a power greater than itself.

Joyce's 'scrupulous meanness' of narrative exposition informs every level of 'Clay'. By restricting his prose to cliché, simple noun-phrases and the staccato rhythms of childhood, Joyce's deft use of free-indirect style mimics Maria's unsophisticated point of view and patterns of speech. The opening page captures her simplicity of mind and childish sense of wonder: the kitchen is 'spick and span', the fire is 'nice and bright' and the entire day tends towards the 'nice evening they would have' at Joe's house (*D*: 76). The restriction placed upon the reader by being constrained to view the world through Maria's eyes is compounded by Joyce's deletion of the particular contexts within which the story's details become explicable. 'Clay' explores its central themes of loss, isolation and spinsterhood by the gradual accumulation of hints and symbolic resonance rather than direct authorial commentary. The story takes place on All Hallows Eve or Halloween, which also falls at the same time as the Celtic festival of Samhain (summer's end) when the fairy folk were supposed to walk the earth. In one Halloween game of divination a ring, coin or nut was baked with bread or cake; whoever received this object with their food could be sure of a future marriage. In another game a blindfolded participant selects items from a saucer; depending upon what was chosen a particular destiny (such as marriage, death or the entry into Holy Orders) was settled upon them. The brilliance of Joyce's method is that these details, once given, enrich the story by conferring upon it further levels of interpretation, but, being withheld, enable 'Clay' to become a narrative of uncanny power and strangeness. The aggregation of isolated details without a general narrative context to explain them diffuses a sense of unease and disequilibrium throughout the tale that is persistently at odds with Maria's cheery sense of social inclusion. Lizzie Fleming's assertion, for example, that 'Maria was sure to get the ring' on Hallows Eve seems incidental until it is read as a symbol of the marriage Maria is never to enjoy (*D*: 77). Similarly a shop assistant mistakenly enquires if it was the 'wedding cake' Maria intended to buy (*D*: 78). Like Maria's lost youth in the 'Dublin by Lamplight' laundry and her lost dreams of love these small narrative incidents offer sporadic clues to her loneliness and emotional isolation. Although their full significance is always enigmatically withheld, a succession of details gradually implies a darker conclusion to Maria's evening journey. Thus when she laughs the tip of her nose almost touches the tip of her chin, like a Halloween witch; at Joe's house she is tricked by the girls into feeling a lump of clay, symbol of death and bare mortality; while her blindfolded selection of clay and the prayer book rather than the wedding ring in the Halloween game indicates her imminent demise. None of the symbolic implications of these details is directly conveyed; instead they bequeath a melancholy undertone to the evening's gaiety. This undertone is perceived but never remarked upon by the other characters; when, at the story's conclusion, Maria forgets the second verse of Balfe's song 'no one tried to show her her mistake' (D: 81). Their reticence is understandable: the missing lines treat of marriage, a maiden besieged by suitors, and a vital connection to life Maria is never to share.

'A Painful Case' occupies a pivotal position in *Dubliners*; it inhabits the space between the tales of 'Maturity' and the three stories ('Ivy Day in the Committee Room', 'A Mother' and 'Grace') that treat of 'Public Life'. In the painful case of Mr James Duffy this space has become an emotional no-man's-land between a loveless past and an uncertain future: the meticulous propriety of the public persona has strangled the life from the inner man of feeling. The transition from 'Clay' is stark: where Maria's days were dreamed away in unreflective innocence, Mr Duffy is consumed by a crippling self-consciousness:

> He lived at a little distance from his body, regarding his own acts with doubt-ful side-glances. He had an odd autobiographical habit which led him to compose in his mind from time to time a short sentence about himself con-taining a subject in the third person and a predicate in the past tense. (D: 83)

Retrospection stands in for the business of living; the predicate of these autobiographical sentences is fixedly in the past tense. Throughout, Joyce's subtle use of free-indirect style captures his protagonist's pompous self-regard and temperamental conservatism. This attitude and this cast of mind are disclosed in the story's opening sentence: 'Mr James Duffy lived in Chapelizod because he wished to live as far as possible from the city of which he was a citizen and because he found all the other suburbs of Dublin mean, modern and pretentious' (D: 82). 'Modern' is the telling signature note; for Mr Duffy the adjective has a necessarily pejorative implication. A style of writing discloses a style of character: Joyce's cool and passionless denotation of Mr Duffy's belongings repro-duces the latter's taste for regularity and order. Each sparse successive detail of his existence hints at an inner life scrupulously withheld from public inspection: the '*Maynooth Catechism*' sewn into his notebook offers a tentative explanation for his aloof retreat from social modernity; his 'complete Wordsworth' suggests the romantic sensibility concealed beneath his haughty disposition. Aspects of his character are revealed by means of a solitary verb or a momentary dissonance of tone: new pieces of music 'encumbered' rather than adorned his music stand; the self-approving archness of his wish to be 'safe from the society of Dublin's gilded youth' merely underlines his stuffiness and social snobbery (*D*: 83, 85). Alone at night he flirts with Nietzschean philosophy and theories of social revolution, but these are just the formless utopian yearnings of an imprisoned soul. Every active principle in Mr Duffy's life is constrained by the remorseless rhythm of the social machine: the departure at the same time each morning for his job at the bank, the midday break at the same pub, the arid evening pleasures into which he is eventually 'set free' (*D*: 83).

Trapped within this paralysed life is a spirit that would escape it; the face Mr Duffy turns to the world 'gave the impression of a man ever alert to greet a redeeming instinct in others but often disappointed'. This longing for emotional reciprocity finds ambiguous expression in his relationship with Mrs Sinico. But here reciprocity soon relapses into self-absorption: the pair may 'entangle' their thoughts, but his is always the dominant tone: 'She listened to all' (*D*: 84). She becomes his 'confessor': the alter ego that permits him the pleasure of contemplating his own hidden nature. The fateful reduction of emotional exchange into the narrow orbit of his self-enclosure is ironically laid bare at the moment that Mrs Sinico forces their relationship to a crisis:

> Sometimes he caught himself listening to the sound of his own voice. He thought that in her eyes he would ascend to an angelical stature; and, as he attached the fervent nature of his companion more and more closely to him, he heard the strange impersonal voice which he recognised as his own, insisting on the soul's incurable loneliness. We cannot give ourselves, it said: we are our own. The end of these discourses was that one night during which she had shown every sign of unusual excitement, Mrs Sinico caught up his hand passionately and pressed it to her cheek. (*D*: 85)

In this bitter epiphany the paralysed soul confronts its own limits: its loneliness is incurable; its nature is a circle returning upon itself. Mr Duffy's carefully cultivated self-image cannot support such an abyssal revelation; he bloodlessly dismisses his companion's embrace as a disillusioning 'interpretation' of his sentiments and abruptly concludes their friendship. With this violent turning inward of outwardly directed feeling Joyce reveals once more the matrix of paralysis; Mr Duffy will find no respite from its tormenting image. It returns to haunt him in the blandly impersonal prose of the newspaper article that relates Mrs Sinico's untimely death. Here in the dully euphemistic language of modern journalese – the bibulous Mrs Sinico who made regular nocturnal flits across

railway tracks is portrayed as being 'rather intemperate in her habits' –
he encounters the reflection of his own rationalisations and evasions
(*D*: 88). Joyce's rhetorical masterstroke appears in the report's studiously
neutral conclusion: 'No blame attached to anyone'. In these five unac-
cented words he sketches an ironic parallel to Mr Duffy's emotionally
neutral, but morally culpable response to the dead woman's desires. The
force of this ironic counterpoint shatters Mr Duffy's serene self-
satisfaction: he travels in the space of five paragraphs from moral recoil
('He had no difficulty now in approving of the course he had taken') to
a terrifying insight into the hellish nature of his solipsism: 'He felt his
moral nature falling to pieces' (*D*: 89). Recoiling savagely from his own
base nature, he returns to the scene of an earlier corruption: he steps at
nightfall into the park and the landscape of a ruined Eden. The image of
'venal and furtive' lovers fills him with lonely despair; the serpentine and
'fiery head' of a goods train glows terrifyingly in the darkness. Existential
hell and paralysed life now disclose themselves in the repetitive rhythms
of Mr Duffy's loveless final vision: 'he felt that he had been outcast from
life's feast . . . he was outcast from life's feast' (*D*: 89–90).

'Ivy Day in the Committee Room' translates existential paralysis into
the political sphere. Its subject and location is overtly political; it takes
place upon a dismal October day in a room where political canvassers
for the 1904 municipal elections gather to gossip and drink. The story
takes place rather than unfolds an action; plot and narrative development
are replaced by an implicit drama of consciousness. The substitution of
modes of consciousness for plot is crucial to Joyce's purpose because 'Ivy
Day' explores the symbolic attachments and affective associations that
now constitute 'political' perspectives upon modern Irish experience. No
action is narrated because for the assembled company no political action
is really possible; their politics is determined by an emotional investment
in the past that renders meaningless any present intervention. The determination of contemporary politics by the accumulated burden of the past
is evident in the witty displacement of the opening sentence; obsessed by
the political legacy of Parnell, the canvassers will, like Old Jack, spend
their time raking over old coals. In the figure of Old Jack the theme of
the dissipation of former energies acquires a visible image: his face now
'lapsed into darkness', he is reduced to a 'crouching shadow' whose
mouth moves 'mechanically' (*D*: 91). The loss of a productive connection between past and present is glimpsed early in his lament for the fractured relationships between fathers and sons. Despite this rupture, the
conversation between the political representatives is dominated by the
past: O'Connor and Hynes canvas for the Nationalist candidate Tierney,

but their bass note is their love for Parnell. Dissenting from the proposed welcome for Edward VII upon his visit to Ireland, Hynes makes clear his allegiance: 'If this man was alive, he said, pointing to the leaf, we'd have no talk of an address of welcome' (D: 94). The reference to the ivy leaf in Hynes' lapel is pointed: politics for these men only has meaning as a symbolic affiliation with historical tradition. The name of Parnell comes to represent a historical moment when political action still had the appearance of value: 'There was some life in it then', concedes Old Jack wearily. However, the incoherence of contemporary Dublin politics appears in the invocation of clerics ('I mentioned Father Burke's name') to buttress the Nationalist ticket. It was the priests, after all, who helped bring Parnell down.

The collective loss of confidence in a new political future transforms ideological division into petty internecine feuding. Tierney is scorned because his father was a shopkeeper; Henchy suspects Hynes of spying for Tierney's rival Colgan; 'hillsiders and fenians' are believed to be colluding with the Crown; Crofton, before his arrival, is 'not worth a damn as a canvasser' (D: 96, 100). Political allegiances are bought or pragmatically exchanged: the Conservatives happily support their rivals the Nationalists to ensure the defeat of Labour. The real nature of political loyalties is exposed by Henchy: 'Nationalism' is sold to the electorate as the credo of stable property prices and low business rates; it can even encompass the visit of a British monarch in the name of an 'influx of money' (D: 102). The allure of capital dissipates the symbolic power of Parnell's name in less than a page. Parnell, for all his charisma, was too morally culpable to lead the Irish to nationhood; however, 'We all respect him now that he's dead and gone.' Hynes cannot at first even recall his verse tribute to Parnell; when it comes it is a hackneyed piece of sentimentalism whose judgements embrace his listeners. The poem transforms Parnell into a redeemer and a Christ; this image reflects darkly upon his inconstant followers who 'befoul and smear' his exalted name (D: 104). In the hush that follows Hynes' poetic hot air the 'pok' of an opened stout bottle sounds the appropriate response.

'A Mother' offers a parable about self-paralysing resentment and small-minded retribution. Mrs Kearney's early life is lived in imaginative rebellion against constricting social circumstance; disdainful of the bourgeois mores of middle-class Dublin she withdraws into 'the chilly circle of her accomplishments' (D: 106). She yearns for a romantic life beyond the familiar rituals of suburban propriety; with the collapse of her romantic hopes she marries the bootmaker Mr Kearney 'out of spite'. Powerless to transcend the impoverished values of her social milieu,

Mrs Kearney transforms herself into their visible representative. Denied the consummation of her romantic desires, she gives her life over to the petty discriminations of social respectability: the decent mother, the 'good wife', the upwardly mobile social schemer (*D*: 135). Too enthralled by her youthful dreams to abandon her romantic hopes, but too weak to bring them to fruition, she chooses to live by proxy through her daughter Kathleen. Sensing a social opportunity in the 'Irish Revival', Mrs Kearney organises Irish classes and piano lessons for her compliant daughter; her reward is a series of piano recitals at the Antient Concert Rooms. Compelled by unforeseen circumstances to countenance a reduction in Kathleen's fee, Mrs Kearney's barely-repressed resentment of the costive manners of polite Dublin society rises explosively to the surface. Unconstrained by the unspoken conventions of social rectitude, she grounds her appeal for remuneration in the language of contract law: 'But she would see that her daughter got her rights: she wouldn't be fooled' (*D*: 115). In the fractious scene at the Concert Rooms that follows, Joyce presents a devastating glimpse of what passes for 'Public Life' in modern Dublin: it takes in the fateful myopia of a woman who will ruin her daughter's prospects in exchange for a minor contractual entitlement, a concert manager who manipulates the conventions of social propriety to evade a contractual obligation, and a reporter distinguished only by 'careful manners' and a 'plausible voice' (*D*: 112). The entire dispute reeks of petty opportunism and the need to maintain social position; as Joyce slyly suggests in the character of Mr O'Madden Burke, the claims of morality are completely displaced by material interests: 'His magniloquent western name was the moral umbrella upon which he balanced the fine problem of his finances' (*D*: 113). Ultimately Mrs Kearney is brought down by her violation of the code she sought elsewhere to uphold; the attribution to her of unladylike behaviour destroys her social reputation. Thus cast down, she becomes the paralysed embodiment of her own inflexible moral law, transformed by the society that rejects her into an 'angry stone image' (*D*: 116).

Where 'A Mother' brings art and the business world into profitless proximity, 'Grace' satirically counterpoints commerce and the spiritual sphere. Here Joyce satirises the way the pragmatic imperatives of business have come to seem indistinguishable from – or even replace – the moral lexicon of religion. The substitution of commercial pragmatism for spiritual wisdom is comically reflected in the confusion of the vocabularies appropriate to each practice. The central character Tom Kernan is a 'commercial traveller of the old school' who 'believed in the dignity of his calling' (*D*: 119–20). His business vocation is represented by the 'grace' of his vestment: a silk hat 'of some decency' and a pair of gaiters. Conversely Father Purdon, the priest called upon by Kernan's friends to lead him back to sobriety, is 'a man of the world like ourselves' (D: 128). The strategies of successful commercial competition now determine every other form of value. Mrs Kernan organises her domestic economy as a game of options and risks: the part of mother presented to her no 'insuperable difficulties' now her sons have been 'launched' successfully upon business careers (D: 121). Even her religious faith is defined as a form of practical utility; belief in the Sacred Heart was the 'most generally useful of all Catholic devotions' (D: 123). The expansive self-confidence of the commercial sensibility absorbs everything it touches; the meeting convened to propel Kernan into a spiritual retreat mutates into an error-strewn disquisition upon ecclesiastical history. Kernan is pressured and flattered into submission; made aware that 'some spiritual agencies were about to concern themselves on his behalf' he discerns the spiritual profit to be accrued in turning himself to account (D: 127). The idea of spiritual profit is pivotal to Father Purdon's culminating sermon; as the gathering's 'spiritual accountant' he is called to open the books of their spiritual life (D: 136). His final appeal is perfectly attuned to the interests of his listeners: in the great reckoning to come of sin and grace, the task of each is to 'set right my accounts' (D: 137). This lesson is gratefully received by a congregation that already resembles a corporate assembly ('Gradually, as he recognised familiar faces, Mr Kernan began to feel more at home'); trousers are quietly hitched, and men kneel 'with care' upon their handkerchiefs (D: 135).

A consummate irony of 'The Dead', the final tale in *Dubliners*, is that what is now perceived to be one of Joyce's most affecting stories takes for its subject the waning of feeling and affect in modern Irish life. For here Joyce presents a world in which the most carefully preserved social rituals retain no vital sense of society and where the most intimate apprehension of passionate life compels us back into communion with the dead rather than into a renewed relation with the living. Joyce's bleak vision of an exhausted Irish culture that substitutes empty ceremony and vapid nostalgia for feeling, art and imagination is symbolised by Gabriel Conroy's bitter experience on the night of the Miss Morkan's annual dance. The occasion of the dance promises to supply a moment of cohesion for the dissipating energies of a dying culture; but every aspect of the evening demonstrates the deathly separation of past and present that denies this culture depth and resonance. From the beginning Joyce's irony simultaneously establishes and undercuts the sisters' role as the custodians of classical Dublin culture: their parties never fall flat and always go off in 'splendid style', where 'style' is gradually revealed to be the petrifaction of a once living sensibility (D: 138). The Morkans' existence in the 'dark gaunt house on Usher's Island', with its haunting echo of Edgar Allan Poe's doomed family, hints at a life that retains no power of creative expression, and this expectation is fulfilled during the course of an evening in which the exchange of living speech is replaced by the performance of ritual gestures and arid proprieties. The unexamined collapse of cultural life into bourgeois sterility is enacted in Mary Jane's piano lessons for the 'better-class families' which take place amid the compendium of clichés that constitute good taste in approved social circles: the self-congratulatory belief in 'eating well', the distrust of fads from 'on the continent' and the faith invested in the respectability of proper names for 'the dignity of family life' (D: 138, 142, 147). Everything considered valuable by the assembled company lies in the past, although the past no longer even functions as a common memory. Joyce underlines this devitalised sense of values in Aunt Kate's consecration of Parkinson as the model tenor of legitimate opera even though she is the only one among them with a discernible memory of his voice. Such unthinking submission to the inherent value of traditional practices reaches its symbolic climax in the discussion of the monks of Mount Melleray:

> He was astonished to hear that the monks never spoke, got up at two in the morning, and slept in their coffins. He asked what they did it for.
> 'That's the rule of the order,' said Aunt Kate firmly.
> 'Yes, but why?' asked Mr Browne.
> Aunt Kate replied that it was the rule, that was all. (D: 158)

Because the authority of a rule lies merely in its repetition, further discussion is pointless, so the lugubrious subject is 'buried' in silence.

Such blank indifference to the relationship between the outward form of a practice and the mode of feeling it is meant to express repeats itself in every phase of Joyce's narrative. It emerges forcefully during Mary Jane's piano recital. What we witness in microcosm in this scene is the modern separation of art from its wider cultural context. A musical vocabulary is frozen into the degraded technique of an 'Academy piece' played out before a captive but increasingly less dutiful audience (D: 146). The impression that the recital affords pleasure only to the performer (and her patron) presents no impediment to its social acceptance; Joyce offers an ironic commentary upon this separation of art from the social world in which it functions in the doleful image of the artist as a 'priestess' absorbed in her priestly gestures without benefit of congregation. Elsewhere the fateful dissociation of art from life is symbolised by

Aunt Julia's schoolgirl embroidery hanging on the walls above the piano. These tableaux, depicting scenes from *Romeo and Juliet* and pictures of the two murdered princes in the tower, interpose the memory of doomed love and frustrated hopes that will become the evening's lasting legacy. But Gabriel, for whom these images will bequeath a lasting and fathomless significance, lets his eyes wander over them without response or recognition.

The deathliness of a moribund and self-regarding culture finds its thematic embodiment in the character of Gabriel Conroy. His bland and urbane exterior obscures the paralysed condition of a life lived at a distance from its vital impulses. Joyce's irony continually exploits this division between Gabriel's image and sensibility to underscore the distinction between what he says and what he will be made to feel. This distinction appears in Gabriel's exchange with Lily, the caretaker's daughter. Lily, it should be noted, is always 'the caretaker's daughter': her servitude and mode of feeling are inappropriate to the self-congratulatory tone of the gathering, and Joyce's narrative ironically reproduces her exclusion by conflating her identity with the broader domestic structure. Casually inquiring as to her romantic situation, Gabriel is discomposed by her bitter retort: 'The men that is now is only all palaver and what they can get out of you' (*D*: 140). His discomposure is tentatively registered; but he expiates this mild regret by subjecting her to more 'palaver' and expediency ('O, Lily,' he said, thrusting [a coin] into her hands, 'it's Christmas-time, isn't it? Just . . . here's a little . . .') and dismissing her from his consciousness.

Gabriel swiftly diagnoses the source of his discomfiture: he had 'taken up a wrong tone' (*D*: 141). His unease extends to the after-dinner speech he is about to deliver to the assembled company: 'He ran over the headings of his speech: Irish hospitality, sad memories, the Three Graces, Paris, the quotation from Browning' (*D*: 151). From the limited perspective afforded by his self-satisfaction, Gabriel reconfigures these middlebrow platitudes into an emblem of his 'superior education' that may well drift 'above the head of his hearers'. However, the definitive sign of his paralysis is that everything remains to him a question of tone; his interest in Robert Browning's poetry is merely the fitting adornment to a 'cultivated' sensibility. Gabriel 'loved to feel the covers and turn over the pages of newly printed books': he shows interest, in fact, in doing everything except reading them (*D*: 148). The pervasive sense that Gabriel exists too easily upon the surface of things is exacerbated by his encounter with Molly Ivors. Their disagreement neatly counterpoints two deadened responses to art and culture that actually constitute the inverse image of one another. Stung by her jibe that he is a 'West Briton', Gabriel reveals himself to be blind to all but the stylistic aspects of art: 'He wanted to say that literature was above politics' (D: 148). Miss Ivors, by contrast, reduces everything to the level of trite political symbolism: she is careful to wear an 'Irish device' for a brooch, read the right newspaper and holiday in the approved local spot (D: 147). Their exchange propels Gabriel to his first crisis of the evening ('O, to tell you the truth,' retorted Gabriel suddenly, 'I'm sick of my country, sick of it!'), but his resentment breathes no life into the discussion (D: 149). What really concerns him is neither art or culture but social respectability; Ivors had 'tried to make him ridiculous before people', which, in this company, is the ultimate transgression (D: 150).

The mortuary chill of Joyce's irony diffuses itself throughout Gabriel's speech, exposing the essential nullity of the values he espouses. His homage to the 'unique' character of Irish hospitality simply mobilises the detritus of a classical education (Paris and the Three Graces) to make a distinctly inhospitable point: the superiority of 'warm-hearted courteous Irish hospitality' to Molly Ivors and the 'new generation' (D: 160). Moreover, Gabriel's strictures upon the 'thought-tormented age' of modernity come a little uncertainly from an admirer of the proto-modernist Browning, whilst his hesitation over the virtues of the 'hypereducated' pushes self-delusion toward epiphany. Each of these statements may be true, within the limited perspective available to Gabriel; but they are also true of *him*. What is also true is precisely what cannot be said: his celebration of the living tissue of tradition is proclaimed over the head of a dying generation. Death is a spectre at the feast ('Poor Aunt Julia! She, too, would soon be a shade with the shade of Patrick Morkan and his horse'); and its presence will overwhelm living duties and living affection (D: 175)

The isolation of this stratum of a decaying Irish culture from the surrounding world is expressed by the central symbol of snow. Oblivious to the living detail of the mundane world, the snow obscures everything it touches, cutting the gathering off from the city beyond. Gabriel is drawn irresistibly to the touch of snow ('How cool it must be outside! How pleasant it would be to walk out alone . . .'); imprisoned within the repetitive gestures of the literary middleman and dutiful nephew, he longs to reclaim a life without duty or responsibility (D: 151). This desire to dissolve historical consciousness inflects the wider culture: snow is, after all, 'general all over Ireland' (D: 176). Yet the impossibility of realising this desire is revealed in the story's closing scene in which Gabriel is confronted by the memory of Gretta's passion for Michael Furey. Despite his reverence for 'tradition', Gabriel is curiously oblivious to the force of memory: both his wife and his life become inexplicable to him in the story's final lines. By faithfully reproducing Gabriel's angle of vision, Joyce's narrative inscribes ironic misrecognition at the heart of revelation. En route with Gretta to their hotel room, Gabriel pictures them galloping to their honeymoon, when what awaits him is a portent of his emotional isolation. The years may not have 'quenched' Gretta's soul, but only because part of her soul resides in the memory of Furey. Stunned by the revelation of her former love, Gabriel enters unwillingly into his epiphany: 'He saw himself as a ludicrous figure, acting as a pennyboy for his aunts, a nervous, well-meaning sentimentalist . . .' (*D*: 173). But revelation affords no redemption; it merely reaffirms his deathly recoil from life. 'Better pass boldly into that other world, in the full glory of some passion,' he reflects, 'than fade and wither dismally with age' (*D*: 176). Such exhausted romanticism provides no escape from self-enclosure: Gabriel's '[g]enerous tears' are also for himself. In the story's closing lines, Joyce's irony inhabits the abyssal distance between Gabriel's partial understanding and the reader's dawning sense of his predicament. At the end Gabriel feels that his soul 'had approached that region where dwell the vast hosts of the dead', but part of his soul has already crossed the border that separates the dead from the living. He cannot apprehend the wayward and flickering existence of the dead because their nullity represents one part of his own being. The exquisite ambivalence of the story's concluding sentences suggests that Gabriel's weariness also expresses the sensibility of his entire culture, as the snow slowly circles the 'dark central plain' and the 'treeless hills of Ireland' to rest upon the 'crooked crosses and headstones' where its youthful passion lies buried.

Further Reading

As so often with Joyce's work, the most concentrated and brilliant stylistic criticism comes from Hugh Kenner. Kenner's *Dublin's Joyce* (1978; first publ. 1955) has a chapter of incisive technical commentary that illuminates the formal qualities, narrative structure and interwoven motifs of the entire cycle of stories. Booth (1961) is acute upon the radicalisation of narrative perspective that led Joyce to abandon *Stephen Hero*, and elaborates upon some of the problems of interpretation produced by his commitment to ironic equivocation and narrative indirection. Two useful collections of essays upon *Dubliners* (Garrett 1968; Hart 1969) examine individual stories within the broader context of Joyce's symbolism, thematic preoccupations and developing narrative technique. Torchiana (1986) explicates the mythic, religious and legendary patterns that Joyce places frequently at the centre of the stories. Atherton (1966) elucidates the biographical and generic dimensions of the stories and analyses Joyce's elevation of a network of significant detail into a resonant symbolic structure. Benstock (1994) focuses upon the cycle's mutually constitutive relationship between text and context in order to show that the significance of each of the stories is determined in part by their inscription within the general context of Irish history, politics and culture. Peake (1977) examines the thematic development and structural unity of the collection; he also demonstrates how the style of the stories is illuminated by the aesthetic theory Joyce later articulates in the character of Stephen Dedalus in *Portrait*. In a similar spirit, although to a different end, Walzl (1982) argues that a number of the stories reflect the Dedalian credo that the survival of the artist depends upon his escape from the constrictive conditions of bourgeois society, including the emotional bond to women and family. In more explicitly theoretical terms, Henke's (1990) reading of sexuality, desire and frustration in *Dubliners* suggests that Joyce incorporates into his fiction an anatomy of male hysteria over the fear of being feminised, whether by individual women, Mother Church or Mother Ireland. Parrinder (1984) analyses Joyce's refinement of fin-de-siècle naturalism, urban realism and the 'slice of life' story pioneered by Guy de Maupassant, and suggests that the collection finds its thematic focus in the reproduction and internalisation of parental, sexual and religious repression.

A Portrait of the Artist as a Young Man (1916)

Joyce's literary career received a major boost in 1914. In this year Grant Richards finally published *Dubliners* and Joyce brought his first novel *A Portrait of the Artist as a Young Man* to completion. *Portrait* took Joyce a decade to write (its concluding words are 'Dublin 1904 Trieste 1914'); neither of his two subsequent and more audaciously 'experimental' novels took him more trouble to bring into focus. The book began in 1904 as a novel 'in some senses autobiographical' entitled *Stephen Hero*, concerning the gradual development of an artistic sensibility from its first awakening in childhood to its mature embrace of continental exile (Joyce 1966: 131–2). Joyce composed about 1000 pages of *Stephen Hero* between 1904 and 1906; he then condensed this draft into a more compact version during the next two years; and this new draft was then thoroughly revised and rewritten as *A Portrait of the Artist as a Young Man* between 1908 and 1914.

The surviving fragment of *Stephen Hero* represents about one-third of the original manuscript. It concentrates, in broad measure, upon the themes subsequently explored in *Portrait*. According to Herbert Gorman, Joyce had in mind:

> an autobiographical book, a personal history, as it were, of the growth of a mind, his own mind, and his own intensive absorption in himself and what he had been and how he had grown out of the Jesuitical garden of his youth. He endeavoured to see himself objectively, to assume a godlike poise of watchfulness and observance over the small boy he called Stephen and who was really himself. (Gorman 1941: 133)

Both *Stephen Hero* and *Portrait* combine elements of the *Bildungsroman* and *Kunstlerroman* traditions. A *Bildungsroman* is a novel describing the gradual education of its protagonist, while a *Kunstlerroman* explores the development of an artistic sensibility. Comparison of the two texts, however, reveals crucial differences between them. Thus *Stephen Hero* draws upon a range of material that is either deleted from, or merely implied within, the narrative of *Portrait*. Examples in *Stephen Hero* of this subsequently excluded or refashioned material include the section upon the death of Stephen Dedalus' younger sister Isabel, Stephen's explicit and extended conversation with his mother about his Easter duty, his abortive 'romance' with Emma Clery and the presentation of his university paper upon Ibsenite drama that symbolises his rejection of nineteenth-century bourgeois and religious morality.

Significant as these differences of theme and emphasis undoubtedly are, the real distinction between *Stephen Hero* and *Portrait* lies at the level of narrative style. Various reasons may be adduced for Joyce's decision to abandon his original conception in about 1908, but his principal problem remained what stance the narrator should assume towards the novel's central character. Joyce gradually came to see that too much of the imaginative energy of *Stephen Hero* was invested in the third-person authorial voice, often at the expense of Stephen himself. This is how he chose to represent Stephen's first attempt at critical writing:

> Stephen's style of writing, [that] though it was over affectionate towards the antique and even the obsolete and too easily rhetorical, was remarkable for a certain crude originality of expression. He gave himself no great trouble to sustain the boldnesses which were expressed or implied in his essays. He threw them out as sudden defence-works while he was busy constructing the enigma of a manner. (*SH*: 32)

Stephen never recovers from this devastating glimpse into his artful construction of an enigmatic 'manner'. All of the mystery implicit in the development of character and self-awareness is immediately dissipated by an authorial voice whose mature vision effortlessly outflanks the mode of consciousness embodied by its protagonist. Reading his paper on Ibsen to a university gathering, Stephen is pictured as 'this heaven-ascending essayist' bent upon an 'eloquent and arrogant peroration' (*SH*: 85). Sometimes aware that the reader's reserves of sympathy for his young noviciate are becoming rapidly depleted, Joyce occasionally imbues Stephen with a quality of insight previously the exclusive domain of his own authorial perspective. Reflecting upon Cranly's exasperation with his apparent indifference over Isabel's fate, Stephen is unable to decide if his friend's conduct 'was to be considered the sign of a deep interest in a human illness or the sign of irritated dissatisfaction with an inhuman theorist' (*SH*: 131). It was under the weight of these contradictions, with Stephen cast alternately as ephebe and ironist, that *Stephen Hero* stalled while Joyce sought a mode of presentation that might bring his thematic concerns more securely into view.

Joyce resolved this problem of narrative perspective in *Portrait* by adopting a style of address that narrowed, almost to a point of imperceptibility, the gap between objective and subjective poles of experience. This is the novel's famous opening section:

> Once upon a time and a very nice good time it was there was a moocow coming down along the road and this moocow that was coming down along the road met a nicens little boy named baby tuckoo . . .
> His father told him that story: his father looked at him through a glass: he had a hairy face.
> He was baby tuckoo. The moocow came down the road where Betty Byrne lived: she sold lemon platt.
>
> > *O, the wild rose blossoms*
> > *On the little green place.*
>
> He sang that song. That was his song.
>
> > *O, the green wothe botheth.*
>
> When you wet the bed, first it is warm then it gets cold. His mother puts on the oilsheet. That had the queer smell. (*P*: 5)

Nothing prepares us for the shock of these lines, which take the ambivalent fluctuation between first- and third-person point-of-view constitutive of free-indirect style and transform it into the structural principle of an entire mode of narration. In these sentences Joyce's prose adopts the apparently impersonal perspective of third-person narrative; but this perspective is continually infiltrated by the questioning consciousness of a barely comprehending child. By maintaining this insistently doubled narrative perspective, Joyce is able both to describe the movement of unformed sensibility towards a sense of coherent identity and, by compelling his readers to see the scene through Stephen's eyes, capture the force and strangeness of a world seen for the first time. Throughout this passage Stephen's sensibility is immersed in the flux of sense experience while represented simultaneously attempting to lend this experience primitive narrative form. His attention fluctuates continually between the allure of an externally imposed narrative ('Once upon a time') and the range of sensuous impressions through which we register the world prior to the mediating structure of language. Each of the five senses is powerfully evoked: sight (the child watching his father watch him); sound (the bedtime story and the song's refrain); touch (the warm and cold bed); smell (his mother and the oilsheet); and taste (lemon platt). But they are evoked within a style that takes the impersonal form of third-person narrative ('His father told him that story') and gradually moulds it to a childish perspective. This perspective enables Joyce to register Stephen's first flicker of self-recognition ('He was baby tuckoo') in an infantile subject/predicate form that exactly reproduces the combination of hesitation and momentary certitude indicative of a consciousness newly aware of language. The same combination appears in Stephen's fondness for clauses that impart pieces of information without establishing any necessary or causal relationship between them ('His father told him that story: his father looked at him though a glass: he had a hairy face') and his unreflective embrace of the vague associative logic of childhood ('The Vances lived in number seven. They had a different father and mother. They were Eileen's father and mother. When they were grown up he was going to marry Eileen'). Language for the boy is suspended ambiguously between nomination and sensual evocation: the 'cachou' his aunt Dante Riordan gives him whenever he offers her tissue-paper may be either a sweet or the phonetic rendering of a sneeze. Joyce takes pains to underline Stephen's sense of both the referential and the sensual power of language because the boy exhibits from the beginning an intense verbal self-consciousness that is fascinated by aesthetic pattern and form. This aspect of Stephen's sensibility becomes evident in the opening scene where he instantly transforms an admonition addressed to him for a childish misdemeanour into a pleasing verbal symmetry:

  – O, Stephen will apologise
Dante said:
  – O, if not, the eagles will come and pull out his eyes.

      Pull out his eyes,
      Apologise,
      Apologise,
      Pull out his eyes.

Apologise,
Pull out his eyes,
Pull out his eyes,
Apologise   (*P*: 5–6)

Stephen's uncanny verbal self-awareness comes to dominate his entire personality; it is this trait that initially isolates him from his peers. His distance from his schoolmates is represented from the beginning as a linguistic difference: 'What kind of a name is that?' rejoins Nasty Roche when informed that he is talking to 'Stephen Dedalus' (*P*: 5). Always a timid and reluctant participant in physical games, Stephen retreats into a vibrant verbal inner world. His life at Clongowes School is determined by his fledgling experiments with language rather than with the establishment of social relationships. Joyce's first depiction of Stephen's life at Clongowes makes this point by deft employment of free-indirect style:

> The wide playgrounds were swarming with boys. All were shouting and the prefects urged them on with strong cries. The evening air was pale and chilly and after every charge and thud of the footballers the greasy leather orb flew like a heavy bird through the grey light. (*P*: 6)

This passage is apt to be read as an example of 'stylish writing' unless attention is paid to Joyce's subtle combination of narrative perspectives. The portentous phrase 'greasy leather orb' obtrudes because it occupies a wholly different register from the accompanying text. Both this phrase and the rather cumbersome simile within which it functions belong to the lexicon of the inexperienced first-time writer: for these few seconds we envisage the scene from Stephen's point of view. This is the first clue Joyce gives that Stephen's intellectual precocity and studied detachment will lead him to adopt a solitary path beyond the crowd. Elsewhere Stephen is captivated by the multiple meanings of words and intrigued by the relationship between language and sensuous experience:

> Suck was a queer word . . . Once he had washed his hands in the lavatory of the Wicklow Hotel and his father pulled the stopper up by the chain after and the dirty water went down through the hole in the basin. And when it had all gone down slowly the hole in the basin had made a sound like that: suck. Only louder.
>
> To remember that and the white look of the lavatory made him feel cold and then hot. There were two cocks that you turned and water came out: cold and hot. He felt cold and then a little hot: and he could see the names printed on the cocks. That was a very queer thing. (*P*: 8–9)

Joyce's elaborate verbal patterning of the Clongowes scenes mimics Stephen's preoccupation with finding a linguistic pattern within which to make sense of new (and often unwelcome) experience. The repetition here of a number of words and phrases – 'cold slimy water', 'how cold and slimy the water had been', 'dirty water', 'suck', 'greasy laces', 'queer and wettish' air, 'cold slime of the ditch' – captures Stephen's reflexive recoil from the physical world. Joyce's intricate verbal design informs the novel's broader thematic pattern. His emphasis upon words like 'water', 'wettish' and 'suck' evokes simultaneously the lost maternal body that Stephen yearns for but is fated to renounce, and the future world of adult sexuality that entices and repels him in equal measure. What is also significant is that the sensations produced in Stephen by these experiences occur at an *affective*, rather than a cognitive, level. One of Joyce's principal interests in *Portrait* was to explore the way ideological concepts like nationalism and religion have their origin in a complex of affects or bodily sensations. An affect describes what happens to us when we receive the impressions of sensible experience: we are attracted to or repelled by certain odours or images, for example, and comforted or alarmed by particular sounds, rhythms or tones. Affections are our primary means of experiencing the world; they describe impulsions and modes of feeling that precede conscious ideas and opinions. As the relationship between certain types of affective response and our perception of the world becomes regular and recognisable, both perception and affect are subsumed beneath *concepts* (such as 'good' food, 'tasteful' perfume, 'proper' speech and 'civilised' manners). Everything we name as our own 'experience' begins in an affective encounter with the sensible world; we then organise affection and perception into concepts, opinions and ideologies that attempt to make the world accommodate our preferred style of living.

The revolutionary innovation of Joyce's style was to describe the construction of a 'character' and a social world from these affective and perceptive origins. An example of this radical stylistic perspective occurs in the school refectory scene. Alone and unhappy in the school refectory Stephen:

> leaned his elbows on the table and shut and opened the flaps of his ears. Then he heard the noise of the refectory every time he opened the flaps of his ears. It made a roar like a train at night. And when he closed the flaps the roar was shut off like a train going into a tunnel. (*P*: 10)

By opening and closing his ears Stephen creates for himself the impression of a train and this impression is linked immediately to the affect of pleasure: 'It was nice to hear it roar and stop and then roar out of the tunnel again.' This pleasurable feeling is then transformed into a series of concepts: railway travel, the school vacation and the safety of home:

It was like a train going in and out of tunnels and that was like the noise of the boys eating in the refectory when you opened and closed the flaps of the ears. Term, vacation; tunnel, out; noise, stop. How far away it was! (*P*: 13)

Stephen's early schooldays are dominated by feelings of fear and insecurity. These feelings reach their apotheosis during his confinement in the Clongowes infirmary. But it is also here that Stephen discovers the unforeseen *pleasure* of self-pity ('It would be nice getting better slowly') and the fantasy of being sacrificed by an uncaring world (*P*: 21). This seemingly incidental infirmary scene is of crucial importance to the novel because Joyce suddenly widens his focus beyond the hapless boy to take in one aspect of the nostalgic discourse of Irish nationalism, with its array of abandoned and sacrificial figures. In Stephen's febrile vision, his own image is momentarily superimposed onto the forsaken body of the abandoned Parnell: 'Parnell! Parnell! He is dead!' (*P*: 22). In one sense Stephen's conflation of his own 'tragic' situation – he has a temporary bout of influenza – with Parnell's political downfall and premature demise reveals his penchant for self-dramatisation. But it also underscores his belief in the intrinsic pathos and value of rebellious independence and prospective self-martyrdom. He first translates this belief into action with his complaint to the rector concerning his mistreatment by Father Dolan; it subsequently becomes central to his artistic credo in Parts 4 and 5 of the novel.

Not the least of the ironies of Part 1 is that Stephen's childish and self-dramatising investment in the pathos of martyrdom constitutes much of what passes for political discussion in adult circles. This connection is made explicit in the Christmas dinner scene. The protagonists of this episode believe themselves to be locked into a struggle over the soul of modern Ireland, but it quickly becomes clear that they are less interested in the abstractions of politics or ideology than the pleasure they derive from establishing their credentials as engaged and virtuous citizens. The emotional violence of Stephen's father's defence of Parnell arises because the image of his 'dead king' symbolises his definitive rupture with the life of expansive vitality he enjoyed before the disappointments of middle age (*P*: 33). Simon Dedalus' entire response to his present life is steeped in nostalgia; on Christmas morning he weeps at the sight of Stephen dressed for Mass because 'he was thinking of his own father' (*P*: 24). And although Stephen's father argues strenuously for a radical separation of Church and state, his representation of Parnell takes on a messianic aspect. 'When he was down they turned on him to betray him and rend him like rats in a sewer,' he laments; to him Parnell is always a redeemer, an outcast, a forsaken one (*P*: 28). To be one of Parnell's number is, for him, to enjoy an unbroken connection with a rebellious Irish spirit in defiance of every opposing influence. This redemptive and pseudo-religious attitude to Irish politics discovers its inverse image in Dante Riordan's deeply political view of the priestly office, which is to denounce renegade politicians in the name of 'public morality' (*P*: 25). This interminable battle between self-justifying certainties is contrasted with Stephen's faltering attempts to align word and world. His imagination is daunted by the transfigurations of religious symbolism ('How could a woman be a tower of ivory or a house of gold?') while continually dissolving its dominant images back into the affective qualities that produce their resonance:

> Eileen had long white hands. One evening when playing tig she had put her hands over his eyes: long and white and thin and cold and soft. That was ivory: a cold white thing. That was the meaning of *Tower of Ivory*. (*P*: 29)

The distinctive feature of the bitter exchanges around the Christmas dinner table is that they reproduce, rather than renounce, this childish fixation upon affect and feeling. Dante's final outburst represents a triumphant emotional vindication of the power of religious sentiment, while Mr Casey's 'Story of the Spit' indicates that 'politics' for the two men remains inseparable from the pleasure of an imaginary revenge upon one's enemies (*P*: 33).

The dinner-party scene affords Stephen his first insight into the capacity of language to provoke and express powerful feeling. The issues at stake in the argument largely escape him, but he 'felt the glow rise to his own cheek as the spoken words thrilled him' (*P*: 32). Joyce continually reconfirms our impression of the limitation of Stephen's perspective by placing the meaning of events just beyond his angle of vision. Stephen senses that his failure to return to Clongowes is determined by the deterioration of his father's circumstances, but this truth is only ever obscurely glimpsed: 'In a vague way he understood his father was in trouble . . .' (*P*: 53). Stephen's awareness of his father's decline leaks ambiguously into the novel; it emerges indistinctly in the scene in which he attempts a poem upon Parnell on the back of one of his father's second moiety notices (*P*: 58). Because the narrative perspective of Joyce's prose is tied so closely to Stephen's point of view, the reader is subjected to many of the limitations imposed by the boy's mode of consciousness. It is not until Stephen accompanies his father to Cork that the disintegration of the family fortunes is firmly established. In this way the movement of the narrative reflects the ebb and flow of Stephen's perception of the world. This perceptual rhythm gives the novel the structure of a musical composition: motifs are introduced, dispersed and then recombined as particular words and images inflect Stephen's imagination. One reason the novel appears to progress in fits and starts is that Joyce's narrative faithfully reproduces Stephen's intense and sudden apprehension of verbal and visual detail. Bored in Cork Stephen closes his ears to his father's desultory ramblings; but a momentary glimpse of the word 'foetus' cut into a desk brings his adolescent turmoil into focus:

> The sudden legend startled his blood: he seemed to feel the absent students of the college about him and to shrink from their company. A vision of their life, which his father's words had been powerless to evoke, sprang up before him out of the word cut in the desk. (P: 75)

Sexuality, writing and vision are densely interwoven in *Portrait*. Literature for the adolescent Stephen not only provides a respite from the privations of family life; by projecting his idea of himself into the books he reads, he begins to devise for himself a heroic and charismatic personality to project outwards into the great life of the world. Drawn to the alluring figure of Mercedes in *The Count of Monte Cristo*, Stephen dreams of meeting in the real world 'the unsubstantial image which his soul so constantly beheld' (P: 54). This image emerges from the stirrings of boyish sexuality; meanwhile the literary representation of this desire gives Stephen his first intimation of *epiphany*. Alone with Mercedes surrounded by darkness and silence, he would be suddenly transfigured: 'He would fade into something impalpable under her eyes and then in a moment, he would be transfigured. Weakness and timidity and inexperience would fall from him in that magic moment.'

The decisive importance of literature in Part 2 is that it enables Stephen to transform his experience into an object for his own aesthetic contemplation. Literature gives the chaotic and affective force of life structure and value: beginning tentatively to record his own experience, Stephen 'chronicled with patience what he saw, detaching himself from it and testing its mortifying flavour in secret' (P: 56). At the same time, however, this self-consciously fashioned aesthetic sensibility slowly detaches Stephen from the social world: he develops a silent and aloof manner and begins to 'taste the joy of his own loneliness' (P: 57). Even at this early stage his sensibility is continually deflected towards sexuality; and it is because of his passion for Eileen that he first attempts some callow Romantic verses in what he takes to be a 'Byronic' style. Writing for Stephen is above all an expression of imaginative *independence*; it places him beyond the call of familial and religious duty and the 'intangible phantoms' of honour (P: 70).

It requires artful intellectual courage to construct a new personality for oneself; but such relentless self-examination can terminate in an arrogant aloofness. Stephen often crosses the border that separates self-fashioning from self-regard, and Joyce captures these moments in sentences that mimic his attempts at high seriousness even as they collapse back into archness and pomposity. 'An abyss of fortune or of temperament sundered him from them,' Stephen observes of his father and his cronies: 'His mind seemed older than theirs: it shone coldly on their strifes and happiness and regrets like a moon upon a younger earth' (*P*: 80). Seemed, indeed. The hackneyed quality of the simile expresses perfectly the callowness of the sentiment. More damagingly, Joyce repeatedly exposes the narcissism at the core of Stephen's sensibility. Such disclosure appears most starkly in the scene in which he is overwhelmed by lust before his fateful encounter with a prostitute:

> He wanted to sin with another of his kind, to force another being to sin with him and to exult with her in sin. He felt some dark presence moving irresistibly upon him from the darkness, a presence subtle and murmurous as a flood filling him wholly with itself. Its murmur besieged his ears like the murmur of some multitude in sleep; its subtle stream penetrated his being. His hands clenched convulsively and his teeth set together as he suffered the agony of its penetration. (*P*: 83–4)

Prostrate before the enervating fires of lust, Stephen is 'penetrated' by his own instinct for gratification. In these ways the narrow circuits of self-involvement evoked in *Dubliners* reassert themselves.

As befits the portrait of an emerging artist, Stephen's need to refashion his experience in aesthetic terms gradually becomes the motive force of the novel. Because of the sustained ambivalence of the authorial point of view, this desire is not merely presented at the level of plot; it also emerges in the style of Joyce's narrative. In a sentence such as 'Stephen's heart began slowly to fold and fade with fear like a withering flower' the narrative voice is pitched equidistantly between Joyce's exterior perspective and Stephen's poeticising sensibility: the artful, but somewhat studied alliteration maintains the type of self-conscious poise Stephen mistakes for self-assurance (*P*: 90). This double perspective enables Joyce to register the pathos of Stephen's apprehension of his artistic vocation while subjecting such pathos to rigorous ironic qualification. The unsettling effects generated by this technique are demonstrated during Stephen's hellish experience at the Jesuit retreat in Part 3. This episode does not simply describe a conflict between the religious and artistic imagination; it also represents a conflict between a stronger and a weaker form of artifice. The Jesuitical voice, with its compelling imagery of damnation and abandonment, is perfectly calculated to arrest and overpower Stephen's imagination; by envisaging hell as a ceaseless torment of the senses, the sermon recasts the tenor of the novel's opening scene in terms of a spiritual death (*P*: 131).

Joyce's irony identifies the limits of Stephen's self-awareness within even his most 'sincere' gestures. During his confessional moments of shame and repentance, Stephen is blinded by his tears. The participle manages to evoke a sense of genuine mortification while implying his lack of real insight into his own need for expiation. The status of Stephen's confession is complicated further by the aesthetic nature of his penitential response which ironically revisits the state of mind that led him to an arrogant isolation as his prayer rises to heaven from his purified heart 'like perfume streaming upwards from a heart of white rose' (*P*: 122). The tone of Joyce's prose gradually assumes the ironic nuances of the short story 'Grace': Stephen, we are told, seemed to feel his soul in prayer 'pressing like fingers the keyboard of a great cash register (*P*: 124). What draws Stephen to the thought of holy orders, apart from a visceral terror of damnation, is the ceremonial and symbolic shape it confers upon the formless chaos of life. Without the shaping ritual of a 'holy rite', he is condemned to an inert and formless passivity: 'In vague sacrificial or sacramental acts alone his will seemed drawn to go forth to encounter reality' (*P*: 134). But Stephen cannot detach the symbol from the servitude it implies: to be numbered within a sodality frustrates his overwhelming desire to be 'elusive of social or religious orders' (*P*: 136). He has, indeed, an almost satanic fear of subordination: he would 'fall silently, in an instant', he acknowledges to himself, if this destiny promised him a proud and independent isolation.

Stephen's rejection of the Church pushes him back towards the university. This decision provokes a rupture with his old life: looking at his mother 'he was made aware dimly and without regret of a first noiseless sundering of their lives' (*P*: 138–9). It is at this point that Stephen finally substitutes a fully-fledged aestheticism for his devotional instincts. Art gives his life an order and a sense of coherence unavailable elsewhere. Walking by the beach, Stephen draws a poetic phrase to his lips: 'A day of dappled seaborne clouds'. Immediately the phrase and the scene appear to him subtly interfused and 'harmonised in a chord' by the creative power of his imagination. In this pivotal passage Stephen is suddenly compelled to contemplate whether it was the subtle rhythms and patterns of descriptive language that continually absorbed his attention or whether he instead 'drew less pleasure from the reflection of the glowing sensible world through the prism of language many coloured and richly storied than from the contemplation of an inner world of individual emotions mirrored perfectly in a lucid supple periodic prose?' (*P*: 140).

Art enables Stephen to draw back from the glimmering and chaotic surface of experience into an ordered and self-conscious inner world. Joyce captures here the essence of Stephen's verbal self-enclosure: those words do not simply *describe* a world; language slowly *becomes* a world with its own character and integrity. The passage begins with Stephen trying out the phrase 'dappled seaborne clouds'; he then begins to move *through* this imaginative landscape which is gradually superimposed upon the physical world he sees around him: 'he raised his eyes toward the slowdrifting clouds, dappled and seaborne' (*P*: 141). Now Stephen stands alone upon the 'trembling bridge' between the social sphere and the higher world of art (*P*: 140). In an ecstatic moment of apprehension he glimpses his vocation: 'A voice from beyond the world was calling' (*P*: 141). The voices of his disporting classmates ('Stephanos Dedalos!') confirm his mythical sense of his inheritance: 'Now, as never before, his strange name seemed to him a prophecy' (*P*: 142).

In the myth of Icarus, Daedalus was a famous Athenian architect and engineer. So highly prized were Daedalus' creative talents that he and his son Icarus were invited to Crete by King Minos in order to construct a dazzlingly intricate labyrinth. Unwilling to allow Daedalus to return home after the labyrinth's completion, King Minos treacherously imprisoned father and son at the heart of the maze. Using a cunning combination of feathers and wax, Daedalus devised two pairs of wings, enabling Icarus and himself to escape the labyrinth and leave Crete. Exulting in his new aerial freedom, and ignoring his father's warning, Icarus flew higher and higher until the warmth of the sun's rays melted the wax that held his wings together. He fell from this great height into the sea and was drowned. Ever since, the fate of Icarus has offered a cautionary lesson to those who 'fly too close to the flame' and risk consuming themselves in the act of living out their dreams of self-transcendence.

The myth of Daedalus and Icarus provides an important narrative context for the development of Stephen's character. Daedalus' fate crystallises two themes that preoccupy Stephen throughout the novel: the responsibility the artist bears to create new forms from the stuff of mundane experience and the danger posed to artistic freedom by every form of external authority. Stephen self-consciously embraces his Daedalian legacy: he knows he must follow his namesake in serving as a symbol of the artist 'forging anew in his workshop out of the sluggish matter of the earth a new soaring impalpable imperishable being' (P: 142). Yet while Stephen identifies himself explicitly with Daedalus' creative vision, he fails to see that his absolute commitment to his artistic vocation threatens to sever his attachment to the broader social world. What Stephen fails to see, Joyce illuminates for his reader by interweaving a series of Icarian references into his ecstatic vision of the physical world. Read in this light, Stephen's 'ecstasy of flight' threatens to take him too close to the sun, where disaster meets those who overreach themselves by renouncing the world ('O cripes! I'm downded!').

Stephen's embrace of his artistic vocation is symbolised by his encounter with the wading girl. His vision of the girl takes the form of an epiphany: a moment of pure aesthetic apprehension in which the lineaments of eternal beauty and grace are suddenly revealed. She is both woman and muse: her stillness, poise and beauty afford Stephen a moment of secular transcendence that alerts him to the possibility of a new and mysterious mode of being. The girl comes to represent the 'wild angel' of 'mortal youth and beauty' that extends to him the promise of a transfigured life. Another kind of life touches his own and transports him beyond merely physical existence; now his soul 'swoons' in its passage towards another mode of life (P: 145). The careful reader will pay attention to this final verb, with its sly allusion to the ecstatic but self-enclosed sensibility of Gabriel Conroy in 'The Dead'; Stephen's slightly over-wrought declaration of intent teeters upon the edge of ironic diminishment. Similarly, it is difficult to accept his subsequent interest in the plays of the contemporary dramatist Gerhart Hauptmann without detecting an echo of Mr Duffy, whose tortured romanticism led unhappily to isolation and sterility. Like Duffy, Stephen's scrupulous aestheticism leads him away from productive engagement with the world; all he sees around him in the teeming Dublin streets are 'heaps of dead language' (P: 150).

The novel's ambivalent attitude to Stephen's vocation is expressed in the transition between Parts 4 and 5. Stephen is displaced, in the space of two pages, from his ecstatic vision of a new world into a bleak parody of communion as he drains his watery cup of tea and sits chewing crusts of dried bread (P: 146). In Part 5 Stephen's intense, but febrile aesthetic self-consciousness comes into conflict with a very different way of thinking about the self: Davin's nationalism. Stephen's disdain for nationalism is reflected in the arch tone of Joyce's prose: the young peasant Davin, he mockingly informs us, worships the 'sorrowful legend of Ireland', while his unsophisticated imagination is governed by the 'broken lights' of Irish myth (P: 151–2). Stephen rejects Davin's appeal to the superiority of national art and culture because it subordinates the imagination to a general and impersonal idea. Davin cannot, Stephen concludes, recognise the singular freedom of artistic creation; his attitude to Irish culture and religion is that of a 'dullwitted loyal serf'. However, Stephen cannot avoid the questions of cultural origins and affiliation completely. His conversation with the English dean of Trinity confronts him with the blithe self-assurance of a people who do not even bother to master their own language before imposing it upon others:

> The language in we are speaking is his before it is mine. How different are the words *home*, *Christ*, *ale*, *master*, on his lips and on mine! I cannot speak or write these words without unrest of spirit. His language, so familiar and so foreign, will always be for me an acquired speech. I have not made or accepted its words. My voice holds them at bay. My soul frets in the shadow of his language. (*P*: 159)

Typically, Stephen registers the impress of colonial servitude in linguistic rather than in social and political terms. Indeed, it is the dean's confusion over the meaning of the word 'tundish' that eventually inflames Stephen's already raw sensitivity. Intriguingly, their ensuing exchange is finely balanced, and the dean, perhaps unknowingly, has the final word: Stephen must avoid 'perishing by inanition' by retreating into an arid world of abstract speculation (*P*: 159). Stephen's elevation of independence of mind above broader social and political commitments meets repeated challenges in the novel's concluding stages; they are exemplified by his dispute with MacCann concerning his refusal to sign a petition advocating general disarmament. Stephen manifests contempt for the pious and redemptive cast of progressive thought: 'If we must have a Jesus,' he complains, 'let us have a legitimate Jesus' (*P*: 166). MacCann's belief in the efficacy of his petition is undoubtedly naïve, but Stephen's vehement response places art definitively beyond moral and political claims. He is, as Davin notes ruefully with an ironic backward glance at the credo of Sinn Féin, 'Always alone' (*P*: 169).

Stephen's extended conversation with Davin reveals his rejection of nationalist cultural politics which is provoked by his refusal to be bound by the debts his forefathers made. In declining Davin's entreaty to be 'one of us', Stephen reprises Ireland's historical betrayal of its rebel leaders: 'No honourable and sincere man,' said Stephen, 'has given up to you his life and his youth and his affections from the days of Tone to those of Parnell but you sold him to the enemy or failed him in need or reviled him and left him for another' (*P*: 170). The precondition for great art, Stephen argues, is freedom from external constraint: the original creative mind must 'fly by' the 'nets of nationality, language, religion' designed to entrap it and ensure its subservience. Stephen does not recognise the irony in the fact that he couches this emancipatory urge in quasi-religious terms because art offers him a new religion of impersonal aesthetic sensibility: 'The artist, like the God of the creation, remains within or behind or beyond or above his handiwork, invisible, refined out of existence, indifferent, paring his fingernails' (P: 181). Joyce, however, signals his distance from Stephen's rapturous speculation by interrupting his discourse with the 'harsh roar of jangled and rattling metal' issuing from a rag and bone cart (P: 175). This ironic distance is rigorously maintained in the description of Stephen's mode of aesthetic creation: 'Towards dawn he awoke. O what sweet music! His soul was all dewy wet.' Free-indirect style ('O what sweet music!') is employed here to dramatise and recast ironically the nature of Stephen's creative exaltation (P: 182). The waking of his soul to artistic inspiration is represented both as a new birth and an adolescent wet-dream, while his mode of morning inspiration dissolves quickly into vapid mysticism: 'A spirit filled him, pure as the purest water, sweet as dew, moving as music.' To his ears lyric poetry is now a new mode of prayer; the rhythms of his villanelle linger in the air like 'incense ascending from the altar of the world' (P: 183). Joyce fashions passages of purple prose to imply Stephen's capitulation to a florid and self-glorifying spiritualism: Stephen now conceives of himself as a 'priest of the eternal imagination, transmuting the daily bread of experience into the radiant body of everliving life' (P: 186). The barely repressed religiosity inspiring his new vocation even informs his renunciation of his mother: his avowal that he will not serve is Satan in a minor key, indebted to the very Christian tradition he renounces (P: 201). On this point Cranly is characteristically astute: Stephen's mind is 'super-saturated with the religion in which you say you disbelieve' (P: 202). Stephen, Cranly judges, does not wish to overcome his religious doubts because he has already displaced religion into aesthetics.

In the final pages of *Portrait* Stephen moves almost imperceptibly from disaffection toward exile. His quest for a new mode of life or of art whereby his spirit could express itself in complete freedom takes him beyond that in which he no longer believes 'whether it call itself my home, my fatherland or my church' (P: 208). From this point he will depend for his freedom only upon 'silence, exile, and cunning'. The narrative of *Ulysses* makes much of 'exile', and mention of the Odyssean virtue of 'cunning' pushes us irresistibly into the world of Joyce's masterpiece. That the end of *Portrait* marks a point of transition between these novels is indicated in several ways. The diary extracts that conclude the novel slip momentarily into the form of interior monologue that constitutes one part of the stylistic triumph of *Ulysses*. The structure of interior monologue represents the grammar or imaginative syntax by which a particular mode of consciousness makes sense of the world. Stephen makes the following diary entry:

> Said religion was not a lying-in hospital. Mother indulgent. Said I have a queer mind and have read too much. Not true. Have read little and understood less. Then she said I would come back to faith because I had a restless mind. This means to leave church by backdoor of sin and reenter through the skylight of repentance. (*P*: 210)

In this passage Joyce reproduces the rhythms of Stephen's thoughts in order to disclose two aspects of his evolving sensibility: the lacerating self-insight that effectively paralyses spontaneous creation, and the aphoristic wit he uses to ward off feeling. Stephen is not a strong enough artist to develop this 'modern' literary style further, but Joyce will subsequently push it to its limits by taking Stephen for his subject. A definitive movement beyond Stephen's point of view is also signalled in his famous declaration of artistic ambition: 'I go to encounter for the millionth time the reality of experience and to forge in the smithy of my soul the uncreated conscience of my race' (*P*: 213). In support of a sentiment that Stephen has always disavowed, these words entwine the drama of individual destiny with the creation of a new national consciousness. They will take Joyce's art far beyond the marmoreal glaze of Stephen's lyric verse towards *Ulysses* and *Finnegans Wake*.

Further Reading

By returning to Joyce's Paris, Trieste and Nola notebooks Scholes and Kain (1965) provide a fascinating glimpse into the compositional history of the novel. In critical terms, the account of *Portrait* presented by Kenner (1987) was crucial in establishing new terms for its reception. Far from endorsing Stephen's self-construction of his own Romantic image, Kenner argues, Joyce consistently views his effusions with an ironic eye. Joyce's ironic perspective upon his protagonist's self-dramatisation indicates here the limits of an aesthetic sensibility that are later parodically exposed in *Ulysses*. Morris (1973) contains a helpful collection of essays upon various aspects of the novel. In one of the most influential poststructuralist readings of Joyce, MacCabe (1978) suggests that Joyce's abandonment of *Stephen Hero* reflects his decisive rupture with the classic realist text. From *Portrait* onward, Joyce gradually stripped away from his fiction the textual metanarrative of classic realism; consequently every subject position – and every position from which an identity might be constituted – is threatened with dissolution into the general play of language. Maud Ellmann (1981) follows MacCabe in developing a reading of *Portrait* influenced by post-structuralist theory; her account displaces conventional discussions of 'character' and motivation to concentrate instead upon the text's constitution of the subject from the presubjective flow of drives, desires and affects. Parrinder argues that the ironic structure of Joyce's narrative and presentation of character enabled him 'both to affirm the romantic myth of artistic genius, and to partially dissociate himself from the arrogance and self-conceit which follows from that myth' (1984: 72). Harkness (1984) explores the connection between Stephen's attitudes and theories and those of fin-de-siècle aesthetes; the ironic tension between Stephen's formal aesthetics and the social and cultural circumstances in which he finds himself is one way by which Joyce exposes the inadequacy of Stephen's theories of art. Thornton (1994) identifies in Joyce's ironic treatment of Stephen a more general critique of the modernist cult of self-contained and self-determining individualism; one crucial entailment of Joyce's 'modernist' style, he argues, is in fact a profoundly 'antimodern' view of reality and the self. Riquelme (1990) suggests that the tension implicit in Joyce's narrative between the modes of realism and fantasy underlines contending and irreconcilable aspects of Stephen's relationship to memory and the perception of finitude. Seed (1992) presents a Bakhtinian reading of Stephen's relationship with the various discourses that constituted turn-of-the-century Irish culture. Coyle (2000) provides a helpful overview of the critical debates that the novel has generated over the last eighty years.

Exiles (1918)

Exiles, Joyce's play first published and performed in 1918, represents his only excursion into drama (if we except the wholly novelistic 'play' presented in the 'Circe' episode of *Ulysses*) and remained relatively neglected until its 1970 London revival. The causes of this critical neglect are not difficult to discern. Although it observes the basic generic protocols of naturalistic drama, *Exiles* never succeeds in breathing life into its dramatic subject. One reason for this dramatic failure is that Joyce makes self-conscious use of the play to refine his *novelistic* portrait of the artist and his responsibilities. On one level, *Exiles* represents Joyce's oblique homage to the drama of Henrik Ibsen that had helped him crystallise his embryonic ideas concerning aesthetic and moral modernity. Thus the play's focus upon the marginalisation of the modern artist, its critique of the sterility of bourgeois culture, and its implied revaluation of contemporary sexual mores provide a succinct rehearsal of Ibsenite themes. At the same time, *Exiles* also appears to spring fully-fledged from the imaginative world of *Portrait*, and Joyce labours to integrate his somewhat dense themes and arguments into the broader emotional texture of the play. These problems of narrative and thematic focus are exacerbated by Joyce's ambivalent attitude to the central artist-figure Richard Rowan. Because Richard is in part a figure of parody, the value of his ethical struggle is never made clear, and the clarity of Joyce's dramatic exposition suffers as a consequence. But the fact that Joyce also sympathises with key aspects of Richard's point of view – he goes so far as to claim in his notes to the play that every man in his audience 'would like to be Richard' – obscures the play's argument and leaves its audience uncertain how, and at whose expense, Joyce's irony ultimately functions (*E*: 164).

The difficulty to interpretation that *Exiles* presents becomes somewhat less pronounced when it is understood to constitute one element of Joyce's more general reflection upon the place of the artist within the culture that produced him. The play was composed between the end of 1913, when Joyce had finished *Portrait*, and the middle of 1915, when he had already begun to draft *Ulysses*. These dates are significant because they suggest that the writing of *Exiles* was one of the ways in which Joyce managed the transition between an (albeit ironically qualified) immersion within the consciousness of an embryonic artist and the confrontation between that consciousness and the exigencies of social reality. Despite its sensitivity to the emotional and moral burden imposed by artistic creation, *Exiles* exposes the limitations of an aesthetic worldview that cannot sustain a productive engagement with the surrounding world. In so doing, it develops Joyce's portrait of the artist beyond the conclusion of his first novel and gestures towards the more exacting imaginative landscape of *Ulysses*.

The play's fundamental contention that 'A nation exacts a penance from those who dared to leave her payable on their return' expresses elements of Joyce's own uneasy relationship with Ireland (*E*: 164). The play takes for its subject the return of the writer Richard Rowan to Ireland with his wife Bertha and son Archie after an absence of nine years. It examines several key Joycean themes: the role of the artist in society, the creative necessity of exile, the nature and limits of personal freedom, and the character of friendship between men. These themes are explored in what Joyce termed three cat and mouse acts in the context of Richard's tortured relationship with Bertha, his sado-masochistic friendship with Robert Hand (whose plan to seduce Bertha Richard tacitly encourages before interposing himself at the last moment), and his attempts to come to terms with the effects of Robert's cousin Beatrice Justice's paralysing infatuation with him. Certainly Joyce's explicatory authorial notes indicate his sympathy with Richard's situation and concerns. In language redolent of Stephen Dedalus' effusions, and which anticipates Richard's own literary mode, Joyce develops a theory of the 'virginity' of the soul. 'Love (understood as the desire of good for another) is in fact so unnatural a phenomenon that it can scarcely repeat itself,' he explains, 'the soul being unable to become virgin again and not having enough energy to cast itself out again into the ocean of another's soul' (E: 163). The difficulty for Joyce (as well as for the audience) is that he never appears convinced how seriously to treat this rather unwieldy theme. The inability of the soul to go forth once more in love, and the lack of spiritual energy this indicates, is personified by Bertha's mental paralysis. She loves Richard, but can find neither a language nor an emotional tone capable of renewing the faltering bond between them; she enters unwillingly into a covert relationship with Robert, but never believes sufficiently in its reality for it to become a test of her feelings for Richard. However, Bertha's failure to establish a vital connection to the world is exactly reproduced in Richard's own spiritual and artistic condition. His friendships are marked throughout by pragmatism and suspicion; his relationship with Archie seems distant and diffident; and he appears to produce very little art. For Joyce the forces of sexual desire and jealousy have a galvanising and redemptive power: Bertha's entanglement with Robert was intended to remind each of them of their latent emotional fidelity to Richard, while the purging of Richard's jealousy constitutes a mystical defence of his spiritual longing for Bertha. Observed from a distance, however, *Exiles* represents Joyce's last great study of paralysis: a world in which the past is unredeemed because the self is never given freely.

The play's uncertain thematic oscillation between redemption and paralysis comes to define the character of Richard Rowan. Richard, Robert declares, has 'fallen from a higher world': his condescension into modern Dublin is designed to overturn its spiritual and moral order and prefigure a new way of living (E: 57). The redemptive – indeed almost messianic – quality of Richard's spiritual revolt is repeatedly emphasised; his friendship with Robert reveals the 'faith of a master in the disciple who will betray him' (E: 58). Joyce accentuates Richard's contempt for an exhausted moral and cultural existence by depicting him as a version of the Byronic hero: his life and art are characterised by 'pride' and 'scorn' (*E*: 22). Crucially, however, Joyce also represents Richard's hubristic romantic attitude as a failure of moral and aesthetic sensibility. Richard not only speaks a different language from everyone else; his words have resonance only for himself. Describing the new union between man and woman his art seeks to inaugurate, Richard asks Robert, 'Even if we are often led to desire through the sense of beauty can you say that the beautiful is what we desire?' (*E*: 55). The echo here of Stephen Dedalus' attitudinising is surely no coincidence, a suspicion strengthened by Richard's continual sense of maternal betrayal: he was estranged from his mother and failed to attend her deathbed. Robert senses that his friend's overwrought rhetoric forms a self-protective screen that enables him to hold at bay the raw contingency of life, an insight implicit in Joyce's arch observation: 'Robert is convinced of the non-existence, of the unreality of the spiritual facts which exist and are real for Richard' (*E*: 165). Lacking the intellectual self-confidence of his friend and rival, Robert's slavish attempts to inhabit Richard's mode succeed only in burlesquing its strained romanticism. Seeking to seduce Bertha, Robert offers his own equation of beauty with desire: 'I think of you always – as something beautiful and distant – the moon or some deep music' (*E*: 39). Too often Robert's speeches appear to be composed of the same faded plush that litters the Rowan living-room. Yet no matter how insistently Robert and Bertha claim that Richard exists upon a different level from others, the recognition that each of the three supporting characters reflects aspects of Richard's personality implicates his mode of being in their poverty of response. Beatrice exudes a passionate intelligence but cannot give herself freely to others; Bertha's emotional covetousness and singularity of purpose leaves her trembling upon the edge of a spiritual vision that never quite comes into focus; while Robert's workaday scheming conceals a romantic desire for self-transcendence that cannot outrun the past. These self-subverting principles of action are not discontinuous with Richard's own; indeed, he comes to exemplify their failure to the highest degree.

The ironic identification of Richard with the repressive limitations of bourgeois Irish culture fatally compromises the gift of freedom he wishes to bestow. The nature and value of this gift elude easy interpretation. To give a thing completely, Richard tells Archie, is also to possess it wholly for oneself: the free expenditure of the self constitutes the true ethical nature of the giver (*E*: 62). The presumptive grandeur of this sentiment exposes it to two forms of objection: this altruistic lesson comes oddly from one who has given virtually nothing to anyone throughout the entire course of the play; and it presupposes that the complete liberty

Richard claims to cede Bertha is itself constitutive of happiness (*E*: 73). Bertha rejects this chimera emphatically: Richard's moral expansiveness is merely a cover for his intellectual affair with Beatrice. She strikes at the core of Richard's moral and aesthetic iconoclasm in more general terms. Complete liberty, Bertha suggests, is only one (and perhaps not the most exalted) form of freedom. There is freedom and self-transcendence also in the development of social relationships. This is a lesson Richard never fully understands, but which glimmers anew in the communion of Bloom and Stephen Dedalus in *Ulysses*.

Further Reading

MacNicholas (1979) provides comprehensive details and commentary concerning the textual genesis and compositional history of the play. Kenner (1987) commits a chapter to *Exiles* that reads it as Joyce's final divestment of the influence of Ibsen and the pathos of the Ibsenite rebel. Tindall (1959) explores Joyce's dramatic reworking of archetypal characters and relationships that recur in his prose fiction. Williams (1968) argues that the play's failure lies in Joyce's inability to translate his practice of narrative indirection from literary into dramatic terms; whereas the vital but incommunicable experience at the heart of 'The Dead' could be implied by the symbolic structure of Joyce's narrative prose, his commitment in *Exiles* to a neutral mode of representational speech drains this experience of all value and resonance. Parrinder (1984) suggests the ways in which the play can be appreciated as a study in the double-binds and paradoxes of sexual permissiveness. Mahaffey (1990) traces the pattern of Wagnerian and Dantesque allusions that inform the play's treatment of human relationships.

Ulysses (1922)

Joyce's second novel, *Ulysses*, began life as an idea for a short story of the same name in 1906. Originally intended for publication in *Dubliners*, 'Ulysses' was projected as the tale of Alfred Hunter, a 'peripatetic Dublin Jew' (Parrinder 1984: 115). The story was abandoned in 1907, as Joyce focused his energies upon the composition of *Portrait*; but the idea about a self-exiled and wandering Jew simultaneously at home and adrift in the modern Irish metropolis never left Joyce, who returned to it once more following the completion of *Portrait* in 1914. By the time *Ulysses* was published in Paris by Shakespeare and Company in 1922, it had grown from its brief embryonic origins into an 'epic' modernist novel of more than 700 pages. Here Joyce developed to its highest point of refinement the experimentation with narrative point of view, interior monologue and stream of consciousness that had preoccupied modern writers such as Dorothy Richardson, Virginia Woolf and Gertrude Stein. His insistence upon representing in *Ulysses* the entirety of modern life from its basis in physical process to its most elevated intellectual expression came at a price; the novel was banned on the grounds of obscenity upon its publication in Britain and the United States. Despite continuing attempts to suppress the novel – and the maintenance of the American ban until 1933 – it was quickly recognised to be a classic of modern literature and established Joyce's reputation as a leading national and international artist.

With *Ulysses* Joyce realised his aesthetic ambition of composing a great epic statement about modern European civilisation. One of the principal functions of epic literature is to inaugurate the foundational narrative of a nation or culture; by employing Homer's *The Odyssey* as an allegorical intertext for the wanderings and tribulations of Leopold Bloom and Stephen Dedalus, Joyce announced his intention to create a new mythos for the modern age. As an Irishman devising a modern prose epic in English, Joyce savoured the irony of an artist from a colonial culture writing the book that would come to define the modernity of the language he inherited. The years he spent writing *Ulysses* were disfigured by the cataclysm of World War One and the beginnings of the Irish Civil War; in the figure of Leopold Bloom Joyce refashioned classical values and virtues to create an image of secular tolerance in a time of violent division. Bloom is, in many ways, a comically reduced Ulysses who substitutes information for wisdom and steadfastness for valour. But like Ulysses he is estranged at once from home and from nation; and like the Greek he was, in Joyce's words, 'subjected to many trials, but with wisdom and courage came though them all' (Budgen 1934: 17). Ulysses' combination of conscientiousness, moral fortitude and supple intelligence marked him out, Joyce noted, as both a 'complete' and a 'good' man: 'Ulysses is son to Laertes, father to Telemachus, husband to Penelope, lover of Calypso, companion in arms of the Greek warriors around Troy and King of Ithaca' (Budgen 1934: 16). Bloom, in turn, is a 'cultured allroundsman': a dutiful (if fantasising) husband, a doting father, a loyal friend, a good citizen, a man of wise passivity and sympathetic demeanour (*U*: 225). Joyce also discerns in Bloom's pragmatic but always sensuous intelligence a point of intersection between Stephen's abstract intellectualism and Molly's corporeal responsiveness. Ultimately it is in the subtle interplay between these three very different modes of consciousness that Joyce's greatest theme declares itself: the representation of the flow and manifold force of life from its affective origins in desire, sensation and sensuous apprehension to its complex manifestation in our ideas of culture, politics and nationhood.

Episode One: Telemachus

The dominant themes of this opening episode are the loss of one's proper place and title and alienation from home, nation and family life. In Homer's *The Odyssey*, Telemachus, Ulysses' son and heir, finds himself alone and friendless while his home is besieged by suitors for his mother Penelope. Counselled by the goddess Athene to live up to his responsibilities and assert his independence ('You should not go on clinging to your childhood. You are no longer of an age to do that'), Telemachus prepares to leave Ithaca and begin his quest to find his father (Homer 1991: 34). Joyce's *Ulysses* begins at 8 a.m. at the Martello Tower at Sandymount Cove, which Stephen Dedalus shares with the medical student Buck Mulligan and Haines, a visiting Englishman. Since the end of *Portrait* Stephen has endured a fruitless sojourn in Paris (where none of his artistic ambitions appears to have been realised) and returned to Dublin during his mother's final illness. Her death proved to be the final point of rupture between Stephen and his family; by refusing to kneel at her bedside he rejected both filial obligation and religious duty. Exiled from the family home, Stephen is no more at ease at Sandymount Cove: while he pays the rent for the tower, Mulligan retains the key, and by the end of the episode Stephen has concluded he can live there no longer. He heads out, instead, onto the Dublin streets toward his encounter with his surrogate father-figure Leopold Bloom.

A number of important themes find symbolic expression in Stephen's exchanges with Mulligan. Like Satan in John Milton's epic poem *Paradise Lost* (1667), Mulligan is a tempter and usurper; unable to create anything of value himself, he substitutes meretricious wit for artistic integrity. He also bears false gifts: like Homer's Trojan horse, his face is 'equine in its length' and 'hued like pale oak' (*U*: 3). Mulligan's parody of the Mass in the novel's opening sentences ('For this, O dearly beloved, is the genuine Christine: body and soul and blood and ouns. Slow music, please') dramatises Stephen's estrangement from religious authority, whilst his observation that 'You wouldn't kneel down to pray for your mother on her deathbed when she asked you' underscores Stephen's fierce resistance to moral convention (*U*: 8). In the act of attempting to usurp Stephen's social and moral authority, Mulligan is also represented

as Claudius to Stephen's Hamlet. Mulligan, like Claudius, takes possession of what is rightfully Stephen's (the key) while accusing Stephen of
suffering from 'General paralysis of the insane' (U: 6). Meanwhile standing at his post 'gazing over the calm sea towards the headland', Stephen,
like Hamlet on the battlements of Elsinore, struggles to maintain his
rebellious independence (U: 9). So routine is Irish subordination to
English colonial authority that it is simply assumed: Haines's bland
remark: 'We feel in England that we have treated you rather unfairly. It
seems history is to blame' captures the blithe self-assurance of imperial
dominion (U: 20). Yet as the caricature figure of the old milk-woman suggests, unthinking reversion to 'traditional' Irish values is no better solution: she is a credulous fool who admires a 'grand' language she cannot
even speak, all the time preferring Mulligan's cheap theatrics to Stephen's
mature reserve (U: 14).

Joyce's prose incorporates aspects of Homeric epic (such as Homer's
stylistic fondness for adjectival conjunctions like 'winedark sea') while
continually extending the range of its symbolic resonance. Mulligan is
variously Claudius, Lucifer and Photius the Heretic; Stephen's image
combines elements of Telemachus, Hamlet and Christ. The uncertainty
of Stephen's image is matched by the ambiguity of his role. He is not
'heroic' in any simple sense: he would not, like Mulligan, risk his life to
save a drowning man. Instead, his epic quest is to remain faithful to the
demands of his own unfettered intelligence. The character and ultimate
destination of this quest, meanwhile, is unknowingly foreshadowed by
Haines: 'I read a theological interpretation of it somewhere . . . The
Father and the Son idea. The Son striving to be atoned with the Father'
(U: 18).

Episode Two: Nestor

The second episode elaborates some of the historical contexts that inform
Ulysses. In *The Odyssey*, Telemachus attempts to discover details of his
father's whereabouts. He encounters the sage Nestor who tells him of
Ulysses' decade-long participation in the Siege of Troy and of the
vengeance wrought by the gods that still prevent him from returning
to his homeland (Homer 1991: 54). In 'Nestor' Stephen engages in a
number of discussions about Irish, European and ecclesiastical history
that continue to define his attitudes towards British and Irish culture.

It is 10 o'clock and the scene has shifted to Mr Deasy's school where
Stephen is employed as a teacher. He is conducting a lesson in classical
history about Pyrrhus and the battle of Asculum. The story of Pyrrhus,

who tried to overthrow the Roman yoke and restore the lost fortunes of Greece, introduces the themes of suffering and exile that preoccupy Stephen and foreshadow his meeting with the outsider Bloom. Stephen has little patience with the plodding narrative history under debate: the apocalyptic strain of his imagination understands history to be determined by the violent collision of blind forces. 'I hear the ruin of all space, shattered glass and toppled masonry,' Stephen reflects at one point, 'and time one livid final flame' (U: 24). The random interplay of historical forces is given structure and coherence only by the achieved form of art. Just as the soul is the ultimate 'form of forms', the end of art redeems history from formless chaos (U: 26). 'History,' Stephen famously declares, 'is a nightmare from which I am trying to awake (U: 34). One reason for this uncompromising position quickly becomes clear: Stephen is haunted by guilt about his mother's death, which resurfaces in his riddle about the 'fox burying his grandmother under a hollybush' (U: 27).

Nestor is represented in a savagely reduced fashion by Mr Deasy. Nestor's advice often fell upon deaf ears; Deasy has no wisdom or good advice to offer. He is a self-regarding establishment insider secure of his position within a corrupt colonial culture. Deasy's ease with the imperial legacy at work in Irish affairs is suggested by 'the tray of Stuart coins, base treasure of a bog' displayed upon his sideboard: 'base', here, also registers Stephen's implied moral judgement (U: 29). Deasy, in fact, represents the type of Protestant Irishman who has internalised the British point of view to the degree that Empire is seen merely as a business proposition. Stephen's interior monologue deftly establishes the connection between Deasy and Haines: 'The seas' ruler. His seacold eyes looked on the empty bay: history is to blame: on me and on my words, unhating' (U: 30). More pointedly, Deasy quotes to Stephen the betrayer Iago's advice to Othello ('Put but money in thy purse'). Stephen recognises that the implication he should abandon art for the safety of the teaching profession is ruinous to his sense of integrity. Never slow to construct general cultural judgements upon the basis of perceived personal slights, he identifies Deasy's intervention as part of the historical loyalist conspiracy against Catholicism: 'The black north and true blue bible. Croppies lie down' (U: 31).

Another reason for the significance of Deasy's character is that it enables Joyce to establish a connection between a style of language and a way of perceiving the world. Deasy's letter to the newspaper concerning the treatment of foot and mouth is a litany of clichés; he writes this way because he is a lazy thinker given to generalisations and received ideas. It is therefore fitting that it is Deasy who offers the first sustained exposition of anti-Semitism in the novel: the Jews, he explains to Stephen, are 'the signs of a nation's decay' that vitiate its 'vital strength' (*U*: 33). These words are the first indication of the repressive forces that impinge daily upon Bloom and that will be challenged by his generous and suffering humanity.

Episode Three: Proteus

Episode three examines the nature of consciousness and perception. It focuses upon the relationship between the multitude of representations of the world our senses encounter and the reality of the world that lies beneath these appearances. Because the episode's emphasis is upon appearance and flux, its dominant symbol is the tides of the sea that present a series of shifting surfaces to our gaze. Homer's section on Proteus concerns itself with the acquisition of knowledge and the fortitude required of the one who seeks it. In order to discover the whereabouts of the Greek heroes with whom he had fought at Troy, Menelaus is forced to grapple with the elusive and shape-shifting Proteus, a god of the sea. Eventually Menelaus manages to pin down Proteus and is given the information he seeks, including the news that Ulysses is presently a captive within the palace of the nymph Calypso (Homer 1991: 79).

Joyce's Homeric analogy seizes upon the idea of the shifting aspects of an ultimate principle (the god Proteus) and employs it as a metaphor for the mind's fluctuating consciousness of the external world. It is 11 o'clock and Stephen is strolling along the beach at Sandymount Strand trying to discern the relationship between the appearance of things and their substantial or unchanging form. He reflects upon the way we perceive the world through its appearance and visible form: 'Signatures of all things I am here to read' (*U*: 37). The speculation to which these thoughts give rise provides *Ulysses* with its first sustained example of interior monologue. Stephen's monologue has a distinctive style that reveals the peculiar cast of his mind. This 'mind style' is dense and allusive; it progresses by a kind of metaphysical wit that yokes together seemingly disparate ideas and sensations. Stephen sees a midwife carrying a bag and imagines the 'misbirth with a trailing navelcord' it might contain (*U*: 38). His mind immediately transforms this image into the entire collection of navel cords that link together the whole of human history. This collection is then converted into the network of a telephone exchange that enables us to ring all the way back home to Eve in 'Edenville'. Stephen's thoughts pass quickly and wittily from idea to idea (unlike Bloom's, which tend to remain at the level of material sensation). Waves impinge upon his consciousness and are pleasingly rendered in language: 'Listen: a fourworded wavespeech: seasoo, hrss, rsseeiss ooos' (*U*: 49). Elsewhere, Stephen's intellectual self-regard pushes him toward pretension: 'Intellectual modality of the visible' is on one level merely a high-sounding phrase for the pre-eminence of sight in our perception of the world (*U*: 37). The purpose of phrases like this is not to advertise Joyce's learning but to place Stephen's speculative preoccupations in a gentle ironic light. These preoccupations are sometimes obtuse and faintly ridiculous, but they are also the signature gestures of a young man struggling to develop his own style of personality. The moments when Stephen admits the hollowness of his own achievements ('Remember your epiphanies on green oval leaves, deeply deep, copies to be sent if you died to all the great libraries of the world, including Alexandria?') win him the reader's sympathy; and it is in moments like these that Joyce satirises his own younger self (*U*: 41).

Another important theme explored in this episode is Stephen's mythic rewriting of his own origins. Stephen believes that he was 'made' not 'begotten': as an artist he is not merely the biological product of his parents, but a fragment of the divine Father, inheritor of a birthright that transcends any human origin (*U*: 38). Lucifer, too, had traces of divinity within him, and Stephen's resolute refusal to submit to any external law retains a satanic dimension. Stephen's proud but iconoclastic intellect will be challenged by his encounter with Bloom, the image of suffering and redemptive humanity. Their meeting is prefigured symbolically in the episode's closing sentences: feeling that there is 'perhaps' someone behind him, Stephen turns and glimpses the three Calvary crosses ('high spars') of a ship shadowing him upon the horizon (*U*: 50).

Episode Four: Calypso

The fourth episode returns to 8 o'clock in the morning, but the scene has shifted from Stephen's wanderings to 7 Eccles Street, the home of Leopold and Molly Bloom. In *The Odyssey*, Ulysses is held captive for seven years by the goddess Calypso until Zeus orders her to release him (Homer 1991: 91). In modern Dublin, Bloom is the emotional captive of Molly, whom he serves by bringing her breakfast before embarking upon his daily rounds.

'Calypso' introduces Leopold Bloom, the modern Ulysses, to the novel. Although Bloom shares certain circumstances with Stephen, Joyce subtly emphasises their differences of temperament and perspective. Both men are, to some degree, exiles: like Stephen, Bloom goes out keyless into the world. Like Ulysses at the siege of Troy, Bloom has also endured a ten-year separation from his wife: he and Molly have not made love since the death of their son Rudy in 1894. Bloom's religious identity as a Jew also underscores his outsider status, although it is never the defining issue for him that it becomes for others. However, unlike Stephen, who inhabits a world of intellectual speculation, Bloom is a sensualist enthralled by the body and its various desires. Bloom's temperamental difference from Stephen is indicated by the style of his interior monologue. Where Stephen's reflections begin characteristically with an idea and then develop onward to the sensations this idea evokes, Bloom's thought tends to proceed in the opposite direction. Shopping at Dlugacz the Butcher's, Bloom's senses are assailed by the sight and smell of meat; his thoughts drift from this immediate sensation to the 'moving hams' of a woman next to him; he then develops this image into a more general vision of the pleasures of youth and romantic life: 'Make hay while the sun shines' (U: 57). His mind cleaves rigorously to material matters (such as how grocers earn their living); he is a realist, despite his weakness for sentimental reverie.

The Bloom household is a monument to fading memories and lapsed desire. Bloom's place in Molly's affections is being usurped by the musical impresario Blazes Boylan: Molly is concealing a letter in Boylan's '[b]old hand' confirming the details of their afternoon tryst when Bloom appears upstairs with her breakfast (U: 61). Meanwhile the triangular relationship between Bloom, Molly and their daughter Milly is reproduced (and mocked) by the 'professional' relationship between Molly, Boylan and Milly. Molly retains a vibrant physical presence for Bloom: upon entering the bedroom his attention is immediately drawn to her 'soft bubs' and the 'warmth of her couched body'. For her part, Molly is replete with native cunning, but remains adrift in the world of language and ideas. She struggles with the meaning of 'metempsychosis' (the idea of the transmigration of the soul by which Joyce alludes slyly to his series of Homeric analogies); 'O, rocks' is her response to Bloom's detailed explanation (U: 62). Her earthy sensuality is suggested by her taste for popular erotic fiction; Bloom, who regards these books with disdain, has tastes that run in a similar direction. Joyce reveals this unacknowledged coincidence of interests by a pun upon Bloom's nickname 'Poldy': Molly has asked Bloom to obtain her a book by Paul de Kock ('Poldy cock'). Yet this punning coincidence serves only to underline the emotional gulf between husband and wife: Molly turns to erotica, not Bloom's body, to satisfy her physical desires.

The infamous final scene depicting Bloom in the lavatory interweaves several important themes. Bloom is both physically and emotionally costive: haunted by the past, he has difficulty opening himself to new feelings and situations. While evacuating himself he reads *Tidbits* before wiping himself with a page of the paper; Joyce permits himself here a pointed comment upon the detritus of much modern journalism, with its crude commercial sensibility and vacuous sloganeering. Ultimately an episode which began with sensual openness concludes beneath the shadow of death: 'Poor Dignan!' (*U*: 67). Bloom's journey toward reconciliation with Molly will require the exorcism of several ghosts.

Episode Five: The Lotus-Eaters

The time is now 10 a.m.; the scene is the streets of Dublin. In *The Odyssey*, Ulysses' crew arrive upon the island of the lotus-eaters and are offered the lotus to eat as a propitiatory gift. Its properties induce in them a narcotic torpor; intent upon gratifying their senses, they 'forget their way home' and abandon their nautical responsibilities (Homer 1991: 139). Only when Ulysses forces them to return to ship do they recover from the effects of their narcotic seduction.

The hedonistic theme of this Homeric episode is reflected in Joyce's prose, which reproduces Bloom's narcotic enthralment to myriad momentary sensual impressions. The tone is set at the beginning of the episode, where he gazes in at the window of the Belfast and Oriental Tea Company and indulges a fantasy of the Far East: 'Not doing a hand's turn all day. Sleep six months out of twelve. Too hot to quarrel. Influence of the climate. Lethargy. Flowers of idleness' (*U*: 69). The lotus-eating theme is symbolised most pithily by the rows of drugs and potions in the chemist's where Bloom goes to buy Molly's face-lotion: 'Drugs age you after mental excitement. Lethargy then. Why? Reaction. A lifetime in a night. Gradually changes your character' (*U*: 81). The torpid sensuality of the prevailing atmosphere only reinforces the pathos of Bloom and Molly's physical estrangement. Bloom unrolls his newspaper and reads the advertising jingle 'What is home without / Plumtree's Potted Meat? / Incomplete. / With it an abode of bliss' (*U*: 72). The language evokes simultaneously the scene of an affectless marriage and a sense of sexual threat: Bloom's home is 'incomplete' without 'potted meat'; but it will become an 'abode of bliss' for Boylan. Here we glimpse the creative power of Joycean irony, which revivifies deadened or reified speech and works against the stultifying effects of business language.

'The Lotus-Eaters' also develops the furtive and self-indulgent aspects of Bloom's character. Bloom wanders to the post office to collect mail addressed to his nom-de-plume 'Henry Flower'. His 'affair' with Martha

Clifford is hardly invigorating; destined to remain unconsummated, it represents a dull reprise of his relationship with Molly. Martha even shares Molly's linguistic uncertainty: 'I called you naughty boy because I do not like that other world' (U: 74). Bloom will never renounce reality for this fantasy relationship: he readily accepts the deferred pleasure of erotic intrigue, but shrinks from the emotional pressure of a sexual affair. Significantly, Joyce suggests that Bloom's narcotic self-seduction and febrile embrace of fantasy is characteristic of contemporary Irish culture in general. As in *Dubliners*, he focuses upon the social function of religion as an opiate for the people that transforms them into unquestioning and obedient souls. In this spirit, Bloom reflects ironically upon the way the Latin Mass 'stupefies' the congregation (U: 77). The religious service works both as a hallucinogen and a narcotic by producing images of transcendence that reinforce our unregenerate human desire to be spiritually redeemed:

> Wonderful organisation certainly, goes like clockwork. Confession. Everyone wants to. Then I will tell you all. Penance. Punish me, please. Great weapon in their hands. (U: 79)

In contrast, Bloom's devotion is to the physical and social body. Men and women are united by common ethical obligations to one another because they share a common flesh. While Bloom's final fantasy-image of his laved body is certainly open to a religious interpretation, he puts his faith resolutely in social relationships. His ethical humanism is not always returned: the confusion over the status of his 'throw it away' remark to Bantam Lyons will confirm his outsider status in the darkness of the 'Cyclops' episode (U: 82).

Episode Six: Hades

It is 11 a.m. and while Stephen is walking upon Sandymount Strand Bloom travels to Glasnevin Cemetery for Paddy Dignam's funeral. This episode mirrors Ulysses' journey to Hades in Book 11 of *The Odyssey*; as Bloom remarks ruefully upon entering the cemetery, 'Whole place gone to hell' (U: 96). The section develops further significant aspects of Bloom's character and underlines his uncertain position within a particular stratum of Dublin society.

Bloom travels to Glasnevin in a cab with Simon Dedalus, Mr Power and Martin Cunningham. His interior monologue offers important insights into his temperament and sensibility. Alongside the inevitable reflections on the mortal passage from cradle to grave, Bloom's meditation ranges across medical science, politics, the advantages of inner-city tramlines and the problems of filial relationships. Bloom is, above all, a *practical* man. He abstains from the general lachrymose sentimentality about Dignam: Dignam, Bloom reflects, brought his death upon himself by taking to drink. One of the first remarks he offers about Dignam at Glasnevin is 'Was he insured?' (*U*: 98). Bloom reveals himself to be an acute judge of character (his sense of Simon Dedalus' contrariness is expertly condensed into seven words 'Noisy selfwilled man. Full of his son'); but his acuity of insight is always leavened by compassion: Simon is 'right' to be full of his son because a son is '[s]omething to hand on' to posterity (*U*: 86). These reflections underscore two of the episode's dominant themes: the futility of living in the past; and the terrible failures of communication and empathy between fathers and sons. The former theme is symbolised by Queen Victoria's anguished veneration of Prince Albert's memory; the latter by Simon's estrangement from Stephen Dedalus and the moving sight of Dignam's bereaved son: 'Poor boy! Was he there when the father? Both unconscious' (*U*: 99).

Bloom's uncertain position within the assembled mourners is repeatedly underlined. The group indulge a casual anti-Semitism by passing derogatory remarks about an elderly member of 'the tribe of Reuben' (*U*: 90). Less explicitly, Power's tactless remark about the cowardice of suicide betrays a basic ignorance of Bloom's family history: Bloom's father poisoned himself some years before, following the collapse of his financial affairs. Bloom is with the group, but he's not wholly *of* it. Meanwhile the pressure of the world outside the cab imposes itself upon him. The pathos of his domestic predicament is wonderfully expressed by his unwelcome consciousness of Boylan: 'He's coming in the afternoon. Her songs' (*U*: 89). Bloom is to be martyred this day and will then rise again. The crucifixion imagery emphasises this symbolic dimension of the novel as the 'white disc' of Boylan's straw hat flashes by the cab window and Bloom reviews the 'nails' upon both of his hands.

Bloom's relative marginalisation within the company of mourners contributes to his outsider's perspective upon the funeral ceremony. As a Jew, the symbols and rituals of Catholicism are something of a mystery to him and his emotional distance from the proceedings is frequently reaffirmed. His unfamiliarity with the local intricacies of Catholic ritual is captured in his inexact representation of the funeral Mass: 'The priest took a stick with a knob at the end of it out of the boy's bucket and shook it over the coffin' (*U*: 100). Consequently, Bloom's response to the symbolic Hell of Glasnevin differs markedly from that of his companions. While Simon Dedalus weeps sentimental tears for his much-neglected wife and Tom

Kernan offers officious remarks about ceremonial niceties, Bloom is unsentimental about bodily decay and the mystery of our ultimate end: 'Once you are dead you are dead. That last day idea. Knocking them all up out of their graves. Come forth, Lazarus!' (*U*: 102). He is unmoved by crass religiosity and the bathetic piety of headstone inscriptions. Instead, the omnipresence of death awakens him once more to the force of physical desire: 'You might pick up a young widow here . . . Love among the tombstones' (*U*: 104). Martha wrote to him that she 'did not like that other world'; nor, glancing around Glasnevin cemetery, does Bloom. The cemetery gate 'glimmered' in front of him; the dead are not going to get him 'this innings' (*U*: 110). He steps through them with alacrity and returns to 'warm fullblooded life'.

Episode Seven: Aeolus

It is noon and both Bloom and Stephen arrive at the offices of the *Evening Telegraph*, although they do not actually meet. Their failure to meet is indicative of the principal theme of the episode: the frustration of hope at the moment of potential success. In *The Odyssey*, the God Aeolus assists Ulysses by gathering into a bag the winds hampering his nautical progress. However Ulysses' crew open the bag looking for 'silver and gold' as they near their destination and are once more blown off course (Homer 1991: 153). Ulysses subsequently returns to Aeolus to request more help, but none is forthcoming.

If the main theme of 'Aeolus' is disappointment, its governing symbol is the lungs. Joyce locates this episode in a newspaper office in order to satirise the inflated and often empty rhetoric of modern journalism, which ceaselessly ventilates 'information' but does not always bring knowledge and truth more securely into view. The conversation in Myles Crawford's office is reminiscent of the political hot air expended in 'Ivy Day in The Committee Room'. Every part of the newspaper print machinery is in constant motion (breathing in and out): much heat is generated, but relatively little light. Joyce's prose style reproduces the typographic layout of newsprint to create an ironic tension between the grandiloquence of newspaper headlines and the text accompanying them. At one point the reader is promised 'Links with Bygone Days of Yore', but connections between the *Telegraph* and the remembered glories of European Catholic culture become increasingly hard to discern (*U*: 134).

Bloom is in the offices of the *Weekly Freeman and National Review* (adjoining the *Telegraph*) attempting to place an advertisement for

Alexander Keyes. He feels oppressed by the thumping of the printing press: 'Smash a man to atoms if they got him caught. Rule the world today' (*U*: 114). As Bloom makes his way to see Councillor Nannetti, business manager of the *Freeman*, his isolation is emphasised once more. Neither Nannetti nor the printer Cuprani lives in his own country, but they are now '[m]ore Irish than the Irish', while Bloom still vainly seeks his countrymen's approval (*U*: 115). The sight of Old Monks the typesetter reading his print backwards reminds Bloom of the fact of his ethnic difference: 'Poor papa with his hagadah book, reading backwards with his finger to me. Pessach. Next year in Jerusalem' (*U*: 118). His alienation from the crowd is subtly expressed by the Keyes advertisement, which presents the punning typographical juxtaposition of two crossed keys. The pun alludes both to the future meeting of keyless Bloom and Stephen and the progress of the usurper Boylan, who will 'cross' Bloom by shattering the illusion of his 'home rule' (*U*: 116).

In Crawford's editorial office Joyce continues to focus obliquely, but insistently, upon Bloom's marginal position. Scant space is provided for Bloom in this scene; he is bumped against the door by each newcomer. Professor MacHugh mutters 'the ghost walks' as Bloom enters the office; Bloom's presence is spectral, like Hamlet's father, and his matrimonial position is also about to be usurped (*U*: 119). The atmosphere in Crawford's office is febrile and unproductive: everyone talks, but no-one listens. Conversation circulates to no particular purpose, like Lenehan's sports pages blown around the floor by the wind. Stephen arrives soon after Bloom departs to continue negotiations with Keyes, but quickly feels himself to be out of place. The entire discussion is now about the past, such as the glorious courtroom performances of Isaac Butt and O'Hagan; meanwhile Bloom's present predicament is ignored. Professor McHugh cautions the assembled newspapermen that they 'mustn't be led away by words, by sounds of words' before extolling at length once more Ireland's distinctive position within the 'catholic chivalry of Europe' (*U*: 126, 128). As the discussion rambles desultorily towards a conclusion, Simon Dedalus' caustic observation 'shite and onions!' threatens to sum up the entire proceedings (*U*: 121). Significantly, Stephen meditates *privately* upon poetry and the responsibilities of language; his sensibility cannot be integrated into this new democracy of commercial opinion. To his ears it is all nothing but '[d]ead noise' (*U*: 138).

Quiet moments of pathos emerge amid this cacophony. When Crawford walks 'jerkily into the office behind, parting the vent of his jacket, jingling his keys in his back pocket' we glimpse both Bloom's dispossession and elements of his domestic despair (*U*: 125). Unlike

Crawford, Bloom is keyless; and the sound of 'jingling' anticipates the bedroom exploits of Molly and Boylan. With the prospect of a successful commission almost in sight, Bloom, like Ulysses, is frustrated: Crawford resists Keyes' newly-inflated demands, telling Bloom that his employer can 'kiss my royal Irish arse' (U: 141). An episode preoccupied with unsatisfied desire eventually finds its appropriate terminus in Stephen's 'Parable of the Plums', with its images of masturbation, spinsterhood and Lord Nelson the '[o]nehanded adulterer' (U: 143).

Episode Eight: Lestrygonians

This episode takes place at lunchtime between and 1 p.m. and 2 p.m. In *The Odyssey*, Ulysses' crew is exposed to the cannibalistic Lestrygonians; one of them is eaten and the lives of the rest placed briefly in peril (Homer 1991: 155). A world away in Dublin, Bloom recoils in horror from the table manners he glimpses in the Burton and seeks refuge instead inside Davy Byrne's. The principal themes of 'Lestrygonians' are food, taste and digestion; the recursive and dilatory style of Joyce's prose is intended to reflect a 'peristaltic' movement 'imitative of the successive muscular contractions which drive nutritive matter along the alimentary canal' (Blamires 1983: 64). Theme and style are seamlessly interwoven in the passage where Bloom speculates whether scientists could create a transparent model of the internal workings of the human body:

> They could: and watch it all the way down, swallow a pin sometimes come out of the ribs years after, tour round the body, changing biliary duct, spleen squirting liver, gastric juice coils of intestine like pipes. (U: 171)

Bloom is abroad once more upon Dublin's streets. His compassionate nature is immediately emphasised: he catches sight of young Dilly Dedalus, her dress 'in flitters', and imagines the strain placed upon families once the mother is gone (U: 145). Bloom's gentleness resurfaces later in his dealings with Mrs Breen, luckless wife of an eccentric husband. His selfless compassion is intrinsic to a broader stratum of theological symbolism within which Bloom is figured as an image of Christ the Redeemer. A YMCA man gives Bloom a throwaway advertisement. Glancing at it, he mistakes the 'Bloo' of 'Blood of the Lamb' for his own name 'Bloom' (U: 144). Moments later he breaks Banbury cakes and casts them upon the Liffey in a symbolic reworking of Christ casting bread upon the waters; and he meditates tellingly upon Handel's *Messiah* at the episode's conclusion (U: 146, 174). In between, Bloom notes the time-ball upon the ballast office, and his thoughts turn to Robert Ball's book on 'Parallax' (U: 147). Joyce employs the idea of parallax, which describes the apparent difference in the position of an object wrought by a change in the position of the observer, to suggest how the meaning of our experience of the world is determined in part by the angle from which we perceive it. The constitutive role of subjective perception in the construction of our social reality helps to explain Joyce's fascination with the interiority of consciousness. Bloom's interest in conceptual problems further distinguishes him from Molly's struggles with 'Met. Him. Pike. Hoses'. His repulsion at the thought of living merely at the level of the bodily appetites is symbolised in the episode's climactic 'Lestrygonian' moment when he enters the Burton: 'His heart astir he pushed in the door of the Burton restaurant. Stink gripped his trembling breath: pungent meatjuice, slop of greens. See the animals feed' (U: 161). A humane vision of life, Bloom decides, requires a judicious balance between the real and ideal: after all, if you treat a woman like a goddess, she will 'put you in your proper place' (U: 168). And surely even a goddess must defecate? With typically exaggerated fastidiousness, he decides to examine this thesis by scrutinising the buttocks of a marble statue.

During Bloom's progress, the past floods in upon him and is rendered in marvellous elliptical fragments. He reflects upon the death of Rudy and the termination it imposed upon his physical relationship with Molly: 'Could never like it again after Rudy. Can't bring back time. Like holding water in your hand' (U: 160). A melancholy meditation upon the seemingly endless cycle of human exploitation and misery – 'Landlord never dies they say. Other steps into his shoes when he gets his notice to quit' – highlights the universality of Bloom's struggle for human decency in a pitiless world before concluding with the terrifying intuition that 'No one is anything' (U: 157). Most movingly of all, Bloom's emotional distance from the day with Molly upon Howth Hill when she pushed seedcake from her mouth into his is captured in four stark words: 'Me. And me now' (U: 168).

Episode Nine: Scylla and Charybdis

The time is 2 p.m. and the scene is the National Library. Joyce's thematic emphasis switches from Bloom's corporeal passion to the bloodless mental landscape of Stephen's intellect. In *The Odyssey*, Homer describes Ulysses' dangerous, but ultimately successful journey between the whirlpool Charybdis and the monster Scylla, whose multiple heads snap down upon passing ships (Homer 1991: 187). Joyce's Homeric parallel works by creating an analogy between these life-threatening hazards and the various forms of rhetoric that threaten to cloud the reader's understanding. On one side of us lies the whirlpool of scholarly arguments proffered by George Russell, John Eglinton and Lyster; on the other side are Stephen's Aristotelian 'dagger definitions' (*U*: 178). We must negotiate our passage by fending off the dangerous seduction of both these forms of partial and motivated disputation.

The recognition that Stephen's arguments also *menace* clear judgement encourages us to inspect them for what they reveal about his character. The subject of the scholarly exchange is Shakespeare's *Hamlet*. Stephen mocks Eglinton's idealised representation of Hamlet as '[t]he beautiful ineffectual dreamer who comes to grief against hard facts' (*U*: 176). He is invited by Eglinton to supply his own interpretation of *Hamlet*, which has already been lampooned by Mulligan in 'Telemachus': 'He proves by algebra that Hamlet's grandson is Shakespeare's grandfather and that he himself is the ghost of his own father' (*U*: 18). Stephen's idiosyncratic reading of *Hamlet* is a testament to his intellectual virtuosity, but it also underlines his obsession with questions of paternity and autonomy. Amid a multitude of other points, Stephen notes that Shakespeare wrote *Hamlet* after his own father's death. Consequently, Shakespeare wasn't a 'son' at the time of the play's composition; nor was he a 'father' because his son Hamnet had already died aged 11 (the same age Rudy would be now had he lived). However, the act of writing made Shakespeare the creative father of his entire family history: father, grandfather, dead son and all his future issue. For writing is a mode of imaginative synthesis by which past, present and future are superimposed upon each other and then reinterpreted anew by the creative intelligence:

> In the intense instant of imagination, when the mind, Shelley says, is a fading coal that which I was is that which I am and that which in possibility I may come to be. So in the future, the sister of the past, I may see myself as I sit here now but by reflection from that which then I shall be. (*U*: 186–7)

The creative struggle of the artist to reinterpret time provides a template for the antagonistic relationship between father and son. Unlike the incontestable physical relationship between mother and child, the connection between father and son is based upon the 'incertitude' of 'the void' (*U*: 199). All that links the two is an 'instant of blind rut'. The son resents the privilege of his father's authorship and the two become joined in a life-long struggle for authority. Writing, Stephen hopefully concludes, enables the son imaginatively to beget his own father and take control of his paternity. Bloom will offer Stephen a kindlier and less fraught vision of the father and son relationship.

Stephen's grandiose theories of authorship and paternity are not to be accepted uncritically; indeed, they are mocked both by him and his audience. 'I think you're getting on very nicely,' Stephen remarks to himself, 'Just mix up a mixture of theolologicophilolological' (*U*: 196). Similarly, Mulligan's parody of Stephen's theories entitled 'Everyman His Own Wife' takes masturbation for its subject (*U*: 208). Despite these mocking overtones, the poignancy of Stephen's isolation remains: he envisages himself as 'Cordoglio', a male version of the king's abandoned daughter Cordelia in Shakespeare's *King Lear* (*U*: 185). His unhappiness curdles into self-disgust at his inability to create art; he pictures himself as Icarus, not Daedalus the artificer and creator: 'Fabulous artificer, the hawklike man. You flew. Whereto? Newhaven-Dieppe, steerage passenger. Paris and back. Lapwing. Icarus' (*U*: 202). Happily the episode's conclusion affords a brighter vision of his prospects. Bloom appears, fresh from inspecting the rear of a statue, and momentarily interposes himself between Stephen and his mocker Mulligan. To the unseeing Mulligan, Bloom is just a 'wandering Jew' (*U*: 209). But for Stephen, Bloom will provide the opportunity for reconciliation with the father and humanity in general.

Episode Ten: The Wandering Rocks

It is 3 p.m. and at the novel's midpoint the scene moves back to the streets of Dublin. In this episode Joyce explores the circulatory system of Dublin's body politic. It is difficult to establish a precise correspondence between *Ulysses* and *The Odyssey* at this juncture, in which case Stuart Gilbert's observation that '[i]n its structure and its *technic* ('labyrinth') this episode may be regarded as a small-scale model of *Ulysses* as a whole' becomes particularly suggestive (Gilbert 1930: 223). One possible parallel between the two texts is that in the *Odyssey* Circe instructs Ulysses to avoid the wandering rocks that imperil ships, and he successfully negotiates his passage beyond them (Homer 1991: 186). In Joyce's hands, this Homeric episode becomes the point of departure for an elaborate exercise in verisimilitude in which he attempts to describe a multitude of urban incidents in the real time it would take his characters to traverse the Dublin streets. The entire episode is lent a degree of formal coherence by its repeated description of the journeys across the city undertaken by the Earl of Dudley and Father Conmee. These two men are glimpsed by many of the episode's other characters and thereby offer a moment of shared experience to a city of drifting souls.

Amidst the kaleidoscopic swirl of incidents and encounters these nineteen short sections present, Joyce develops various elements of character and thematic structure. The fourth section offers an insight into the poverty and disarray of the Dedalus household and the impending disaster of the 'throwaway' incident (*U*: 218). Section five slyly juxtaposes Boylan's purchase of 'ripe shamefaced peaches' for his tryst with Molly and the 'darkbacked figure' – Homeric epithets both – of Bloom. Bloom maintains a persistent but unacknowledged presence in many of these vignettes. He appears vestigially in Lenehan's account of his erotic fumbling with Molly in the back of a cab (Bloom is pictured in the same scene droning on about the position of the stars). Yet Lenehan is forced to admit that Bloom, like Ulysses, is a 'cultured allroundsman' and that 'there's a touch of the artist' about him (*U*: 225). Bloom always remains exposed to Joyce's ironic gaze: searching for erotic fiction for Molly, he lingers over *Sweets of Sin*, a novel that describes a love triangle similar to his own. But Bloom's generosity in subscribing five shillings to the Widow Dignam Fund is contrasted favourably with the parsimony of Jimmy Henry and Long John Fanning, and elicits from John Wyse Nolan the observation that 'there is much kindness in the Jew' (*U*: 236). Elsewhere section thirteen presents one of the novel's most poignant and revealing episodes. Here Stephen is pictured peering through a jeweller's window and brooding upon his own discouraging situation. Feeling himself torn between an artistic vocation and the relentless pressures of the social world, he is compelled to acknowledge the consequences of his own crippling interiority. Suddenly the pitiable sight of his sister Dilly clutching her French primer for his approval casts him outward from his private imaginative reverie into an unwelcome engagement with the surrounding world. 'She is drowning,' he realises, but *still* he cannot help her, because his narcissism represents every claim upon his sympathy as a limit to his independence. Paralysed by his inability to respond to the emotional demand she places upon him, his imagination subtly reverses the relation between them, until, by the scene's conclusion, she is drowning *him*: 'She will drown me with her, eyes and hair. Lank coils of seaweed hair around me, my heart, my soul. Salt green death' (*U*: 233).

Episode Eleven: The Sirens

The time is now 4 p.m. and the place is the bar of the Ormond Hotel. The subject of this episode is seduction and the dangers that may befall those lured from their proper path. Joyce's Homeric inspiration is Ulysses' encounter with the Sirens, whose ravishing song lures men to their death; to resist this deadly temptation Ulysses stuffs the ears of his crew with 'beeswax' and has himself tied to the mast until the ship passes out of the Sirens' range (Homer 1991: 190). Joyce represents the Sirens' power of seduction through an array of musical forms (his technical virtuosity develops multiple correspondences between linguistic and musical styles) and the blowsy charms of the barmaids Miss Douce and Miss Kennedy. However, the key elements of the Homeric story are ironically reconfigured: Boylan makes no attempt to resist temptation; and Molly is temporarily seduced away from Bloom through no fault of his own.

The episode opens with a virtuoso orchestral presentation of the fifty-seven motifs that Joyce will combine within his stylistic symphony. The narrative begins by contrasting the barmaids' frank and open sexual flirtatiousness with Bloom's private and furtive mode of erotic fantasy (his thoughts return repeatedly to Molly's body, women's underwear and the contents of *Sweets of Sin*). 'Sirens' also provides our first sustained encounter with Molly's lover Blazes Boylan. His physical charisma is immediately apparent, and Miss Douce begins to flirt with him: 'Smack. She let free sudden in rebound her nipped elastic garter smackwarm against her smackable a woman's warmhosed thigh' (*U*: 256). Boylan may be the 'conquering hero', but Bloom, paradoxically, is an 'unconquered hero': his defeat is enacted at the sexual, not moral level (*U*: 254). As Boylan leaves the bar to keep his appointment with Molly the jingling sound of his harness echoes the sound of Molly's bedsprings to signal Bloom's downfall: 'Bloom heard a jing, a little sound. He's off. Light sob of breath Bloom sighed on the silent bluehued flowers. Jingling. He's gone. Jingle. Hear.' (*U*: 257).

The main body of 'Sirens' develops a number of musical motifs to underscore the pathos of Bloom's isolation. Richie Goulding chatters excitedly about a song from Bellini's La *Somnambula* (an opera exploring a woman's sexual downfall) while Stephen's father Simon Dedalus rehearses a melancholy air from Flotow's *Martha*. As Simon's song about a lost Martha surges to its climax, Bloom's identity merges with those of Simon and Lionel (Flotow's singer) into the common name of the abandoned man 'Siopold' (*U*: 265). When Boylan arrives at Bloom's house to enact his usurpation, the 'cockcock' note of betrayal is sounded (*U*: 271). Alone on the street as the clock strikes 4, Bloom is left in despondent solitude: 'Four o'clock's all's well! Sleep! All is lost now' (*U*: 277).

Episode Twelve: The Cyclops

The time is 5 p.m. and the scene is Barney Kiernan's Tavern. In *The Odyssey*, Ulysses struggles with the enormous one-eyed Cyclops

Polyphemus. In order to escape the Cyclops' clutches, Ulysses blinds Polyphemus ('So seizing the fire-point-hardened timber we twirled it in his eye') and has then to evade a boulder flung at him by the sightless beast (Homer 1991: 147). Joyce's modern version of this incident substitutes rhetorical for physical violence. Bloom is forced to contend with the ideologically one-eyed Citizen, a bigot blind to all other points of view. In this episode Joyce employs parody and narrative inflation to expose and ridicule the outlandish claims and absurd self-importance of a puffed-up nobody. His hyperbolic style works by inhabiting a particular language or way of seeing the world (the language of journalism, law, science, nationalist politics and so on) and then satirising its claim to account for the entirety of human experience. The purpose of this satire is to underline Joyce's belief that the subordination of different opinions and points of view to systematic or totalising accounts of human experience results in intolerance, repression and violence. Against these intolerant myths of identity and origin, he pits Bloom's lonely, inclusive and embattled humanity.

The Cyclopean note is struck in the very first sentence when the sweep nearly takes out the narrator's eye (U: 280). The narrator and Joe Hynes go to Barney Kiernan's where they encounter the Citizen sitting with his monstrous dog Garryowen. The Citizen's size and sense of self-importance are satirised by the narrator's reproduction of a ludicrous list of 'Irish' heroes that includes 'Captain Nemo', 'Thomas Cook and Son', and 'Dick Turpin' (U: 285). Joyce's comically self-undermining lists playfully expose the Citizen's lack of discrimination and his willingness to tailor evidence to support his narrow sectarian beliefs. His blinkered prejudice is reflected in his complaint that there are too many English names in the births, marriages and deaths columns of the *Irish Independent*. The tavern atmosphere is a lethal combination of menace, ignorance and drunken sentimentality: Alf Bergan is still under the impression that Dignam is alive, and Terry the barman weeps piously when Bergan's mistake is rectified. Joyce mocks their credulousness by an abrupt swerve into the language of spiritualism (U: 288). When Bloom appears, he is immediately distinguished by his reverence for fact and empirical detail; soon 'Herr Professor Luitpold Blumenduft' is providing a scientific explanation of post-execution tumescence (U: 292). Bloom and the Citizen engage in an argument about Irish revolutionary politics, but Bloom's interventions go unremarked; Joyce burlesques the entire exchange in his rendition of the execution of a revolutionary ('Quietly, unassumingly Rumbold stepped on to the scaffold in faultless morning dress') that satirises the cheap sentiment and threadbare clichés of some political rhetoric (*U*: 295). Throughout his disputes with the Citizen, Bloom is consistently figured as the voice of *restraint*. He speaks equably of the graceful virtues of lawn tennis; his interlocutors prefer the physical conflict of boxing. This difference in sporting taste is indicative of a difference in attitude to life: physical violence is a fundamentally one-eyed affair (the boxer Bennett's 'right eye was nearly closed'); Bloom's two eyes remain resolutely open (*U*: 305). No agreement between the parties is possible when the Citizen begins his xenophobic assault upon outsiders, speaking contemptuously of 'half and half' breeds and the 'syphilisation' of English culture (*U*: 307, 311). Bloom speaks out forlornly against 'perpetuating national hatred among nations'; and it is Bloom, not the Citizen, who offers a generous and inclusive definition of citizenship and nationhood: 'A nation is the same people living in the same place' (*U*: 317). As the episode moves toward its sinister conclusion, Bloom's ethnicity becomes a dominant theme. 'That's the new Messiah for Ireland' sneers the Citizen upon learning that Virag is the original Bloom family name (*U*: 323). Temporarily marooned within an environment where intelligence is outflanked by stupidity, it is no surprise that Bloom is brought low by a simple piece of ignorance. While he is briefly absent at the courthouse, a false report is spread that Bloom is collecting his Gold Cup winnings. Bloom replies to the Citizen's anti-Semitic abuse with a proud defence of the glories of Jewish intellectual and spiritual history; but his defiant claim that 'the Saviour was a jew and his father was a jew' provokes in his interlocutor the desire to 'crucify' that 'bloody jewman' (*U*: 327). As Bloom is hustled out of the tavern, the cyclopean Citizen hurls an object at him (a 'Jacob's' biscuit tin acts as a comically reduced boulder), but his aim is impaired when he is momentarily blinded by the sun. In the final scene the car transporting Bloom and his retreating company is transformed into Elijah's chariot: 'Bloom Elijah' rises above the Dublin streets symbolically to herald the coming of the son of God (*U*: 330).

Episode Thirteen: Nausicaa

It is now 8 p.m. and the scene is the rocks on Sandymount shore. In *The Odyssey* Nausicaa, daughter of King Alkinoos, arrives at the shore with her maidens to wash linen. The maidens disport themselves and inadvertently awaken Ulysses, who has been washed up upon the shore following a tempest at sea. The women are thrown into confusion, but Nausicaa assumes control, clothes Ulysses and takes him home to recuperate (Homer 1991: 110). Joyce's handling of this Homeric episode is characteristically ironic: Gerty Macdowell, unlike Nausicaa, offers only the briefest respite for 'the stormtossed heart of man', and Bloom remains alone and at a considerable distance from home (*U*: 331).

After the violent climax of 'Cyclops', style and tone relax to reflect the sprawling reverie of a young woman at twilight. Gerty is a relatively unsophisticated girl whose desires appear decked out in the representations of popular culture. Joyce satirically reproduces her mental style by adopting the cliché-ridden and dreamy romanticism ('The summer evening had begun to fold the world in its mysterious embrace') of sentimental women's magazines (*U*: 331). His prose retains an ambivalent tone: Gerty is faintly ridiculous, self-regarding and self-dramatising; but she also yearns for a life beyond her mundane surroundings. Joyce's language captures both these aspects of her social and psychological reality. His deft employment of free-indirect style registers both the pathos of her investment in her own image ('The waxen pallor of her face was almost spiritual in its ivorylike purity though her rosebud mouth was a genuine Cupid's bow') and her attempt to give this image emotional and spiritual dignity (*U*: 333). A combination of motifs evokes a parallel between Gerty and the Virgin Mary: Gerty's hands are of 'finely veined alabaster', she retains a 'queenly *hauteur*', she wears 'blue for luck' and functions as the 'ministering angel' of her home (*U*: 333, 335, 339). Gerty is a curiously worldly version of Mary: when she finally becomes aware of Bloom's rapt adoration of her legs, religious and erotic vocabularies intertwine as she utters the 'cry that has rung through the ages' (*U*: 350). But Joyce's irony is not only at Gerty's expense; it encompasses the broader Irish culture that pays lip-service to religious icons while satiating itself with the sensuous things of this world.

Gerty's relative lack of sophistication is apparent in her naïve assessment of Ulysses Bloom ('she knew he could be trusted to the death, steadfast, a sterling man, a man of inflexible honour to his fingertips'); flattered by his attention, she gradually exposes her thighs and underclothes to his gaze (*U*: 349). Her overestimation of Bloom's virtues is revealed in his self-absorbed response to her lameness: 'Glad I didn't know it when she was on show' (*U*: 351). Sentimental idealism in *Ulysses* is always forced to confront the harsh realities of life. Joyce represents the barrenness of their encounter in biological terms: Gerty is gradually made aware of her approaching menstrual period ('that thing must be coming on') while Bloom masturbates furtively at a distance (*U*: 345). As Gerty moves off down the beach, Bloom momentarily recalls the lyric 'Those lovely seaside girls'. The song reminds him involuntarily of Molly's tryst with Boylan and the coincidence that his watch stopped at the hour of their meeting. The pain inflicted upon him by this realisation is starkly conveyed: 'Was that just when he, she? Oh, he did. Into her. She did. Done. Ah!' (*U*: 353). Boylan gets the 'plums' while Bloom gets the 'plumstones' (*U*: 359). Realising that it is the anniversary of the month when he and Molly first courted on Howth Hill, Bloom dreams of a return to those heady days. But he also knows that it is futile (and dangerous) to live in the past: 'She kissed me. My youth. Never again.' As Bloom tires and his thoughts drift, the episode ends with the 'cuckoo' announcing Molly's betrayal of her husband (*U*: 365).

Episode Fourteen: Oxen of the Sun

The time is now 10 p.m. and the location is the maternity hospital at Holles Street. In *The Odyssey* Ulysses and his crew visit the Isle of the Sun. Ulysses explicitly warns his starving crew against killing the sacred oxen of the isle for food, because they are fertility symbols cherished by the gods. However, when he falls asleep his men disobey him and strike the oxen down. The gods are quick to punish this transgression: a thunderbolt strikes Ulysses' ship and all lives except his own are lost (Homer 1991: 196). Joyce's comic parallel describes a less calamitous crime against fertility by detailing the boorish behaviour of a group of drunken students in the proximity of women in childbirth. That this 'sacrilegious' offence is viewed far less seriously in *Ulysses* is evident from the fact that 'Oxen' also symbolises a key moment of birth and regeneration in the novel. For it is in these pages that Joyce describes the first substantive encounter between Bloom, the sonless father, and Stephen, the fatherless son.

Joyce's concern here with birth and regeneration famously determines the literary style of the episode. In a virtuoso exhibition of pastiche and parody, he develops a series of correspondences between the biological gestation of a foetus and the historical constitution of a language. Thus the episode begins with a dense and convoluted Latinate prose passage representing a period before the 'English' language had properly come into being, and develops by way of a multitude of forms and vocabularies towards the styles of contemporary expression. These intervening forms include Anglo-Saxon, Middle English, early modern romance, Shakespearean song, John Bunyan's allegorical prose, eighteenth-century literary journalism and political oratory, the Gothic novel and the nineteenth-century prose of Charles Dickens and John Ruskin. Intriguingly, Joyce also suggests that this succession of historical styles also represents a mode of cultural decline. As we move from the nineteenth century into the present day, literary expression disintegrates into a chaos of slang, advertising-speak, cod psychology and incommensurable professional jargons. Whilst idioms and professional vocabularies jostle one another ceaselessly in the marketplace of opinion, we are presented with more and more information and less and less knowledge.

Throughout this episode, Bloom is distinguished by his compassion and restraint. He embodies the '[s]tark ruth of man', and he alone of the company is constantly concerned for the condition of Mrs Purefoy (*U*: 368). Bloom's abstemiousness is favourably compared to the increasingly intoxicated Stephen, the 'most drunken' of the students (*U*: 371). His compassionate nature leads him to adopt a paternalistic attitude towards the younger man 'for that he lived riotously with those wastrels and murdered his goods with whores' (*U*: 373). This attitude compels him to follow Stephen to 'Bawdyhouse' and into the hell of nighttown (*U*: 406).

Episode Fifteen: Circe

It is now midnight and the location changes to the streets and brothels of the 'nighttown' district. In *The Odyssey*, Ulysses' men are invited to a feast where they 'were given evil drugs and enchanted' by the goddess Circe who then transforms them into swine with her wand (Homer 1991: 157). Assisted by the god Hermes, who supplies him with a potion to protect him from Circe's sorcery, Ulysses sets out to recover his crew. In the ensuing struggle Circe attempts to ensnare Ulysses, but he overpowers her, compels her to return his men to their human form, and is subsequently taken to her bed. Joyce's bleak reworking of this Homeric episode discloses a nightmarish and hallucinatory landscape upon which men are transformed into beasts by both the cruelty of others and the enactment of their own repressed desires. Joyce's ability to create a narrative syntax and a series of images to portray the irrational movement of the unconscious mind distinguishes one aspect of the revolutionary innovation of his writing. Ironically, it is within this space of violent juxtapositions and terrifying nocturnal revelations that Bloom assumes moral responsibility for Stephen and become the surrogate father to a fatherless son.

The nightmarish quality of nighttown is quickly established. The inhabitants are grotesques; malign voices whisper anonymously from shadows, while an idiot with St Vitus Dance – a form of degenerative nervous disorder characterised by spasmodic movement of the body and limbs – is cruelly abused by children. A drunken Stephen imagines himself and Lynch to be St Peter and St John, but his '[p]ornosophical philotheology' expresses his latent bestial nature (*U*: 411). Bloom is shocked (although secretly fascinated) by this environment; his inner turmoil is gradually externalised until his fears and fantasises constitute the psychological reality of the world around him. In the phantasmagoria that follows, Bloom's repressed desires, social pretensions and profound yearning for social inclusion are relentlessly exposed. He encounters the ghost of his father, who chastises him for his spendthrift nature; his various lurid fantasies about Molly and street prostitutes also recall his interest in sexual squalor and trash erotica. At one point the swirling street scenes are suddenly reconfigured into a courtroom scene: here, at the 'hellsgates' of Judgement Day, the trial begins of Bloom's moral being (*U*: 427). All the rebuffs and frustrations Bloom has suffered now return to haunt him. His plaintive defence of his moral rectitude ('I am doing good to others') has little effect as his latent femininity and secret masochism are uproariously revealed (*U*: 430). Bloom recoils from the evidence of his longing for self-abasement by establishing the compensatory fantasy of himself as the political and moral Messiah of the new Bloomusalem. In the new moral order of Bloomusalem his generosity and wisdom are permanently upon display. Bloomusalem abruptly disintegrates when Bloom is accused of harbouring an onanistic obsession; a clue to his redemptive character is provided, though, by the subsequent denunciation of him as a false Messiah and his abandonment to the civil and religious authorities (*U*: 469). Rejected once more, Bloom slinks away to the bestial den of Bella Cohen's brothel, where he discovers Stephen playing the piano and talking high-sounding nonsense. In the brothel, the satirical courtroom image of Bloom as the 'new womanly man' acquires a much darker hue (*U*: 465). Upon Bella Cohen's arrival, Bloom sinks into a series of unconscious (and therefore unstructured) erotic fantasies in which his repressed carnal nature is lent a ghastly imaginative life. Infatuated with Bella, and wholly submissive to her authority, Bloom bends to kiss her shoes; his dehumanisation continues as he metamorphoses into a beast and kneels upon all fours before her. Throughout this transfiguration, Bloom's wish to invert sexual roles and identities is given full figurative expression: Bella is accordingly transformed into the masculine 'Bello' while Bloom's character is insistently feminised. In Bloom's surreal sado-masochistic fantasy 'Bello' rides upon him, violently penetrates him and forces him to wear female underclothes until he finally admits that he is 'Not man. Woman' (*U*: 501). A mock-funeral is then held for Bloom to commemorate the death of his old sexual nature. Within the novel's complex symbolic economy, one version of Bloom's existence has come to a close; he will later be reborn as Stephen's father.

The theme of apocalypse and resurrection is also underscored by Stephen's brothel experience. Assailed once more by the ghost of his mother, Stephen asserts his desire to be liberated from the past in the credo 'Non serviam' and smashes the chandelier with his ashplant (*U*: 541). This violent sundering of the present from the past culminates in a symbolic apocalypse in which time's 'livid final flame' leaps amid the 'ruin of all space, shattered glass and toppling masonry' (*U*: 542). The vulnerability of the position into which Stephen has placed himself by his defiant renunciation of filial and domestic bonds is quietly and movingly emphasised. Thus in one of the novel's key symbolic moments, Bloom accepts temporary paternal responsibility for Stephen, shrewdly assessing the damage to Bella Cohen's apartments and settling the bill; subsequently he defends Stephen's interests once more when, in a scene that underscores the implicit violence of imperial authority, the younger man is assaulted by drunken British soldiers (*U*: 558). The unlikely union of Bloom and Stephen was symbolically prefigured in the enigmatic aside 'Jewgreek is greekjew. Extremes meet' (*U*: 474). This reconciliation of seemingly discordant world-views is effected when the Hebraic Bloom enters into dialogue with the acolyte of Greek intellectual culture. In the episode's final pages this meeting accrues broader symbolic overtones. Arising from the pavement, Stephen, like the crucified Christ, has 'no bones broken', while Bloom, gazing upon his miraculously risen companion, is blessed with a vision of his dead son Rudy (*U*: 563, 565). Upon each of these different levels, the father and son are reconciled.

Episode Sixteen: *Eumaeus*

The time is 1 a.m. Bloom and Stephen make their way to the Cabman Shelter at Butt Bridge. The Homeric episode Joyce reworks here explores themes of homecoming and recognition. Eventually arriving home in Ithaca, Ulysses comes in disguise to the hut of the 'noble swineherd' Eumaeus (Homer 1991: 211). He develops an elaborate story to conceal his identity, but ceases to dissemble when Telemachus appears. Together at last, father and son prepare their revenge upon Penelope's suitors. Joyce's version of this episode maintains an ironic distance from the epic account: his theme is *misrecognition*. Bloom is not, after all, Stephen's father, and only dimly perceives his character; and Stephen will remain an incongruous presence in Bloom's household.

The lateness of the hour and the exhaustion of the two men are reflected in the periphrastic style of Joyce's prose: a style, that is, characterised by a series of rambling digressive sentences replete with a loose syntax and a profusion of subordinate clauses. Ulysses' evasions to Eumaeus are mirrored by the stream of falsehoods uttered by the sailor W. B. Murphy whose tall tales concerning the legendary marksmanship of Simon Dedalus bear no relation to reality. Murphy's fantasy that he saw Simon touring 'the wide world with Hengler's Royal Circus' only serves to reinforce the fact that Simon is no Ulysses to Stephen's Telemachus (U: 579). Eumaeus is loosely embodied in the figure of the former 'Invincible' Skin-the-Goat, although the latter has merely transformed loyalty to the past into an excuse for a narrowly sectarian politics. The conversation of Bloom and Stephen with Skin-the-Goat accentuates once more their temperamental differences. Skin-the-Goat's views and character offer a passable imitation of the Citizen replayed in a minor key. His 'forcible-feeble philippic' represents Ireland as 'the richest country bar none on the face of God's earth' reduced to beggary by a perfidious Albion (U: 595). Notwithstanding his distaste for such monological accounts, Bloom's response is a masterpiece of even-handed diplomacy. Because the conduct of international affairs is subject to a host of unknown and unforeseeable developments, he reflects, it is 'highly advisable in the interim to try to make the most of both countries' (U: 596). 'It is hard,' Bloom continues, 'to lay down any hard and fast rules as to right and wrong but room for improvement all round there certainly is' (U: 597-8). Bloom's equable liberalism is exemplary under the circumstances, but it fails to escape Joyce's comic irony; Bloom is so careful to respect every side of an argument that his politics risks being drained of positive content. In contrast, Stephen's narcissistic individualism effortlessly (and arrogantly) transcends the workaday demands of political engagement: 'But I suspect,' Stephen interrupted, 'Ireland must be important because it belongs to me' (U: 599).

Stephen's response reminds us that, despite their temporary association, the two men inhabit very different mental worlds. Bloom demonstrates his 'patriotism' by his tolerance, secularism and concern for social justice; Stephen's sole commitment is to his private aesthetic ambition. Joyce's ironic and ambivalent treatment of their attitudes extends itself to the broader epic context. Bloom may be momentarily characterised here as 'our hero', but, as the narrator of the scene concludes wearily about the nationalist dream of Parnell's imminent return, you can never wholly reoccupy the ground you once possessed: 'Still, as regards return, you were a lucky dog if they didn't set the terrier at you directly you got back' (U: 604).

Episode Seventeen: Ithaca

It is 2 a.m. and the two weary travellers conclude their odyssey at 7 Eccles Street. In *The Odyssey*, Ulysses and Telemachus successfully rout Penelope's suitors and reclaim Ithaca as their own (Homer 1991: 328). Joyce's comic vision tempers the violence of this epic encounter by representing it as the (often hilarious) collision between two styles of perceiving the world. 'Ithaca' offers Joyce's most acute juxtaposition of Bloom's secular, pragmatic and autodidactic world-view with Stephen's intellectually rigorous, if self-regarding, aesthetic intelligence. This meeting of minds is conveyed in a detached analytical style modelled upon the deductive procedures of formal logic and the call-and-response method of the Catholic catechism. The apparent omniscience of Joyce's authorial point of view, which transcends the merely human sphere while providing a minute dissection of its characteristics and motivations, humorously suggests the Olympian point of view of the Greek gods. The comic comparisons between diverse phenomena evoked by this mode of presentation highlight the incongruity of Bloom and Stephen's personalities and opinions, but they also suggest the lasting importance of those human qualities that this Olympian view so conspicuously lacks. For it is in this tentative and partial exchange of perspectives and sympathies that Bloom's humanity momentarily reawakens Stephen's over-reaching intelligence to the value of earthly things.

Amid the welter of this episode's detail, certain key themes crystallise. Arriving home, Bloom discovers that, like Stephen, he is keyless. At one level, the identities of the two men gradually merge throughout the episode until they become 'Blephen' and 'Stoom' (*U*: 635). But at another level, their temperamental differences hold them apart: Bloom takes Stephen seriously; Stephen always views Bloom ironically. This difference in perspective is revealed in other ways: Stephen, for example, conceives of himself grandiloquently as labouring beneath a 'matutinal cloud'; to Bloom he is merely drunk (*U*: 620). When Stephen offers Bloom his densely symbolic 'parable of the Plums', Bloom immediately calculates ways in which he can convert the younger man's talents into commercial gold. Yet despite this divergence of views, each man occasionally recognises in the other qualities necessary to the completion of himself. In Bloom's words, Stephen heard 'in a profound ancient male unfamiliar melody the accumulation of the past'; in Stephen, Bloom recognised 'the predestination of a future' (*U*: 642). This movement of communion and self-revelation forms one part of the broader theological pattern within which father and son are joined in a new spiritual union. As Stephen refuses Bloom's offer of a bed for a night and prepares to leave, he holds aloft his ashplant (his symbolic cross) and drunkenly quotes the 113th psalm. Joyce celebrates this passage from spiritual bondage into Paradise in one of his most ravishing sentences: 'The heaventree of stars hung with humid nightblue fruit' (*U*: 651).

Bloom's odyssey is over. Comforting himself with the knowledge that 'as a competent keyless citizen he had proceeded energetically from the unknown to the known through the incertitude of the void', he proceeds to bed (*U*: 650). Like Ulysses, he has endured a lengthy separation from his wife, but the episode's final pages hint at a possible reconciliation. Evidence of Boylan's presence lies all around, but 'Everyman' Bloom looks for solace to the heart's constancy, rather than the vagaries of desire. Kissing the 'plump mellow yellow smellow melons' of Molly's rump, Bloom settles for the night (*U*: 686).

Episode Eighteen: Penelope

After the formal scholarly examination of phenomena in 'Ithaca', the final episode immerses us in the preconscious mind of Molly Bloom. Joyce's exploration of Molly's sensibility adapts the stream-of-consciousness technique and suspends the grammatical structures of prose in order to convey the allusive associational logic of her dream-thoughts. Molly's 'monologue' is therefore reproduced in eight gargantuan sentences completely devoid of punctuation. Grammar confers a logical structure upon the obscure world of preconscious motivations; by removing it Joyce intended to submerge his readers in the primal flux of human instinct and desire. The motif of flow in 'Penelope' also assumes a theological significance: the water (or chamber music) Molly makes in her chamber-pot symbolises the waters of baptism and renewal, while her menstrual blood evokes the blood of Christian passion and redemption. Amid the drift of images and narrative fragments, defining elements of Molly's personality swim into focus. She is mentally agile (although not given to intellectual abstraction), streetwise and supremely confident of her centrality to the Bloom household. She can be censorious (particularly of other women); but she is also generous, and loyal to Bloom, despite her adulterous liaison with Boylan. Her hostility to politics notwithstanding, experience has made a feminist of Molly: her thoughts return repeatedly to the question of personal autonomy and the constraints placed upon the expression of female desire. She is resolute, self-assertive and passionate: a woman to captivate a lover or keep a household of suitors at bay.

Molly's mental toughness appears in various guises. She sees straight though Bloom's subterfuges (the returning Bloom 'came somewhere Im sure'), and she has no time for Milly's girlish intrigues (*U*: 691). She is scornfully dismissive of Bloom's laborious attempts to educate her ('if I asked him hed say its from the Greek leave us as wise as we were before') and takes an appropriately cynical view of his lascivious love-letters (*U*: 696). The motor of human relationships, in Molly's eyes, is desire; the slavishness of male desire enables women to run rings around them. Certainly there is no shame in sexuality: 'what else were we given all those desires for Id like to know' (*U*: 726–7). She resists what she sees as the masculine world of politics and abstract ideas: it was delusions like these that killed her former lover Mulvey. Molly embraces the physical pleasure Boylan gives her, but disdains his male brutishness and swagger. The physical body is one more way in which the odds are stacked against women; the world would be a better place if women took control of it. Despite his peccadilloes and permanent air of abstraction, Bloom, Molly recognises, is decent and gentle and kind. Her summation of her feelings for him combines love and knowingness in equal measure ('that was why I liked him because I saw he understood or felt what a woman is and I knew I could always get round him'): she will give him one more chance to restart their relationship (*U*: 731). As her monologue swells to its conclusion, the memory of their first lovemaking prefigures Bloom's homecoming and a new sexual future: 'yes and his heart was going like mad and yes I said yes I will Yes' (*U*: 732).

Further Reading

Although published only eight years after the appearance of *Ulysses*, and inevitably superseded in some of its critical judgements, Gilbert (1930) repays scrutiny. It combines lucid accounts of the style, rhythm and structure of Joyce's prose with detailed readings of its constituent episodes. Budgen's (1934) record of his Zurich friendship with Joyce provides fascinating glimpses of Joyce's method of composition and the broader aesthetic and cultural questions that inform *Ulysses*. Kenner (1987) devotes an important chapter to the relationship in the novel between styles of rhetoric and modes of consciousness; a second book (1978) charts the novel's stylistic transition from naturalism to parody; while a third (1980) offers a critical discussion of the entire work. Levin draws attention to the dialectical relationship at the heart of the novel between its 'epic symbolism' and its 'naturalistic atmosphere' (1944: 66). Adams highlights another important aspect of the novel's style: the tension between the semantic richness of its symbolism and the accumulation of flat and often inexplicable surface detail that tears 'a series of holes in the pattern of reader-information' (1962: 26). Thornton (1961) supplies an exhaustive compendium of Joyce's network of allusions. Blamires (1988) provides a detailed page-by-page paraphrase of the novel, reworking its myriad details into a coherent linear narrative; his volume remains a useful point of departure for the first-time reader. Charting the influence upon Joyce's work of writers such as Homer, Dante, Shakespeare and Flaubert, Goldberg examines the 'classical temper' of his art: an aesthetic that 'accepts the ordinary world of humanity as the primary object of its attention' in order to express a 'moral as well as an artistic ideal, an ideal of spiritual completion and impersonal order' (1961: 32). Reading *Ulysses* within the context of modern phenomenology and modernist narrative experimentation, Steinberg (1979) establishes useful distinctions between Joyce's employment of spoken monologue, interior monologue and stream-of-consciousness technique. Gottfried (1980) sustains a minute examination of Joyce's syntax and its virtuoso manipulation of traditional rhetorical paradigms. Lawrence (1981) suggests that the novel's multiple syntactic displacements gradually rewrite the conventions of the novel by marking a transition from the presentation of character to a self-conscious concern with the impersonal proliferation of rhetorical styles. Employing the post-structuralist theories of Jacques Derrida and Jacques Lacan, MacCabe (1978) examines Joyce's subversive rethinking of the relationship between desire, politics and subjectivity. Attridge explores the ways Joyce's extraordinary 'linguistic and generic inventiveness' demonstrates the 'peculiar capacity of literature to engage with crucial intellectual, ethical and political issues without attempting to resolve them' (2000: xiv). In a similar spirit, Fairhall (1993) examines the effects of nationalism, colonialism and World War One upon Joyce's work and considers the ways in which *Ulysses* compels us to rethink the relationship between narrative fiction and historiography. A different historical context and cultural milieu is invoked by Segall (1993) and Vanderham (1998) who provide comprehensive accounts of the American trial of *Ulysses* and its centrality to contemporary debates concerning censorship and literary value. Senn (1995) offers numerous valuable insights into the novel's style, syntax and intellectual structure.

Finnegans Wake (1939)

Finnegans Wake has some claim to be the least read major work of Western literature. It typifies for many people the perceived division between the demands of modernist experimentation and the sensibility of the general reading public. One reason for this judgement is the novel's notorious difficulty. *Finnegans Wake* begins, in a sense, where *Ulysses* ends. Having completed his epic of modern civic life by exploring the subconscious desires and dream-thoughts of a Dublin housewife, Joyce undertakes – in one of *Finnegans Wake*'s many dimensions – to parody and rewrite a number of Western cultural archetypes in the language of a drunken and dreaming Dublin publican. The difficulty of Joyce's last novel is also exacerbated by the fact that it marks no clear internal transition between realist and post-realist modes of representation.

Notwithstanding the many problems of interpretation with which *Ulysses* confronts us, it at least begins in a highly wrought but still recognisably realist style before proceeding to revolutionise the forms of modern prose. However, the depiction of the Fall of Man with which *Finnegans Wake* begins admits no meaningful distinction between the moment of creation and the Tower of Babel; from the opening sentence of the novel the myriad languages of humanity are scattered across the text. In order to begin to make sense of these words, we have, from the very first moment, to suspend our conventional expectation of what literature is and develop new protocols of reading. This process takes both time and interpretative labour, and any brief introduction to Joyce's novel is inevitably overwhelmed by the extraordinary detail and richness of his narrative. Acknowledging this caveat, the following remarks are offered with two guiding principles in mind. The reader has, after all, to begin *somewhere*; and the initial commitment to grapple with Joyce's riddling text is more likely to be renewed once a few basic principles of plot and exposition are securely established.

Finnegans Wake is, then, at one level, the story of a family. This family consists of a Dublin publican H. C. Earwicker, his wife Anna Livia Plurabelle, their twin sons Shaun and Shem and their daughter Isabel. These five principal characters are supplemented by a range of other figures. These include Kate the pub maid, Joe the pub handyman, Isabel's twenty-eight female attendants (for twenty-eight and one make twenty-nine and Isabel is a leap-year girl), the twelve pub-goers who offer a choric commentary upon the main action and double as the twelve biblical apostles, and the four old men known as 'mamalujo' (a contraction of Matthew, Mark, Luke and John, the names of the four New Testament disciples). Also lurking in the shadows are the two girls and the three soldiers who witness Earwicker's hotly-denied 'crime' and fall in Phoenix Park. Meanwhile down by the River Liffey, two old washerwomen wash out the family's dirty laundry in the fading light of evening.

In Joyce's allegorical and analogical schema every character is both individually distinct and an aspect of a larger totality. Earwicker is a Dublin publican, but he also becomes an archetype of Adam, Christ, Caesar, Wellington, Cromwell, the legendary Irish hero Finn MacCool and a plethora of other identities. Earwicker's initials 'HCE' also stand, as Joyce notes wryly, for 'Here Comes Everybody' (FW: 32). In narrower terms, he embodies the fate of the builder Tim Finnegan, eponymous hero of 'The Ballad of Tim Finnegan', who falls drunkenly to his death from a ladder only to be resurrected at his wake by a dash of spilt whiskey. Like Tim Finnegan, Earwicker is a builder of cities (but also of nations); like Adam he falls; and like Christ he rises once more. Similarly, Anna Livia may be a publican's wife, but she is also Eve, the Virgin Mary, the pagan goddess Isis and the little hen who gathers fragments from the midden-dump of history. Ultimately all the characters of the *Wake* are aspects or projections of this original couple. The three children, for example, are both individuals in their own right and emanations of the 'forced payrents' or first parents (FW: 576). The perpetual opposition between the anarchic Shem the Penman and the authoritarian Shaun reflects in part the opposition between an artist and the society that tries to control him; but it also expresses the schism between two halves of Earwicker's discordant personality. The nightmarish figure of the 'cad' who accosts Earwicker in the second episode combines traits of Shem and Shaun: he thereby becomes an external projection of Earwicker's inner guilt and anxiety. In the same way, the three soldiers in the Park are also Earwicker and his two sons, while the laughing girls double as Anna Livia and Isabel. Isabel is both Anna Livia's daughter and a younger version of Anna Livia herself; Kate, meanwhile, represents Anna Livia in her declining years. Earwicker's inability to maintain a proper distinction between his wife's various aspects is perhaps the source of all his difficulties: both he and his sons yearn incestuously for Isabel, and this displacement of the sexual economy engenders many of the family's conflicts. It is also a feature of the broader Oedipal drama that drives the narrative of *Finnegans Wake* in which the two sons strive to replace the father and stamp their own image upon the history of their times.

Much of the novel's action takes place in the suburb of Chapelizod (home of Mr Duffy in 'A Painful Case') on the western side of Dublin. However, it is impossible to speak simply of 'place' in *Finnegans Wake* because place is also a *character* in the novel. The initials 'HCE' take on many meanings ('Here Comes Everybody', 'Haroun Childeric Eggeberth' and so on) including the landscape of 'Howth Castle and Environs' (FW: 3). Earwicker's mythic personality is also represented by the Hill of

Howth, Phoenix Park, the Wellington Monument and much else besides. Similarly Anna Livia is also the River Liffey (the River of Life, water of female generation and the particular river that flows through Dublin up into Howth and Dublin Bay). Individuals, places and archetypes are brought together in a narrative of the falling, rising and regeneration of a family, a people and a culture.

The plot of a narrative as notoriously complicated as *Finnegans Wake* is open to many kinds of interpretation. While commentators have advanced various different readings of the plot, all of them reveal the same basic paradigm: the narrative describes a fall, a 'death' or meta-morphosis, and a resurrection. As long as this fundamental pattern is kept in mind, the differences between accounts of the novel only add to its richness and range of resonance. The principal point of disagreement between commentators upon the *Wake* concerns the novel's dream-structure. When reading the novel are we immersed in the dreaming sub-conscious of Earwicker or is he merely one of the characters through which Joyce's narrative unfolds? The first position was famously estab-lished by Edmund Wilson who claimed that 'we are introduced, at the very beginning, into Earwicker's drowsing consciousness, and we have to make what we can of the names, the shapes, and above all, of the voices, which fill that dim and shifting world' (1931: 230). Other critics, noting the difficulties that Earwicker's variable state of consciousness through-out the novel poses for this conjecture, argue that the *Wake* is the product of a dreaming consciousness that lies outside – but which momentarily represents itself within – the novel's narrative world. Recalling that Joyce allegedly told an interviewer that *Finnegans Wake* was ' "about" Finn lying dying by the River Liffey with the history of Ireland and the world cycling through his mind', Clive Hart suggests, 'There is no reason to doubt the accuracy of this report, which would seem to establish the important point that Joyce thought of *Finnegans Wake* as a unified dream-whole centred on a single mind' (Hart 1962: 81). By interpreting the novel as the narrative projection of a consciousness situated outside the novel that is focalised by a series of characters within its pages, the problem of Earwicker's relative state of consciousness is removed and the primary contrast between a day's activities and the 'larger mythic pat-terns' they symbolise brought into sharp relief (Hart 1962: 85). A third, and perhaps more persuasive, reading regards the entire novel as the dream or collective unconscious of Western culture from its Old Testament origins in the fall of Adam (who, like Earwicker, commits a 'crime' in a garden) to the contemporary moment of modern history (Tindall 1969: 19). In this account, *Finnegans Wake* is nothing less than a new creation myth in which the tensions and divisions within a particular family come to represent the conflicts and emancipatory dreams that engender different versions of human society and culture.

In another sense, the story of *Finnegans Wake* is also the story of Joyce's twenty-year labour to develop a style and a mode of narrative presentation with which to represent the dreams, desires and repressions that constitute the 'unconscious' of modern culture. Such reference to the 'unconscious' inevitably invites comparisons between Joyce's writing and the psychoanalytical research of Sigmund Freud. This comparison is not entirely misplaced. Although Joyce had only a passing acquaintance with Freud's work – not just young girls, it seems, were 'easily freudened' – he shared Freud's belief that the associative patterns of language and dream constituted the royal road to the unconscious (*FW*: 115). For Freud, the unreal symbolic narratives of dream and our 'slips' or acts of conversational misspeaking opened a temporary gap through which our unconscious desires and fears might inscribe themselves within the rational structures of daily life. In an analogous spirit, Joyce's 'nightynovel' created a labyrinthine dream-language in which he offered a gloriously comic (but also deeply serious) version of the fall of mankind (*FW*: 54). Because the story of the Fall transcends national cultures, Joyce's style draws necessarily upon a multiplicity of languages. His book of the wake is a polyphony of up to sixty-five languages in which English, Irish and French rub shoulders with Danish, German and Italian. *Finnegans Wake* also makes use of the three classic effects of the Freudian dream-work – condensation, substitution and displacement – to convey its sense of 'feeling aslip' (*FW*: 597). It is these devices that create the impression for his readers of a continuous shuttling between the unconscious and the waking mind. 'You mean to see,' a character inquires in the final episode, 'we have been hadding a sound night's sleep?' (*FW*: 597). Joyce's novelistic technique has other distinctive traits. Because he intends every particular textual incident to acquire its manifold significance by reference to the various mythic narratives that envelop the novel, his style develops analogically from individual details to general contexts. Its method is to present 'someone imparticular who will somewherise for the whole' (*FW*: 602). Yet within this larger analogical movement, Joyce experiments continuously with different modes of narrative organisation. At one level the structure of *Finnegans Wake* is borrowed from musical composition: it states, elaborates and varies particular motifs before combining them in complex new relationships. At another it develops the cinematic 'monthage' (or montage) principle of the juxtaposition and superimposition of images pioneered by Joyce's friend Serge Eisenstein

(*FW*: 223). *Finnegans Wake* rustles throughout to the 'flickerflapper' of the movie-screen (*FW*: 266).

One other crucial stylistic feature of the novel – Joyce's adoption of a cyclical historical narrative – becomes more readily explicable by reference to the work of the Italian philosopher, philologist and historiographer Giambattista Vico. Vico's *The New Science* (1725) presented an original and highly idiosyncratic philosophy of history. By attempting to excavate the layers of social and political history concealed within mythological narratives, Vico claimed to have discovered an ideal eternal history through which the particular history of each individual nation must pass. He argued that there is a fixed and definable cyclical progression within human societies. Each society proceeds through three distinct ages: the Divine Age (when people believed themselves living under divine government), the Heroic Age (when heroes ruled the earth by virtue of strength within aristocratic social structures) and the Human Age (when the equality of human nature was represented by the political principle of democracy). Human society, according to Vico, moves progressively through each stage before entering a '*ricorso*' (a period of dissolution and reversal) and beginning the entire cycle again. Each historical stage has its own historical symbols and modes of representation. The Divine Age is born when primitive man, terrified by a thunderstorm, creates a divine personality to account for this shattering primal force; retreating into his cave, he creates the ideas of 'religion' and 'family' which he then elaborates in grunts, gestures and rudimentary fables. The Heroic Age is distinguished by wars, duels and aristocratic alliances; speech has now developed to employ figures such as metaphor, allegory and poetic figures, and 'marriage' becomes the governing symbol of an age increasingly preoccupied with status and the reproduction of authority. The Human Age of democracy and popular government is symbolised by 'burial' because it contains within it the seeds of its own destruction; for in our own democratic age a communicative schism begins to appear between the abstract language of social élites and the debased discourse of the common people. This schism provokes a social and political crisis, popular democracy collapses, and a *ricorso* begins the entire cycle again.

Joyce was undoubtedly influenced by this Viconian schema, and several of its distinctive features find their way into *Finnegans Wake*. Joyce was attracted to the idea of a cyclical history in which the repetition of the 'seim anew' opened the text of history to original new perspectives upon experience, and the novel famously begins (as in traditional epics) *in media res* (or in the middle) before looping back at its conclusion to the beginning once again (*FW*: 215). In Joyce's 'whole-mole millwheeling vicociclometer' everything returns subtly to alter everything that has already gone before (*FW*: 614). He was also drawn to Vico's idea that the cyclical progression between historical periods could be embodied in the lives of national heroes; the capacious character of Earwicker is composed accordingly of many different historical archetypes. Yet although *Finnegans Wake* makes considerable use of the symbols of marriage, burial, religion and the family, it is a mistake simply to map Joyce's narrative onto Vico's tripartite structure. From Vico, Joyce took exactly those elements he needed: the bare outline of a cyclical structure, a delight in national characteristics, a fascination with etymology and neologism, and a conviction that mythology contained profound clues to our historical and social nature. His real interest, though, lay in how the repetition of the same desires, dreams, fears and social structures produced each man and woman in their irreducible human particularity. In Joyce's hands, the cyclically repeated traces of a universal history reveal to us both what is common in our humanity and what is distinctively our own. As he puts it early in the novel, 'It is the same told of all. Many. Miscegenations on miscegenations' (*FW*: 18).

Part 1: First Narrative Movement (pp. 3–29)

The novel begins with a particularly dense seven-page overture that introduces some of the main characters and principle themes (including an early version of the fall of Earwicker). After this opening, the episode has three points of main narrative focus: the story of Willingdone's Waterloo, the tale of Mutt, Jeff and the Prankquean, and Anna Livia's discovery of the letter (which is also *Finnegans Wake)* in the midden-dump. None of these characters and incidents is clearly defined; such definition as they acquire comes through the novel's insistent patterns of repetition.

Although the prologue is compressed and difficult to explicate, some help is at hand. Joyce's letter of 15 November 1926 to Harriet Shaw Weaver provides a partial gloss to the novel's opening page; from the hints that he supplies, we may glean valuable insights into his style and thematic concerns. We begin with 'riverrun', which continues from the novel's last words ('A way a lone a lost a loved a long the') and alludes to both Anna Livia (the Liffey, the river and mother of life and regeneration) and Earwicker (the roaring sea that takes the river that is also Anna Livia into his arms on the novel's final page). The river runs past the church of 'Eve and Adam' (note the inversion: 'Eve' comes first; a fall must come before a rise and a transfiguration) and into Dublin Bay where it returns ('recirculation') back to 'Howth Castle and Environs'. Already Joyce's punning concentration of language is evident: 'commodious' signifies a convenient or well-judged route, a Roman emperor and a 'commode' (chamber-pot) for evacuated waste; 'vicus' refers to locality in general, the Vico Road by Dublin Bay in particular, and Giambattista Vico, a presiding spirit throughout the novel. Like Vico's history of 'recirculation', the *Wake* has the narrative rhythm of a cyclical return. 'Howth Castle and Environs' is the geographical locality where much of the narrative unfolds; but as the letters 'HCE' suggest, this landscape is also the body of Earwicker. The next paragraph, which details the seven things that have not yet ('passencore') happened at the time of Eve and Adam, affords numerous examples of Joyce's punning displacements and compressions. Thus we discover Sir Tristram's 'penisolate' war: a peninsular war, a solitary pen and an isolate penis (and the *Wake* has much to say about writing, loneliness and desire). 'Venissoon' combines 'very soon' with the 'venison' with which a 'kidscad' (Jacob) deceives (or 'buttended') a 'bland old Isaac' in the Book of Genesis. 'Buttended' also contains a punning reference to Isaac Butt whose leadership of the Home Rule Party was 'ended' by the 'kid' Charles Stuart Parnell. Meanwhile the 'sosie sesthers wroth with twone nathandjoe' does much work in short order: the argument of two girls with a man prefigures Earwicker's troubles in the Park; the compound term 'twone' alludes to the merging of two things into one later exemplified by the civil (dis)union of Shaun and Shem; meanwhile the inversion of 'Jonathan' in 'nathandjoe' locates Joyce in the Irish tradition of political satire associated with figures such as Jonathan Swift.

A paragraph then introduces Finnegan-Earwicker himself. He is a builder (a mason or 'maurer'), a creator of cities and a lover of women (*FW*: 4). Yet his identity, like so much in the *Wake*, is multiple. He is a 'pentschanjeuchy chap' (Punch and Judy and the 'pentateuch' or first five books of the Old Testament) who lived before 'guennesses' (Genesis and Guinness) and 'exodus'; he is also an archetype of the fallen Adam and the risen Christ ('Phall if you but will, rise you must') and another version of Earwicker, this man of 'hod, cement and edifices'. He built cities and towers, but he was brought down by this 'municipal sin business'. It appears he was building the Tower of Babel: the edifice was composed of 'one thousand and one stories, all told' (*FW*: 5). It is also said that, like Adam, Earwicker was punished for a 'collupsus of his back promises'. Whatever his circumstances, he climbed his ladder 'Phill' of drink, fell off and died (*FW*: 6). A wake is held for the 'overgrown babeling' whose enormous body stretches from Howth ('Bailywick') to Chapelizod ('shopalist'). A roaring good time is had by all before his guests 'quaffoff his fraudstuff' and devour his body (*FW*: 7). In the same spirit we, Joyce's readers, participate at the wake by devouring the stories telling of Earwicker's fall and rise.

A swift detour takes us to the 'Willingdone Museyroom' (a compound of the Wellington Monument and the Magazine in Phoenix Park). Outside are three soldiers (who double as Earwicker and his twin sons Shaun and Shem) and two girls (who double as Anna Livia and her daughter Isabel). The soldiers are being raucously obscene while the girls 'minxt the follyages' or urinate in the bushes (*FW*: 8). Perhaps Earwicker is watching furtively; perhaps this is his 'municipal sin'. The story of Willingdone's conflict with 'Lipoleum' (Napoleon) is turned into an Oedipal family romance: the soldiers and girls take Lipoleum's side and unhorse their father as Lipoleum wins this version of the battle. Meanwhile a little bird skips across the battlefield collecting debris: Anna Livia is this custodian of historical remains. Instantly transformed into a little hen, she gathers the shards of history into her 'nabsack' (*FW*: 11). The waste ground she crosses is the midden-dump that contains the scattered fragments of human history; in this dump she discovers the letter that symbolises all letters (and all literature). Joyce's structural principle of superimposition is evident here: just as Earwicker is both the fallen Adam and a sleeping publican, Anna Livia is the hen of the dump and a sleeping publican's wife. Both of them are also contained *in* the dump: what Joyce uncovers there is the story of Everyman and Everywoman. The history of this family (which is also Irish history and a history of the world) is recorded intermittently throughout the novel by four historians (who also represent the four evangelists), 'mamalujo'. We may, as readers, be 'abcedminded', or keen to read in a straightforward order, but if we make the effort to 'stoop' and attend closely to this new 'allaphbed', we will discover a new history of mankind in its glittering fragments (*FW*: 18). *Finnegans Wake* will take us from the 'felix culpa (fortunate fall) of a 'feonix culprit' (culprit in Phoenix Park) to a new ascension (*FW*: 23).

Second Narrative Movement (pp. 30–47)

This is one of the earliest episodes to be written and it is noticeably less dense than the first. It is, however, an episode of crucial importance because it presents the encounter between Earwicker and the cad upon which so much in the novel turns. This encounter between an older and a younger man introduces one of the novel's dominant themes: the

Oedipal struggle between fathers and sons for prestige and authority. The episode opens with an introductory passage describing how Earwicker came by his name. One day the king was out leading a 'hunting party' when he came across Earwicker catching 'earwuggers' or earwigs (*FW*: 31). The king then transformed this 'earwugger' into an 'earwigger' and named him for his occupation. This, at any rate, is one version of the 'narratives' detailing Earwicker's origins. Because Earwicker's identity is insistently plural – he is, we recall, both the original father and an embodiment of humanity in general – it is not the *only* version. Earwicker's pub-friends offer another interpretation of the 'sigla HCE': for them the initials of this 'imposing everybody' stand for 'Here Comes Everybody' (*FW*: 32). This seems a more appropriate appellation for our 'folksforefather' (*FW*: 33). Yet despite his imposing reputation, Earwicker has, it appears, committed a heinous sin. The circumstances remain enigmatic, but certain 'wisecrackers' have been quick to read a 'baser meaning' into them. For a while Earwicker lay under the 'ludicrous imputation' of 'annoying Welsh fusiliers in the people's park', although the case remains unproven. But the soldiers ('shomers') continue to accuse him of 'having behaved with ongentilmensky immodus opposite a pair of dainty maidservants in the swoolth of the rushy hollow whither' (*FW*: 34). Earwicker, that is, spied upon two young women as they urinated in the park. The themes of voyeurism, desire and (the making of) water recur throughout the novel. Although he claims to be '[G]uiltless of much laid to him', Earwicker's general behaviour arouses suspicion. One 'happygogusty Ides-of-April morning' he was walking through Phoenix Park, site of his 'alleged misdemeanour', when he met a 'cad with a pipe' who asked him the time (*FW*: 35). Replying that it was twelve noon, Earwicker then launched into an unnecessary defence of the 'hakusay accusation againstm' (*FW*: 36). Nonplussed by this exchange, the cad reported it to his wife; she passed it onto her priest; and from there the story is generally circulated until it is turned into 'The Ballad of Perrse O'Reilly' ('perce-oreille' is French for 'earwig') by the 'illstarred beachbusker' Hosty (*FW*: 40).

Several points should be noted here. Earwicker's encounter with the cad occurs at Easter; his trial and fall have a clear symbolic correspondence with the Christian passion. However, Easter is also the date of the 1916 Easter Rising (or 'fenian rising') in Ireland; Earwicker's fall also represents Ireland's submission to imperial dominion (*FW*: 35). The cad's identity, meanwhile, is a compendium of literary personalities (including Yeats, Swift, Eliot and Joyce himself). He is a 'littlebilker': a writer, artificer and fraud (*FW*: 37). As the cad's persona suggests, writing in

Finnegans Wake is seen as a dangerous and transgressive force because it continually generates new perspectives upon historical truth and social morality. At the same time, writing is also one of the supreme activities of humankind. Our identity is, after all, partly the product of mythic and historical narratives; writing enables us to imagine the world perpetually anew.

Third Narrative Movement (pp. 48–74)

In this episode the 'nightynovel' is almost completely immersed in dream (*FW*: 54). Following the logic of dreams, names and identities coalesce and 'reamalgamerge' (*FW*: 49). The cad's story continues to circulate, but only a few basic details remain constant: Earwicker fell and Anna Livia revived him. Everything else is merely 'pillow talk and chithouse chat' (*FW*: 57). Earwicker may well be guilty but, like all fallen men, he is 'human, erring and condonable' (*FW*: 58). In this sense he resembles Parnell and Caesar; but he is also an archetype of the pagan god Osiris who was torn 'limb from lamb'. Fleeing Dublin and its rumourmongering, Earwicker (like Joyce) settles in Trieste where he marries a 'papishee' (*FW*: 62). Yet still he is subjected to the gossip of 'Errorland'. A lecturer (a representative of Shaun, like every lecturer in the *Wake)* now intervenes, presenting one more version of the cad's story. Through Shaun's mouth the cad insists that he was merely attempting to enter the pub after hours; his hammering upon the door inadvertently made such a 'battering babel' that he brought Joe, the handyman (followed by Isabel and a furious Anna Livia) to the door (*FW*: 64). This chaotic and indistinct scene dissolves to show a hen scratching out fragments of a letter from the midden-dump. The image is a sign of renewal and regeneration: the salvaged fragments will eventually become *Finnegans Wake*.

Fourth Narrative Movement (pp. 75–103)

We are still in the night(mare) world of the previous episode. Appropriately enough, the language in which this world is disclosed to us is 'nat language at any sinse of the world' (*FW*: 83). Joyce's punning compression of themes is fully displayed here: 'nat' is 'not' but also Danish for 'night'; 'since' approximates 'sense' but simultaneously introduces time, history and process into the way we make sense of the world. The Fall was, after all, a fall into history, mortality and the corruptibility of the flesh. In this episode Joyce interconnects themes with bewildering speed. The narrative begins with Earwicker trapped in his pub, still dreaming of the two girls who have undone him. Self-pity prompts his observation that he has endured the exile of Adam and Christ's agony of abandonment because of the 'wordwounder' cad (*FW*: 75). A bizarre metamorphosis then presents a dead Earwicker in a coffin-submarine. While he sleeps for 1,000 years, the world continues upon its chaotic path: soldiers fight one another, conflicts unfold and religious schisms deepen. The scene then switches abruptly to the dump, where rubbish accumulates and Isabel and her twenty-eight girls conduct their 'school for scamper' (*FW*: 80). As the girls cross Dublin by tram, Earwicker sifts through versions of the cad's story, trying to discover his own role in these now infamous events. Unfortunately this deductive labour is not his alone; Joyce transports us suddenly to the trial of Earwicker at the Old Bailey courthouse in London. This nightmare courtroom is in anarchic disarray: the charge against the accused is unspecific, while witnesses, lawyers and the prisoner blur continually into one another. Significantly, this legal conflict is also represented as a conflict within the family: the prosecutor resembles Shaun and the defence lawyer Shem. Eventually Earwicker's fragile identity splits apart under the strain of his examination and his consciousness is amalgamated with those of his two sons. Although what remains of Earwicker is ultimately acquitted – for this courtroom permits no proper adjudication – the judges conclude by expressing their contempt for him. In thematic counterpoint, the narrative focus switches to Kate (an older version of Anna Livia) and her dump-museum, wherein lie all the glittering fragments of the world. The accumulation of fragments implies renewal and a new historical sense; Joyce's prose employs 'backwords' (backward words) to suggest the possibility of a new cycle and a new beginning. HCE therefore momentarily becomes ECH. These 'tristurned initials' are 'the cluekey to a worldroom beyond the roomwhorld' where a city is being built after a fall (*FW*: 100). Down by the river, meanwhile, the washerwomen speculate about Earwicker's scandal and the history of his beleaguered family. It was Anna Livia, they remind us, who 'shuttered' her husband after the fall, gathered his fragments and 'waked' him from his stupor (*FW*: 102). Now her story takes centre stage.

Fifth Narrative Movement (pp. 104–25)

This episode concentrates on the letter the hen digs up from the dump. Because the letter symbolises writing, literature and textuality in general, the fifth narrative movement is full of literary allusions. The hen's letter has a complex symbolic function in the novel: as a product, like all writing, of the Fall and the global dissemination of languages, it reminds us of a lost paradisial unity; but the richness of its internal detail also suggests the cultural glories that writing and literature make possible. The introductory passage hails Anna the 'Allmaziful' (mazy and merciful) for presiding over the letter: the letter itself is a 'mamafesta' or manifesto concerning the 'Mosthighest' Earwicker (*FW*: 104). This section is followed by an extended lecture delivered by a representative of the New World – Shaun, in one of his loquacious incarnations – upon the letter's origins and the character of Shem the Penman, Shaun's brother and rival. Shem represents one (slightly self-regarding) aspect of Joyce's nature: he is a writer, a punster, a forger and the creator of worlds through words. Joyce exploits the lecture to satirise various academic and critical approaches to literature: Marxism, psychoanalysis and formalism are inspected in turn and found wanting. The lecturer's 'Extorreor Monolothe' revisits the scene of the letter's discovery: it was dug up by the hen one April, but her chick Kevin (yet another version of Shaun) claimed credit for it (*FW*: 105). In this context, the figure of Kevin/Shaun is a parody of T. S. Eliot: Joyce always maintained that the style of *The Waste Land* was indebted to *Ulysses*. Preserved in the dump, the letter, like every text, incorporates omissions and ambiguities that present formidable problems of interpretation. These difficulties are exacerbated by the fact that Shem has stained the letter with tea. Like all writers, who compose second-order worlds out of language, Shem is a forger who transfigures everything he touches. A thunderclap ends the lecturer's digression upon Shem and returns him to Anna Livia and the letter. Anna Livia's concern is simple: she wants to discover the truth about her husband's encounter with the soldiers and the two girls. Her attitude to this affair is unflinching: life must be seen 'foully' with all its 'smut' (*FW*: 113). Typically, her interests are quickly overridden by those of other people. The lecturer abruptly dismisses her in order to vent spleen upon Shem – he's merely an ear that repeats all he hears; he has neither originality nor an eye for detail – and incompetent readers of literature. In the lecture's swirl of claim and counter-claim, the 'chaosmos' of the letter and the *Wake* become one (*FW*: 118). Only Joyce's ideal reader (that 'ideal reader suffering from an ideal insomnia') might hope to decipher it (*FW*: 120).

Sixth Narrative Movement (pp. 126–68)

This episode consists of a twelve-question quiz asked of Shaun by the 'twelve apostrophes' or pub-patrons (*FW*: 126). The questions combine elaborate formality – the first alone runs for thirteen pages – with linguistic improvisation, pun and wordplay indicative of the entire novel's 'artful disorder'. Several exchanges are of particular significance. The first question put to Shaun concerns Earwicker's nature. His father, Shaun replies, is 'larger than life' (FW: 132). Indeed, he includes *everybody*: 'you and I are in him' (FW: 130). Earwicker is variously a faller, a riser, a builder, a hero, a king, a giant, a pope, an emperor, the Hill of Howth, a tree, a fish and a lover of women. He also combines certain crucial symbolic functions: he is both Adam, the first tailor of fig-leaves, and the tree of life (FW: 126). He built a city and founded the house of Man. In accordance with Joyce's Viconian theme, Earwicker 'moves in vicous cicles yet remews the same' (FW: 134). To sum up: he is the legendary Irish hero Finn MacCool. In answer to the oblique second question about his mother, Shaun avers that Anna Livia is the Liffey that streams through Dublin 'for river and iver, and a night' (FW: 139). Shaun's reply to question three sharpens Joyce's allegorical schema: the pub motto is the motto of Dublin (FW: 140). His response to question seven suggests that the twelve questions and pub drinkers are also the twelve apostles; question eight reveals the twenty-eight 'maggies' to be aspects of the nature of Isabel and Anna Livia (FW: 142). What, question nine inquires of Shaun, would the 'fargazer' staring into the 'course of his tory' (and *Finnegans Wake)* actually see? A 'collideorscape!' answers Shaun: an apparently chaotic landscape where fragments collide with one to another to form new modes of perception (FW: 143). Isabel appears to answer the tenth question in order to emphasise her resentment of her father and his incestuous desires: Earwicker is 'seeking an opening and means to be first with me as his belle alliance' (FW: 144). Question eleven poses to Shaun a crucial issue: if the 'fain shinner' (sinner and Sinn Féiner) Shem begged you to save his immortal soul, would you? 'No, blank ye', Shaun replies, before offering a defence of his decision: to reject Shem is to uphold the claims of space against time and eye against ear (FW: 149). Yet despite Shaun's best efforts, the division between these qualities cannot be consistently maintained in *Finnegans Wake*. In response to the final question 'Sacer esto' Shaun is compelled to admit 'Semus sumus!': Shem and I, we are the same (FW: 168).

Seventh Narrative Movement (pp. 169–95)

This episode focuses upon the figure of Shem the Penman. Appropriately enough, considering that Shem is a habitual forger of texts and identities, his own identity is profoundly unstable: he also takes on, in this passage, the attributes of Earwicker, the cad and those of Joyce himself. Certainly Joyce's own biography is interwoven with Shem's history. Hounded out of Ireland by the forces of moral orthodoxy, Shem takes refuge at the 'beerlitz' (Berlitz) School where he appears to spend his exile cooking and evacuating his bowels (*FW*: 182). He looses from his 'unheavenly body' a 'quantity of obscene matter not protected by copriright in the United Stars of Ourania'; *Ulysses*, we recall, was condemned as obscene and then pirated in the United States (*FW*: 185). Shem, like Joyce, writes constantly (and the episode is crammed with punning references to Joyce's own work) in order to create a 'cyclewheeling history' (*Finnegans Wake*) that explores what is 'common to allflesh' (*FW*: 186). The book of the Wake is also the Book of the World.

Eighth Narrative Movement (pp. 196–216)

The story of Anna Livia now returns to centre stage. Anna Livia is the River Liffey flowing through Dublin; as the mother of 1,001 children she is also the stream of life that enables each generation to renew itself. The renewing river of life is the central theme; Joyce puns continually upon river-names throughout the episode. Anna Livia, then, is not merely a wife and lover; she is the Great Mother of a 'litter' that includes every one of Joyce's readers (*FW*: 202). Consequently her influence extends from the past to the present and into the future: 'Anna was, Livia is, Plurabelle's to be' (*FW*: 215). Despite Joyce's masterful evocation of Anna Livia's riparian character, the narrative content of the episode is relatively slight. Down by the Liffey the washerwomen wash out Earwicker's dirty linen ('Scorching my hand and starving my famine to make his private linen public') and gossip about his relationship with Anna Livia (*FW*: 196). Earwicker, the women tell us, was placed under 'loch and neagh' (an Irish river, but also 'lock and key') and brought to trial where he was accused of 'illysus distilling' (*FW* 196). The product of his illicit trade was *Ulysses*, the obscene and irreligious book (a 'mess' that burlesqued a Mass) that he composed on the 'Reeve Gootch' (Left Bank or Rive Gauche) in Paris (*FW*: 197). In this regard, Shem the Penman is clearly his father's son. Meanwhile in a pool by the river ('trouved by a poule in the parco!'), Anna Livia discovers another letter describing the 'salt troublin bay' or Dublin Bay (*FW*: 201). She quietly places this letter in her 'shammy mailsack', another incarnation of the 'nabsack' described in the first episode (*FW*: 206). The contents of this letter are of little intrinsic significance, but the 'mailsack' is an important symbol: it is here that Anna Livia places the fragments she collects in order to preserve the old world and make a new world possible. The theme of rebirth is underscored by the washerwomen's refrain: 'Wring out the clothes! Wring in the dew!' (*FW*: 213). The famous final part of the passage, which Joyce selected for his recorded reading, is a paean to the life-giving properties of the river of life which carries the past into the future and makes the 'seim anew' (*FW*: 215). The fall of night at the end of this episode brings Part 1 of *Finnegans Wake* to a conclusion.

Part 2: Ninth Narrative Movement (pp. 219–59)

The lilting rhythms of the previous narrative movement provide little preparation for this episode, which constitutes one of the most opaque and convoluted passages of writing in the novel. Because of the complexity of Joyce's wordplay, it is worth noting that the narrative action is reasonably uncomplicated. The episode begins at the 'Feenicht's Playhouse' near Phoenix Park where the children, including Isabel's attendants, are staging a play entitled *The Mime of Mick, Nick and the Maggies* (*FW*: 219). During the play, Isabel poses a riddle to Shem by visual clues and theatrical gestures ('all the airish signics of her dipand-dump helpabit') which completely befuddles him (*FW*: 223). The answer to the riddle, it appears, is 'heliotropic', but Shem's weak eyes make him a poor candidate for 'gazework' (*FW*: 224). Humiliated after his first failure ('he displaid all the oathword science of his visible disgrace'), Shem flees into exile where he spends his time writing (*FW*: 227). His period abroad is not unproductive: while in France he publishes his 'farced epistol to the hibruws' (a hilarious image of *Ulysses* composed by Saint Paul) which infuriates British public opinion: 'the old sniggering publicking press and its nation of sheepcopers' (*FW*: 228–9). Following his third failure to solve Isabel's riddle, Shem tries in desperation to disguise himself as her favourite 'Toffey Tough' Shaun, but his brother is quickly upon the scene to expose the fraud (*FW*: 249). Now the twins fight one another ('each was wrought with his other') like the biblical brothers Cain and Abel; the girls flitter around them, confident that the process of 'naturel rejection' will enable the stronger boy to emerge (*FW*: 252). During this contest, Earwicker has already called 'enthreat-eningly' from the pub-door: dinner is ready and the play must end (*FW*: 246). While the other children begin their evening round of dinner, homework and bed, Shem remains resentfully apart. A clap of thunder echoes the slamming of the pub door, bringing to an end this ironic evocation of the divine Viconian age of family and religion.

Tenth Narrative Movement (pp. 260–308)

In this episode we pass out of the daylight world towards night and the heaviness of sleep. The gradual passing of the daylight world is reflected in the density and opacity of Joyce's style. As we slip into nocturnal darkness, identities become further unsettled, locations more abstract and generalised, and the details of plot and narrative action increasingly obscure. Joyce ironically exacerbates this unsettling of everyday perspective by presenting this part of the story as a formal academic dissertation. For this episode assumes the form of a scholarly treatise complete with footnotes and a slew of marginal commentary. At first glance, Joyce's adoption of a scholarly template might appear appropriate to the ostensible subject of the episode, which concerns the children's attempt to complete their evening homework. In practice, however, the effect is the reverse: by couching their childish deliberations and incessant gossiping within the austere framework of scholarly inquiry, Joyce comically exposes the degree to which their real concern is not with mathematics, algebra or history, but rather with the drama of sexual difference and the dynamics of the family unit. Joyce's joke is not, however, only at the children's expense. The novel's bewildering wordplay and creative commingling of different levels of reference also reveals the futility of every analytical attempt to provide a singular and absolutely coherent explanation of the meaning of human experience. To this end, our fragmentary reading of Joyce's language is frequently anticipated by the text itself, which outruns exegesis by offering simultaneously two or three possible interpretations of the passage under discussion.

The text of the homework exercise is annotated by Shem, Shaun and Isabel. Their style of commentary reflects their individual style of personality. Shaun's commentary, located in the right-hand margin, is fearsomely abstract and wilfully obscure; Shem's annotations, which occupy the left-hand margin, are much lighter and mirthful in tone: 'Ideal Present Alone Produces Real Future', he notes at one point, in perfect mockery of Shaun's high-brow obscurantism (*FW*: 303). After a passage without marginal commentary, the twins surreptitiously exchange sides. Isabel's contributions appear mainly in the footnotes, which offer much pithier insights into the proceedings than those yielded by her brothers' more learned disputation. While the twins act out the son's rebellion against the father (they metamorphose at one point into 'Bruto' and 'Cassio' in their struggle against 'Sire Jeallyous Seizer', the father who has jealously stolen their mother from them), it is Isabel who explores most purposefully the 'gramma's grammar' of sexual difference and Oedipal desire

(*FW*: 281, 271, 268). Meanwhile the twins' excursion into algebra and geometry barely conceals their Oedipal frustration: their analysis of 'ann aquilittoral dryankle' (Anna and an equilateral triangle) makes explicit the correspondence they see between geometrical triangles and the topography of the maternal genitals (*FW*: 286). Warming to this theme, Shaun conducts a geometry lesson ('I'll make you to see figuratleavely the whome of your eternal geomater') in which the earth comes to represent the 'whome' of the Earwicker family (*FW*: 296–7). Employing their 'doubling bicurculars' (Dublin-eyes as well as the double-eyes of the compass-circles), the twins isolate Anna Livia's 'triagonal delta' and 'safety vulve' (*FW*: 295, 297). Shem is delighted with this primal discovery, but he receives a 'mooxed' reaction from Shaun, who insists that his brother is 'gaping up the wrong palce' (*FW*: 299). Shaun at this point is a thinly-disguised version of Joyce's brother Stanislaus; he advises Shem Joyce to abandon his impecunious novelistic career and find employment in a brewery. Joyce delights in exposing the implicit violence of this arid bourgeois morality: when Shem entreats his brother to consider writing himself, Shaun punches him to the ground (*FW*: 303). Picking himself up, Shem forgives his brother, even though Shaun (now momentarily reconfigured as T. S. Eliot), not his more talented twin, received the 'Noblett's surprize' or Nobel Prize for Literature (*FW*: 306).

Eleventh Narrative Movement (pp. 309–82)

This episode, which takes place in Earwicker's pub, is concerned with two extended pub yarns: the stories of the Sailor and the Tailor, and of Butt and the Russian General. Both stories reinforce some of the novel's key themes; Earwicker's response to them provides revealing glimpses of his character and situation. An unnamed speaker begins the first tale while Earwicker serves drinks to the assembled company. A sailor inquires of a 'ship's husband' (a shipping agent) where he might have a suit made (*FW*: 311). He is directed to 'Kersse', the tailor, who has taken a tailoring business over from 'Ashe and Whitehead', At Kersse's, the sailor asks for a suit for 'his lady her master' consisting of a 'peer of trouders under the pattern of a cassack'. A deal is agreed, whereupon the sailor helps himself to a 'fringe sleeve' and departs. Outraged by this theft of material, the tailor yells 'Stolp, tief', but the sailor continues on his voyage for 'Farety days and fearty nights' (*FW*: 312). This allusion to Noah reminds Earwicker of the Book of Genesis and his own fall from the 'top of the ladder' (*FW*: 314). When the story resumes, the returning sailor objects at his 'second tryon' to the tailoring of the 'civille row faction': a Savile Row dispute becomes a metaphor for the Irish Civil War (*FW*: 320). Although the 'baffling yarn sailed in circles', its solution is significant. In order to resolve their dispute, the tailor proposes the reconciliation of their two families by marriage: the 'nowedding captain' will marry 'Nanny Ni Sheeres' the tailor's daughter (*FW*: 325, 328). In this way division is overcome by a new family understanding and feuding opposites are reconciled.

The story of Butt and the Russian General develops through a dialogue between Butt (another incarnation of Shem) and Jeff (Shaun). Serving as an Irish private in the British Army, Butt chances upon a Russian general crouching and defecating. The general represents an easy kill, but Butt 'adn't the arts' to shoot him (*FW*: 345). Butt only musters the resolve to fire when the general wipes his backside with a 'sad of tearfs' (*FW*: 346). As so often in Joyce, patriotism, an unreflective veneration of national soil and violence are inextricably linked. Butt's hostile response to a stranger in an open landscape recalls the cad's challenge to Earwicker: the two men, and with them the two brothers, will eventually merge into the composite figure of Buckley.

The symbolic overtones of these two stories provoke an outburst from Earwicker. He has been reading a 'suppressed' book (*Ulysses* comes to mind) which reminds him of the episode with the two girls ('one which I have pushed my finker in for . . . another which I fombly fongered freequuntly'); these admissions unite the drinkers against him (*FW*: 357). Earwicker protests his innocence: he is incapable of 'unlifting upfallen girls' even though they 'bare whiteness against me' (*FW*: 363, 364). His defence falls upon deaf ears; the unconvinced assembly departs. Feeling rejected and misunderstood, Earwicker finishes the dregs of the abandoned drinks before falling insensible to the floor (*FW*: 382). The noise of his fall awakens Kate, who finds Earwicker 'just slumped to throne' at her feet. Guilt has been explored and a fall has occurred, but in *Finnegans Wake* a rise is always possible. The 'myterbilder' (a compound term which links master-builder to master-forger to suggest Earwicker may well be composing or dreaming the narrative of *Finnegans Wake*) may have 'fullen aslip' but a new day will rouse him (*FW*: 377).

Twelfth Narrative Movement (pp. 383–99)

A brief section, and one of the first to be composed, this episode comes as a welcome relief from the opacity of its predecessor. Its subject is the writing and (mis)interpretation of history. The episode is narrated in turns by the four speakers who comprise the composite group

'Mamalujo'. Momentarily abandoning their traditional evangelical function, the disciples direct their 'gastspiels' towards the historical 'matther
of Erryn' (*FW*: 393, 389). At least as significant as the content of their
new gospel is the order in which its individual narratives are presented:
Joyce reverses the traditional gospel order so that the speakers now
appear in the sequence John, Luke, Mark, Matthew; and reversal, in
Finnegans Wake, always suggests the possibility of renewal and new
beginnings. The central narrative strand of this episode is the tragic myth
of Tristan, Iseult and King Mark. This myth records the journey of the
heroic knight Tristan to Ireland to escort Isolde, Mark's intended, back
to Cornwall. Aboard ship, Tristan and Isolde drink a love-potion prepared by Isolde's mother for her daughter and Mark, and the two fall in
love. Turned into an outcast by his love for Isolde, Tristan is fatally
wounded in combat; he dies before Isolde can arrive to give him succour,
and she dies of grief by his side. Joyce relocates the central elements of
this myth (Cornwall becomes Chapelizod) and identifies Shaun with
Tristan and Earwicker with Mark in order to underscore the son's
Oedipal rebellion against the father: 'Where the old conk cruised now
croons the yunk' (*FW*: 387–8). Much of the rest of the episode deals satirically with the uncertain status of historical narrative as it is passed down
through the ages. The confused and repetitive ramblings of the four nar-
rators inspire little confidence. The past, to them, is 'all puddled and
mythified' (*FW*: 393). But what else can we expect from four old men
(and by extension an Irish Catholic culture) too immersed in 'bygone
times' to see the present for what it is (*FW*: 386)? Completely in thrall
to their own interests, their history of 'Erryn' quickly becomes obscured
by a welter of age-old religious concerns: the nature of the Eucharist,
the problem of divorce and the divisive cultural experience of the
Reformation (*FW*: 384).

Part 3: Thirteenth Narrative Movement (pp. 403–28)

It was appropriate that Part 2 ended with Shaun in the ascendancy
because Part 3 is largely his book. The father is for a time put aside; the
son takes his place. In ironic homage to Shaun's exalted self-image, Joyce
casts him in the thirteenth episode as Jesus the Postman bringing the good
news in a letter from America. During this episode Shaun follows the
fourteen Stages of the Cross while answering questions about his divine
mission or 'heaviest crux' (*FW*: 409). To emphasise the incongruity of
Shaun's pious fraud, Joyce presents him undertaking his mission floating
down a river in a Guinness barrel. Unabashed, Shaun still insists upon

the dignity of his calling: it was laid upon him 'from on high' by high-level 'Eusebian Concordant Homilies' (Earwicker disguised) of the Church (*FW*: 409). Now he undertakes his 'vacation in life' down in the 'nightmaze' (the world and the *Wake*) where he parades the 'relics of my time' and sings the Lord's Prayer (*FW*: 411). In response to an obscure question about 'Biggerstiff' Swift and his 'Two venusstas' (Jonathan Swift and Vanessa) Shaun delivers his fable of the Ondt (ant) and the Gracehopper (*FW*: 413). This fabular battle between insects pits space (the Ondt is also Shaun) against time (the Gracehopper is also Shem). Amid the myriad puns upon insects, politics, philosophy and religious rituals, a conflict develops between the Ondt's repressive moralism and the Gracehopper's social extravagance. The Gracehopper spends his time at parties and shopping for 'housery' for female insects (*FW*: 414). Worse, he lavishes his attention upon 'bilking' or composing artworks (*FW*: 416). But the Gracehopper is doomed to inhabit the social margins in the stultifying bourgeois world dominated by the Ondt's values. The Gracehopper's marginalisation and exile is then comically represented as he is forced to roam the world in search of basic sustenance while the Ondt smokes a 'spatial brunt of Hosana cigals' and is waited upon by four 'houris' (*FW*: 417). In Shaun's self-satisfied fable, business profits are elevated above aesthetics and the artist is left to apologise for his own creations. Shaun's censorious attitude extends to the 'shemletters' (the narrative of *Finnegans Wake*): he cannot read out this 'filth' and the lies it contains about his parents (*FW*: 419). To Shaun's consternation, however, the distinction he insists upon between Shem and himself is put once more into question. Asked whether his own 'slanguage' resembles Shem's own, Shaun the fabulist expresses contempt for his brother's second-rate 'wordsharping' (*FW*: 421–2). In fact, he blusters, the best of Shem's work is 'partly my own'. Shem's writing is for the most part 'a copy . . . the last word in stolentelling' (*FW*: 424). Despite his antipathy toward art and artists, Shaun could compose the 'blurry wards' evoking the 'Book of Lief' much more imaginatively than Shem (or Joyce) if he so desired (*FW*: 425). And with this self-subverting riposte, he sails off down the river in his barrel.

Fourteenth Narrative Movement (pp. 429–73)

Shaun's barrel arrives at St Bridget's 'nightschool' where he delivers a sermon to Isabel and her twenty-eight attendants (*FW*: 430). Shaun (now magically transformed into the lover 'Jaun') sermonises in favour of tra-ditional values: like many religious authoritarians, he is obsessed with the social and moral etiquette of women. His sermon completed, Shaun Jaun celebrates Mass (running once more through the Stations of the Cross) and rails against the permissive effects of music and literature. However, his puritanical remarks are undermined by his preoccupation with erotica and female underwear: 'For if the shorth of your skorth falls down to his knees pray how wrong will he look till he rises?' (FW: 434). Significantly, Jaun's warnings against sexual licence and the malign influence of his brother insist that Shem is, like Earwicker, a 'general omnibus character' (FW: 444). Jaun counsels Isabel against incestuous relations with Earwicker and Shem, but relaxes the prohibition where his own interests are concerned: he will teach her 'bed minners'. Once she accepts Jaun, he tells her, the two of them will become holy instructors and 'circumcivicise all Dublin country' (FW: 446). In the meantime, Jaun prepares for his holy ascension 'for 'tis a grand thing (superb!) to be going to meet a king!' (FW: 452). This spiritual journey is also a family drama: loathe to leave Isabel unsupported, Jaun cedes her grudgingly to Shem's care. Shem may be a maverick, but he remains Jaun's brother: the 'shadow of a post' (FW: 462). But now Jaun must prepare to ascend unto Heaven. Mourning the loss of their 'sunflower', the girls commence a 'to-maronite wail' (FW: 470). The episode's dense final pages conflate two mythic narratives. The girls' liturgical chorus 'Oasis . . . Oisis' figures Jaun as Osiris: a god torn to pieces, but then reconfigured by a mother's care. But Jaun is also an archetype of Christ, the redeemer, who will rise again when he 'retourneys postexilic, on that day that belongs to joyful Ireland, the people that is of all time' (FW: 472). Upon his return the 'devil era' (the factional politics of de Valera and the New Irish State) will be over, the brothers will merge together into a new Father, and the 'west shall shake the east awake' (FW: 473).

Fifteenth Narrative Movement (pp. 474–554)

Having undergone his spiritual odyssey, we find Shaun lying 'dormant' on a mound that will later be revealed to be the dump where Anna Livia discovered the letter (FW: 474). Except that Shaun is no longer Shaun (or Jaun): he has 'metandmorefussed' into Yawn (FW: 513). In the first part of the episode Yawn's 'soul's groupography' is examined by the four old men 'mamalujo' (FW: 476). Yawn's individual psychology is also a 'groupography' because he contains each member of the Earwicker family within himself. As he later admits, 'I have something inside of me talking to myself' (FW: 522). One by one Anna Livia, Isabel and Kate emerge from Yawn's unconscious depths; Earwicker's self-disclosure takes longer and is much more enigmatic. Throughout, Yawn presents a formidable puzzle to his examiners: he appears as a giant baby screaming with 'ear-piercing dulcitude' (*FW*: 474). Yawn is, in every sense, an Oedipal riddle (a 'crossroads puzzler') waiting to be solved (*FW*: 475). The puzzle he poses appears to involve the entire condition of mankind, and so his questioners institute a 'star-chamber quiry' to get to the bottom of him (*FW*: 475). A series of questions bring the solution to Yawn's riddle no closer: in exasperation Luke demands 'Are we speachin d'anglas landadge or are you sprakin sea Djoytsch?' (*FW*: 485). What the four men really want is information about Earwicker, that 'twicer' (both Christ and Adam), who was born in a stable, fell from the Magazine Wall and was subsequently imprisoned. A section follows on Earwicker's crimes, which is brought to an abrupt conclusion when Anna Livia emerges from Yawn's depths to defend him. Her defence honestly acknowledges Earwicker's weaknesses ('I will confess to his sins and blush me further'): it may be true that he put his 'pennis in the sluts maschine' of the two girls, but he always adored Anna Livia, and in return she loves him still (*FW*: 494–5). Obsessed with Earwicker, the inquisitors demand an account of his fall and wake: 'Recount!' (*FW*: 496). Yawn retells these now familiar stories and describes how the 'illassorted first couple' Earwicker and Anna Livia first met (*FW*: 503). He also admits his own complicity in these crimes: like his father, he 'bopeeped' at the two girls (*FW*: 508). His interlocutors are scornful of these extenuations: Earwicker's defence (and *Finnegans Wake*) is 'the hoax that joke bilked' (*FW*: 511). Anna Livia now returns to give her own version of her marriage to Earwicker: she loved him, despite his shortcomings, and he gave her three children. Undeterred, the four men quiz Yawn about his 'epic struggle' with his father (*FW*: 515). This Oedipal contest is reconfigured as the dispute between Earwicker and the cad, who 'mardred' the 'author' (father) with his 'pocket browning' (*FW*: 516–17). All is not lost, however: Earwicker will rise once more to walk amongst us ('Handwalled amokst us'): 'O bella! O pia! O pura' (*FW*: 518). The men reject Yawn's 'cock and a biddy story' (*FW*: 519). He should get himself 'psychoanolised' (*FW*: 522). Preening before her mirror like 'Nircississies', Isabel then rises up through Yawn to offer her testimony (*FW*: 526). Whilst it is true that her father had 'wickred' designs upon her, she frustrated him by wearing 'boyproof knicks' (*FW*: 527). Anyway, she has no eyes for her father: she is helplessly in love with her own reflection.

But now it is the moment for Earwicker to appear in his own defence: 'Arise, sir ghostus!' (*FW*: 532). He insists that he is 'as cleanliving as could be' and that he has always loved his 'littlums wifukie'. There is no reputable evidence against him: only the slanders of the 'outcast mastiff' cad (*FW*: 534). He rejects all allegations of a 'shrubbery trick' with the two girls (*FW*: 538). Because of the constant vilification he has endured, he has vowed to 'discontinue entyrely all practices' (*FW*: 537). In a crucial passage of his defence, Earwicker extols his virtues as a primal father and builder of cities. When he arrived in Ireland from Denmark, he recounts, the land was a 'hole' and a 'bog' (*FW*: 539). Upon this waste-land he built a fortified city of 'magnificent distances'. Now Dublin has hospitals, centres of commerce, 'Big-man-up-in-the-Sky scraps' (sky-scrapers), factories, a zoo and a police-force (*FW*: 543). All of these developments stem from Earwicker, 'your sleeping giant' (*FW*: 540). He also established universities and 'polled ye many' in a new democratic state (*FW*: 551). Did his interrogators but know it, he is a national hero receiving 'omomonious letters' and 'widely-signed petitions' praising his 'monumentalness' (*FW*: 543). Yet despite his pre-eminence amongst men, Earwicker is incomplete without his mate; the episode therefore concludes with a hymn of praise to 'Fulvia Fluvia' Anna Livia (*FW*: 547). His devotional address is characteristically earthy in tone ('with all my bawdy did I her whorship'); but so 'streng' were they both made when his 'malestream' entered her 'shegulf' that their relationship remains a mutual support and delight (*FW*: 547).

Sixteenth Narrative Movement (pp. 555–90)

This episode takes us back to the Earwicker bedroom. The four old men are still present ('therenow they stood, the sycomores, all four of them') as presiding spirits (*FW*: 555). A brief scene recalls to us Earwicker's late night pub collapse: Kate climbs down the stairs to discover Earwicker naked on the floor with the 'clookey in his fisstball' (*FW*: 557). Scenes then establish themselves and dissolve with great rapidity. The question is reasonably asked: 'Where are we at all? and whenabouts in the name of space?' (*FW*: 558). From the pub floor, we are transported abruptly back to the courtroom, where Earwicker is found guilty of 'those impu-tations of fornicolopulation with two of his albowcrural correlations' (*FW*: 557). The description of the Earwicker marital bed as the 'bed of trial' suggests that Earwicker's moral trial has its origin in the Oedipal economy of the family (*FW*: 558). To underscore this point, Earwicker and Anna Livia are discovered abed in the 'First position of harmony' by one of their children (*FW*: 559). As the couple slump into a 'second posi-tion of discordance', Earwicker evinces rage at this intrusion upon his exclusive marital territory (*FW*: 564). The Oedipal theme continues as

Anna Livia leaves her bed to comfort a weeping child terrified by a vision of Earwicker (the 'bad bold faathern') as a predatory black panther (*FW*: 565). The child's interruption impairs Earwicker's subsequent sexual performance; his memory of the upstanding 'Wellington memorial' makes his current detumescence ('O my bigbagbone') harder to bear (*FW*: 567). To cheer himself, he creates a compensatory fantasy proclaiming his vitality and charisma. As an Irish tricolour is unfurled, Earwicker's hod is 'hoisted' once more, and he is knighted (and put back together) by the king: 'Arise Sir Pompkey Dompkey' (*FW*: 568). Ladies wave from balconies and 'the two genitalmen of Veruno' is performed in his honour (*FW*: 569). But this fantasy cannot keep the family's Oedipal tensions at bay: they resurface with savage force in a nightmarish play describing 'unnatural coits', sexual violence and 'incestuous temptations' (*FW*: 572–3). These bleak images of unnatural sexuality are then reinforced by the extended history of the court case of Tango Ltd, which involves multiple puns upon contraception. The tone changes with the insertion of a hymn to God on behalf of 'Big Maester Finnykin' and Anna Livia, our 'forced payrents' (*FW*: 576). The tone of this hymn, which focuses upon Earwicker's 'doublin existents', is equivocally poised: the observation that he is 'rounding up on his family' is arch as well as admiring (*FW*: 578). Yet whatever his detractors allege, Earwicker built and cultivated the land ('that ever gave his best hand into chancerisk') that made a decent civic life possible (*FW*: 582). The mood lightens gently as Earwicker and Anna Livia make love: Earwicker is finally 'in momentum' and has his 'wick-in-her' (*FW*: 582–3). The cock then crows to usher in the dawn. In bed, the children gossip about their father's crimes, real or imagined. Earwicker, Shaun asserts, is a 'chameleon' who assumes many different identities (*FW*: 590). His father's shape-shifting quickly acquires an archetypal significance: Earwicker has a 'seven days licence', (like Adam in the Creation), his fortunes 'misflooded' (like Noah), and he kept 'slate for accounts his keeper was cooking' (like Moses with the Ten Commandments). Crucially, Earwicker is also a version of the crucified redeemer: a man 'crossbugled' by three 'buglehorners' (*FW*: 589).

Part 4: Seventeenth Narrative Movement (pp. 593–628)

The final episode brings with it a new morning. The sun and the Son are rising: 'Array! Surrection!' (*FW*: 593). Earwicker is about to awaken and the pub to reopen. News of Earwicker's renaissance (he is a 'newman') spreads far and wide (*FW*: 596). As the household revives, thoughts flicker back to the night just passed: 'You mean to see we have been hadding a sound night's sleep?' (*FW*: 597). Certainly, but by dint of this dreamscape 'the streamsbecoming' of all life has been revealed in 'tittle-tell tattle'. Anyway, the night and the wake are now over: 'Every talk has his stay' (*FW*: 597). Intimations of the East and the rising sun now subtly infuse Joyce's prose: 'Lotus Spray!' (*FW*: 598). Light is gradually shed upon the entire 'pantomime', revealing the old man of the sea and the old woman in the sky to be 'Father Times and Mother Spaceis' (*FW*: 600). Here Joyce's allegorical archetypes come into relief: Anna Livia ('Innalavia') is a 'pool' standing beside the 'river of lives'; Earwicker came to 'Libnud' (Dublin) from an 'accorsaired race' of Danish invaders where he experienced a sexual and aquatic fall: he's seduced by a cataract and 'Caughterect' (*FW*: 600). Yet because this fall yielded children, new life and renewal, it was also a fortunate fall: 'Goodspeed the blow!' 'Kevin' (by now an amalgam of Shem and Shaun) will now rise to supplant his father and 'somewherise for the whole' (*FW*: 602). Meanwhile an exhausted Earwicker seeks 'the shades of his retirement' (*FW*: 607). It is time to wake from dreaming and the *Wake* and to come downstairs for tea. The twins (disguised as Muta and Juva) continue to discuss Earwicker and discover, in the fact of their common paternity, much shared ground. They will, however, always represent antagonistic principles (creativity and social order): their temporary 'unification' is doomed to fracture into 'diversity' and the 'instinct of combat' (*FW*: 610).

As the novel moves to its conclusion, it is still haunted by the big questions: 'What has gone? How it ends?' (*FW*: 614). The answer to the first question is: everything, from the first atom to the end of creation. For *Finnegans Wake* (Joyce's 'wholemole millwheeling vicociclometer') offers 'letter from litter' an outline of the 'sameold gamebold adomic structure of our Finnius the old One': the Father, his children and their countless descendants (*FW*: 614–15). The letter from the litter also introduces another letter from Anna Livia which presents one more (highly qualified) defence of her husband. It reprises key themes and motifs: in the cyclical structure of the *Wake* 'Themes have thimes and habit reburns' (*FW*: 614). Anna Livia protests once more against the 'Mucksrats' that hold their own 'trespasses' against Earwicker (*FW*: 615). The 'direst of housebonds' he may well be, but he did not deserve the 'mean stinker' of a plot confected by his enemies *(FW*: 617). However, his 'grand fooneral' is about to take place; then Earwicker will wake and 'redress' the conspirators. It is now time for the 'herewaker' to get himself up 'erect, confident and heroic' (*FW*: 619). With this affirmation of renewal, 'Alma Luvia, Pollabella' passes into her final monologue: 'I am leafy speafing' (*FW*: 619). As we follow her 'goolden wending' from Chapelizod and out into Dublin Bay, her meandering narrative ranges across the novel's central themes. At its heart is the character of Earwicker, which she represents as mercurial (his moods change, like the twins, in a 'twinngling of an aye'), maddening and charismatic (*FW*: 620). The Fall may have come but the 'Pheonix' will rise and Anna Livia will take once more 'the owld Finvara for my shwalders' (*FW*: 621). The final pages accordingly describe the genesis of a new cycle, but this creative movement demands the passing away of the old order before it can come into being. In this sense, Anna Livia's reconciliation with Earwicker is a union that inevitably brings one part of her life to an end: she is 'near to faint away. Into the deeps' (*FW*: 626). Throughout this passage, her husband remains both passionately desirable and terrifyingly strange to her. No longer merely Howth Castle and Environs, he is transformed at last into the sea into which she flows. When their streams meet ('Where you meet I') he will overpower her, as he did once before when he came 'darkly roaring' to 'perce me rawly' (*FW*: 626). Even as she speaks, Earwicker is 'changing': he is both her young 'sonhusband' and the waters of her own eclipse (*FW*: 627). Yet Anna Livia knows that her eclipse is the precondition for the world's regeneration: afterwards Earwicker will take a 'daughterwife from the hills again' who is 'Swimming in my hindmoist' (*FW*: 627). The new queen replaces the old queen: 'Anyway let her rain for my time is come.' In lines of exquisite pathos, Anna Livia is shown 'passing out. O bitter ending.' But as she goes back to her 'cold mad feary father' and his 'therrble prongs', she brings with her the 'keys' to his rebirth: 'Finn, again!' (*FW*: 628). The cyclical structure of Joyce's prose reproduces this regenerative movement as the novel's last words anticipate its first ('riverrun') and renew the same once more.

Further Reading

No doubt because of the sheer complexity of *Finnegans Wake*, criticism of the novel took some time to establish itself. The exception was the collection of essays produced by Joyce's friends and supporters *Our Exagmination round His Factification for Incamination of Work in Progress* (Beckett et al. 1929) which appeared during the text's composition. Although superseded by more recent studies, Campbell and Robinson's explication of the *Wake*'s general architectural design as 'a mighty allegory of the fall and resurrection of mankind' (1947: 13) proved influential in early critical discussion. The most suggestive and brilliantly compressed introduction to Joyce's radical new style is, however, to be found in Kenner (1987); here the philosophical, rhetorical and lexical layers of the novel are laid bare for the first time. Three works published in the following five years continued this labour of elucidation: Glasheen (1956) tabulated the appearance of the *Wake*'s characters and shed light on their archetypal origins; Atherton (1959) presented a useful guide to the intertextual dimension of the novel by describing the literary, philosophical and religious allusions woven into its narrative texture; while Litz (1961) returned to Joyce's drafts and proof-sheets to illuminate his compositional method and design. Drawing upon these various bodies of work, Hart (1962) undertook a thorough re-examination of the book's internal organisation which clarified key elements of the *Wake*'s dream-structure, spatio-temporal framework and cyclical mode of narrative development. An important strand of *Wake* criticism concerns itself with the creative and compositional process that brought the text into being; Hayman (1963) has made signal contributions to this area. In the hope of finding a point of connection between the *Wake* and the 'ordinary reader', Burgess (1965) produced a simplified and unpretentious introduction to the novel's characters, locations and stylistic variety. Tindall (1969) provided a considerably more ambitious and sophisticated version of this introductory schema; his reader's guide combined detailed readings of individual passages with a more comprehensive sense of the novel's thematic development and structural cohesion. An important interpretative advance in *Wake* studies was marked by McHugh (1976) which examined Joyce's manuscript sigla to demonstrate the interdependence of the novel's syntactical and thematic patterning. McHugh (1980) later extended these insights by creating an indispensable word-for-word annotation of the language of Joyce's epic. Norris (1976) presented an intriguing semiological analysis of Joyce's 'decentered' text informed by Freudian psychoanalysis, structuralist linguistics and deconstructive philosophy. MacCabe (1978) also drew upon the insights of post-structuralist linguistics and deconstructive philosophy to rethink the novel's insights into the relation between politics and language. Among recent studies, Hofheinz (1995) has employed the techniques of structural narrative analysis to examine how the *Wake*'s comic revisions of Irish historiography highlight what is politically at stake in the act of cultural self-representation.

Chapter 3

Criticism

Introduction

This section focuses on the critical responses that Joyce's work has evoked over the years. Although the scope and complexity of Joyce's writing has provoked a sometimes bewildering variety of interpretations, the history of its critical reception may be divided into two main phases. The first phase, broadly encompassing the period between the publication of *Ulysses* in 1922 and the early 1960s, comprises contemporary attempts to come to terms with the literary, cultural and political challenge of Joycean modernism and the gradual emergence of Joyce's status as a 'classic' modernist writer. A considerable number of these documents are gathered in Robert Deming's two-volume collection *James Joyce: The Critical Heritage* (1970). The second phase, stretching from the 1960s to the present day, is notable for the explosion of literary and cultural theory over the last forty years. Joyce's fictive exploration of questions of textuality, gender, sexuality, colonialism, nationalism and the unconscious has made him a subject of continuing fascination for a broad range of literary critics and cultural theorists. The sheer volume of critical writing on Joyce makes what follows necessarily selective; the subsections are intended to provide a guide to landmark episodes in Joyce criticism and key examples of the different ways in which his work is currently being read.

First Responses

Considering the violent critical debate and division Joyce's work would precipitate, the early reviews of his first publication *Chamber Music* are a study in tranquillity. Two of the first reviewers, Arthur Symons and Thomas Kettle, celebrated the formal control, tonal delicacy and rhythmical suppleness of Joyce's poetry while taking care to emphasise his aesthetic distance from the 'Celtic movement' with which he would often be associated (Deming 1970a: 36). What excites Kettle in *Chamber Music* is the intense literary self-consciousness with which Joyce reworks and simplifies aspects of French symbolist poetics whilst leaving 'no trace of the folklore, folk dialect, or even the national feeling that have coloured the work of practically every writer in contemporary Ireland' (Deming 1970a: 37). Nowhere in Joyce's poetry, Kettle assured the anxious reader, is there 'any sense of that modern point of view which consumes all life in the language of problems'. The implication that Joyce had already separated himself from a modern aesthetic that was too pre-occupied with problems of language will come as a surprise to readers familiar with *Ulysses* and *Finnegans Wake*, but those developments lay years into the future, and Joyce was gratified by Kettle's eulogising tone (Ellmann 1983: 261). Extending the lineage of Joyce's poetic antecedents to include the Elizabethan and Jacobean lyricists, Arthur Symons, the critic who did so much to introduce the innovations of French symbolist verse to an anglophone audience, singled out for attention the symbolist richness of Joyce's poetry. Symons discerned this symbolist inheritance in Joyce's ability to evoke the numinous and ineffable quality of an experi-ence before it is subsumed by everyday attitudes and sentiments. Such scrupulous commitment to the evocation of 'tiny, evanescent things', Symons observed, is particularly to be welcomed in a young Irishman 'who is in no Irish movement, literary or national, and has not even any-thing obviously Celtic in his manner' (Deming 1970a: 38).

Unsurprisingly, some of the most perceptive early criticism of *Chamber Music* was penned by those reviewers able to consider the stylistic strengths and weaknesses of Joyce's poems in the light of his subsequent fiction. Thus an unsigned review contained in the March 1919 number of the *New Republic* speculates that if we may judge Joyce's personality by 'the zest and spontaneity of his plays and novel, it is fair to say that he was in verse a shadow of himself and others, a dilettante playing a safe and pleasant game' (Deming 1970a: 44). While the rhythmical skill, formal dexterity and musicality of the lyrics is to be admired, their studied archaism and too obvious indebtedness to Dante Gabriel Rossetti and W. B. Yeats lends them a faintly antiquarian quality. What chiefly distinguishes these lyrics is an unusual mode of narratorial indirection, a 'disembodied third person' perspective which will come to characterise Joyce's prose fiction (Deming 1970a: 45). Writing in 1930 when the first instalments of *Work in Progress* were already in circulation, Morton D. Zabel also outlines the deficiencies of Joyce's lyric poetry before underlining the importance of this lyric impulse to his mature prose. Although *Chamber Music* bears only a superficial verbal resemblance in Zabel's estimation to the poetry of the 'Celtic twilight' with which it is sometimes compared, the volume is weakened by a 'deliberate archaism and a kind of fawning studiousness which attempt to disguise the absence of profounder elements' in its design (Deming 1970a: 46). Yet Joyce's subsequent refinement of his lyric technique in *Pomes Penyeach* – influenced, Zabel suggests, by the 'inferential subtlety of the Symbolists' and a reading of Rimbaud and Meredith – enabled him eventually to assume 'his own poetic character for the first time' (Deming 1970a: 47). Crucial to this new poetic character is a style distinguished by a pronounced alliteration, the persistent periphrasis of compound-terms and a creative power to 'order the material of allegory'. But the remarkable aspect of these new stylistic elements, Zabel reminds us, is that they found their most resonant expression in the diction and form of *Ulysses* rather than in his lyric verse. Far from being abandoned in the sprawling discursive structures of his prose fiction, Joyce's lyric mode is responsible for many of his fiction's most powerful effects; it makes itself felt with particular force, Zabel concludes, in passages like the river symphony at the beginning of *Work in Progress* where Joyce needed to sound an emotional depth more profound than the surface delights of parody and satire (Deming 1970a: 48).

Early reactions to *Dubliners*, as so often in pre-war responses to Joyce's fiction more generally, combine a tentative recognition of the range and quality of its stylistic effects with a moral recoil from its unsavoury depiction of the more 'sordid' and unprepossessing aspects of life. A foretaste of this response is provided by an unsigned review in the *Times Literary Supplement* of June 1914, which acknowledges that despite being too comprehensive for its theme, the collection's title is nevertheless typical of a book 'which purports, we assume, to describe life as it is and yet regards it from one aspect only'. Although the review proffers the key stylistic insight that 'Shunning the emphatic, Mr Joyce is less concerned with the episode than with the mood which it suggests', it quickly becomes clear that the 'one aspect' to which the author is deemed to restrict himself is not a rigorously qualified handling of point of view but an undue partiality to the drab and mean side of life, an issue the reviewer deems trivial when treated at any length (Deming 1970a: 60). A more positive review from the *Athenaeum* of the same month praises Joyce for the vivid naturalism of his stories, his skill both of observation and technique and his exactness of characterisation, before concluding with the pious hope that henceforth Joyce may attempt 'larger and broader work, in which the necessity of asserting the proportions of life may compel him to enlarge his outlook and eliminate such scenes and details as can only shock, without in any useful way impressing or elevating, the reader' (Deming 1970a: 62).

In a perceptive review of *Dubliners* in the *New Statesman* Gerald Gould allows himself the now obligatory reservation concerning the moral disposition of the stories before astutely identifying that capacity to disclose a subject without implying an attitude toward it that underpinned Joyce's subtle extension of naturalism (Deming 1970a: 63). Too much can, in truth, be made of the initial resistance to what the *Athenaeum*'s anonymous reviewer called the 'more sordid and baser aspects' of Joyce's subject matter (Deming 1970a: 61). The majority of even the most morally censorious reviewers found much to impress them in the quality and restrained exactitude of Joyce's prose; the unsigned review of *Dubliners* in the July 1914 issue of *Everyman* which concluded that, 'Wonderfully written, the power of genius is in every line, but it is a genius that, blind to the blue of the heavens, seeks inspiration in the hell of despair' sounds the authentic note of Joyce's original notices (Deming 1970a: 64). What was required now was a critical perspective able to range beyond a moral register in order to comprehend the stylistic and technical breakthrough announced by Joyce's fiction. Not for the first time in relation to Joyce's work, this perspective was supplied by his friend and supporter Ezra Pound. Pound's review of *Dubliners* in the *Egoist* of 1914 situated Joyce's work for the first time in the modern realistic tradition inaugurated by Flaubert. Like Flaubert, Pound argues, one of Joyce's defining qualities is that he 'writes a clear, hard prose' that 'carefully avoids telling you a lot that you don't want to know'. Joyce's terse, economical prose 'presents his people swiftly and vividly, he does not sentimentalise over them, he does not weave convolutions'. What distinguishes Joyce as a contemporary of continental writers is his exclusion of unnecessary detail which enables him to convey the quiddity of a particular experience without submerging its potentially universal element beneath a mass of local contingencies (Deming 1970a: 66–8).

Pound's critical support for Joyce's work would continue for the next decade. That such support was necessary is demonstrated by Edward Garnett's now famous reader's report upon *A Portrait of the Artist as a Young Man* for Duckworth and Company, which was considering publishing the novel. Garnett's report typifies both the defensiveness and the ambivalence of many Edwardian responses to Joyce's work. This ambivalence reveals itself in Garnett's choice of adjectives and adverbs: *Portrait* is 'unprepossessing', 'unattractive', 'formless', 'unrestrained', 'unconventional' and too concerned with 'ugly' words and things; but it is also 'ably written', interesting and 'well drawn' (Deming 1970a: 81). What Garnett descries, Joyce's uncompromising subject matter aside, is a stylistic virtuosity turned to no definite account; incontrovertibly well written as it may be, Joyce's plotless and enigmatic novel nevertheless renders interpretation impossible in 'conventional' terms. These stylistic peculiarities have, Garnett suspects, cultural as well as specifically aesthetic implications because they establish a barrier between the (presumably well-educated) 'publisher's reader' and the 'ordinary man among the reading public' unversed in the subtleties of the avant-garde. Here in microcosm is a preliminary glimpse of the modernist 'culture wars' within which Joyce's work would play so prominent a part. Pound's polemical response to Garnett's guarded criticism celebrates, rather than simply defends, Joyce's novel by strenuously championing a rarefied idea of aesthetic value over the claims of 'ordinary' taste:

> Hark to his puling squeek. too 'unconventional.' What in hell do we want but some change from the unbearable monotony of the weekly six shilling pear's soap annual novel . . . (Ellmann 1966: 372–3)

Some critics, following Pound's lead, detected in *Portrait* a stylistic advance beyond both Edwardian and naturalistic fiction. Diego Angeli, in an commendatory review Joyce was doubtless delighted to translate from Italian for the pages of the *Egoist*, declares that with this novel the Irishman had shown himself to be a writer who has 'found a way to break free from the tradition of the old English novel and to adopt a new style consonant with a new conception' (Deming 1970a: 114). Swelling this chorus of praise, W. B. Yeats wrote that the chapters of *Portrait* that he had read in the *Egoist* had convinced him that Joyce is 'the most remarkable new talent in Ireland to-day' (Deming 1970a: 80). However well-intentioned, Yeats' unduly specifying phrase 'disguised autobiography' to describe the novel was to become symptomatic of a strain of criticism which, when confronted with *Portrait*'s stylistic dislocations, chose to transform it into the autobiography of a diseased imagination. Reinforcing Garnett's injunction that *Portrait* needed to be 'pulled into shape and made more definite' in order to stand a chance with its readers, these critics made sense of the novel by relegating Stephen Dedalus to the sidelines and reading the book as Joyce's confession of his own moral baseness and loss of spiritual conviction (Deming 1970a: 81). Complaining that the novel's 'brutal probing of the depths of uncleanness' has 'the coarseness in places of a young man who is wilfully coarse', the reviewer in the *Literary World* left it open to the magazine's readers to decide the identity of the young man in question: 'Whether it is self-portraiture we do not know, but it has the intimate veracity, or appearance of veracity, of the great writers of confessions' (Deming 1970a: 91). Abjuring such subtlety, an unsigned review in the *Everyman* of 23 February 1917 entitled 'A Study in Garbage' discerned in the novel an admirable synthesis of author and subject before concluding that 'Mr Joyce is a clever novelist, but we feel he would be really at his best in a treatise on drains' (Deming 1970a: 85).

Whilst acknowledging that Joyce would 'bring back into the general picture of life aspects which modern drainage and modern decorum have taken out of ordinary intercourse and conversation', H. G. Wells' review of *Portrait* for the American *Nation* focused upon Joyce's startling and experimentalist approach to paragraph and punctuation which, although not altogether to Wells' own taste, recreates the 'growth of a rather secretive, imaginative boy in Dublin' with powerful intensity (Deming 1970a: 86–7). Two features of Wells' review would resonate down the years: his assertion that Joyce, like his countryman Jonathan Swift, suffered from a 'cloacal obsession' helped create an image of the novelist in the public mind as the writer of obscene and scatological books; while Wells' attentiveness to the sensory and affective qualities of Joyce's prose would be developed by a number of post-war critics (Deming 1970a: 86). Wells' review also represents one of the first ideological appropriations of Joyce's work for a particular political end: a liberal critique of the political limits of 'extreme' Irish nationalism. Making a direct appeal though the pages of the *Nation* to the 'American observer', Wells argues that the novel's unquestioning portrayal of a culture in which 'the English are to be hated', coupled with the refusal of any of its characters to recognise 'that a considerable number of Englishmen have displayed a very earnest disposition to put matters right with Ireland', reveals how much narrower and meaner of spirit is the 'extreme Irish "patriot" ' than the 'English or American liberal' (Deming 1970a: 88).

Ulysses **and After**

'If this spectrum of various critical light seems a bit bewildering to the contemporary reader,' observes Robert H. Deming, we must understand that the generation of critics which greeted *Portrait* was 'not prepared for a realistic-impressionistic novel which had an artist-hero who was so personally cathartic, whose mind recorded significant as well as insignificant details and impressions in a combination of the symbolic and the realistic and in a form so candidly personal' (Deming 1970a: 11). Critical interest in *Portrait* gradually dissipated in the years following the novel's publication; such interest as still remained was then swallowed up by the furore surrounding *Ulysses* which began to be published in the *Little Review* in 1918. Few novels have divided critical opinion as violently as *Ulysses* when it finally made its appearance in 1922. This observation barely does justice to the reception of a work that was reviled, celebrated, legally examined, banned, pirated and reinterpreted as a modernist 'classic' within twenty years of its publication. The anticipatory tremors of this literary and cultural *cause célèbre* can be felt in George Bernard Shaw's appalled reaction in a 1921 letter to Sylvia Beach refusing her appeal for a subvention to support the novel's publication. Condemning the novel as a 'revolting record of a disgusting piece of civilisation', Shaw concluded that all that could be said for the book was that Joyce had at least had the courage to attempt to rub the nose of the human subject in its own filth (Deming 1970a: 189–90).

S. P. B. Mais mined a similar vein of disgust in a March 1922 *Daily Express* review. His remarks typified a recurrent theme in early criticism of *Ulysses*: the combination of moral distaste for the novel's subject matter and incomprehension of its stylistic method. Our first impression of the novel, he proclaimed, is that of 'sheer disgust' while our second is irritability because 'we never know whether a character is speaking or merely thinking' (Deming 1970a: 191). However, an early entry on the other side of the critical ledger was made by Valéry Larbaud who, in an address to a Paris conference in 1921 heavily influenced by conversations with Joyce, offered a concise introduction to Joyce's innovatory approach to style, form and characterisation. Larbaud's text constitutes one of the first attempts to trace the stylistic genesis of Joyce's fiction in its development from *Dubliners* onwards. Taking care to distinguish Joyce's writing from mainstream nineteenth-century realism and the great masters of naturalism, Larbaud discovers antecedents for Joyce in the tradition of Flaubert and Maupassant before going to considerable lengths to stress the centrality to his work of a symbolic method. Part of the challenge of *Portrait*, he argues, lies in its fluctuation between a 'real' and a 'symbolic' level of narration: the name 'Stephen Dedalus', for example, denotes both a particular personage and a chain of symbolic associations linking the martyr St Stephen to the mythical figure Daedalus, the name of the creator of the Labyrinth and father of Icarus. This typology of symbolic correspondences will be recreated in *Ulysses*; in fact Joyce's symbolism will 'actually be the plot of that extraordinary book' (Deming 1970a: 256). The stylistic advance of *Portrait* and *Ulysses* over *Dubliners* is characterised both by the elaboration of this symbolic method and the substitution of interior monologue and dialogue for narration:

> We are more frequently carried to the essence of the thought of the characters; we see these thoughts forming, we follow them, we assist at their arrival at the level of conscience and it is through what the character thinks that we learn who he is, what he does, or where he is and what happens around him. (Deming 1970a: 257–8)

Larbaud's careful exposition of Joyce's method is clearly designed to forestall the dismissive response of the reader unable to make sense of *Ulysses*. The point, he patiently explains, is not to let ourselves be swept away by the sheer motility of impressions but to utilise the 'key' or network of symbolic and Homeric correspondences that disclose the basic plan of the novel. Only when we grasp *Ulysses* as a recreation of the *Odyssey* and come to understand the symbolic significance of Bloom and Stephen within its revised mythic framework does the novel's range of resonance become apparent. However, despite Larbaud's praise for Joyce's achievement in extricating the character of Ulysses from both the *Odyssey* and the mass of scholarship that threatens to obscure it, his own concerted emphasis upon *Ulysses* as 'a book which has a key' that it is our critical task to discover itself laid the groundwork for the scholarly industry that has overtaken Joyce and sometimes substituted the minutiae of interpretation for the pleasure of reading (Deming 1970a: 260–1). Exhortations like 'If one reads *Ulysses* with attention, one cannot fail to discover this plan' risk turning literary criticism into a moral duty (Deming 1970a: 261). The sharpness of his analysis notwithstanding, the reputation of *Ulysses* was compromised as much as it was enhanced by Larbaud's interpretative labours.

These preliminary responses pushed the stakes high. A rather more nuanced critical perspective, combining admiration for the novel's virtuosity with principled reservation about its achievement, was to be found in the reviews of John Middleton Murray and Arnold Bennett. Writing in the *Nation and Athenauem* of April 1922, Murray takes aim at Larbaud's somewhat exalted critical register before advancing his own more restrained opinion. The genius of Joyce's method, Murray suggests, lies in describing consciousness not only as it reveals itself in waking thought but on the very fringe of its sentience. Against this, *Ulysses* is too long and too unselective in its incorporation of data to prevent its form being overwhelmed by the sheer pressure of contingent detail. Murray's final judgement is an ideological *tour de force*, a remarkable harnessing of aesthetic radicalism for conservative cultural ends. Although upon one level *Ulysses* represents a prodigious act of artistic liberation from the shackles of moral and social conventions, Joyce's literary rebellion may in fact ultimately serve to remind other writers of the artistic limits beyond which it seems profitless to venture: 'It may help them to free themselves of inhibitions which are really destructive of vitality, and, at the same time, make it easier for them to accept those which are the conditions of civilization, and perhaps of art itself' (Deming 1970a: 196).

Arnold Bennett's review from the same year offers praise and condemnation of *Ulysses* in equal measure. Acknowledging frankly that Joyce is an astonishing and original literary phenomenon, Bennett singles out for celebration his originality of conception, wit in execution, verbal invention and prodigious humour. The best portions of the novel, such as 'Circe' and 'Penelope' are, Bennett asserts, immortal. Unfortunately, these sections constitute only a fraction of the whole. Two serious objections to the novel in Bennett's eyes are, contra Larbaud, its arrogant refusal to offer the reader an obvious plan to navigate its labyrinth and its 'pervading difficult dulness' (Deming 1970a: 220). Joyce, Bennett continues, 'seems to have no geographical sense, little sense of environment, no sense of the general kindness of human nature, and not much poetical sense. Worse than all, he has positively no sense of perspective' (Deming 1970a: 221). There is, finally, something low minded and inartistic about Joyce's reckless immersion of his reader in a welter of seemingly trivial detail. A true original Joyce may be, but with his wilfulness he has 'made novel reading into a fair imitation of penal servitude'.

Bennett's objection, intended in howsoever sincere a spirit, that Joyce lacked both a geographical and poetic sense and any feeling for human kindness indicates that *Ulysses* was already open to every kind of misinterpretation. After all, later critics have reiterated Joyce's claim that a map of Dublin might be reconstructed from the novel's minute reproduction of details, while its portrayal of the 'everyman' Leopold Bloom has often been read as a triumph of humane and disinterested sympathy. The need was clear for a more thoroughgoing engagement with Joyce's literary objectives and accomplishment; it arrived in the form of T. S. Eliot's short essay 'Ulysses, Order and Myth', which appeared in the *Dial* of 1923. Eliot's essay represents a signal contribution to the early critical reception of Joyce's work. Studiously detaching his reflection upon *Ulysses* from the furore provoked by its alleged obscenity and incoherence, Eliot redirects critical attention to two of the innovatory features of Joyce's novelistic method: its maintenance of a continuous parallel to the *Odyssey* and its employment of appropriate styles and symbols to characterise each of its episodes. The radical innovation of *Ulysses*, Eliot contends, is to manage the transition from a 'narrative' to a 'mythical' method (Eliot 1980: 483). This transition has a twofold significance. By building his novel upon so carefully elaborated a mythical foundation, Joyce breathes new life into the form of the novel, the vitality of which otherwise ended with Flaubert and with James in the decades before *Ulysses* was published. More significantly, Eliot claims that the purpose of Joyce's new 'mythical method' reveals itself in a highly particular attitude to modern history and culture:

> In using the myth, in manipulating a continuous parallel between antiquity and contemporaneity, Mr Joyce is pursuing a method which others must pursue after him. They will not be imitators, any more than the scientist who uses the discoveries of an Einstein in pursuing his own, independent, further investigations. It is simply a way of controlling, of ordering, of giving a shape and a significance to the immense panorama of futility and anarchy which is contemporary history. (1980: 483)

Eliot's essay offers a sober and sympathetic view of *Ulysses* at a time when Joyce's reputation was a matter of considerable dispute, but his main conclusion is open to serious objection. Certainly Joyce believed that the purpose of all good art was to give a shape and a significance to the flux of human experience, but the view of the world that envisaged contemporary history as an 'immense panorama of futility and anarchy' belongs more to the Christian resignation of Eliot's *Four Quartets* than the landscape of *Ulysses*. There is, after all, a world of difference between the perception of universal historical 'futility' and the words of affirmation that bring *Ulysses* to its conclusion.

As might be expected from a body of work that threatened to revolutionise the form and practice of the modern novel, Joyce's fiction simultaneously excited and divided the sympathies of other major modernist writers. In these circumstances it is perhaps unsurprising that two of the writers most publicly supportive of his work, T. S. Eliot and Ezra Pound, were poets with little to fear from the large shadow Joyce's innovations was casting over the terrain of modern fiction. In an essay upon *Ulysses* composed in 1922, Pound returned to the comparison with Flaubert outlined in his reflections upon *Dubliners* and *Portrait*, declaring Joyce to be by this stage in his development the superior writer. *Ulysses*, he continues, exemplifies to the highest possible degree Flaubert's narrative concision, concentration of theme and image, epigrammatic wit and subversion of linguistic cliché. But where Flaubert's fiction is weakened by a relatively static and inflexible mode of narrative exposition, *Ulysses* exhibits an unrivalled narrative and perceptual dynamism (Deming 1970a: 265). Ominously, though, even Pound's tireless sympathy was stretched to breaking point by the early instalments of *Work in Progress*.

The ambivalence felt by contemporary prose writers towards Joyce is perfectly expressed in Virginia Woolf's reflections upon *Ulysses*. Her essay 'Modern Fiction' is initially generous in its praise for Joyce, at least insofar as his work develops the mode of stylistic impressionism she took to be modernism's authentic expression. The fragments of *Ulysses* so far published suggest to Woolf that Joyce's flickering interior revelation of consciousness already has the makings of a masterpiece (Woolf 1925: 190). Yet despite the stylistic and indeed 'spiritual' advance marked by Joyce's technique, the novel ultimately fails in comparison to the fiction of Conrad and Hardy for reasons Woolf finds increasingly difficult to establish. Were it merely a matter of the 'comparative poverty of the writer's mind' – a view Wyndham Lewis would not be slow to endorse – the relative weakness of Joyce's work might easily be explained; but could, Woolf haltingly suggests, the defects lie elsewhere: in the 'angular' effect upon the reader produced by Joyce's emphasis upon 'indecency' and the claustrophobia of a method that locates us within a self which, 'in spite of its tremor of susceptibility, never embraces or creates what is outside itself and beyond?' (Woolf 1925: 191)? Perhaps sensing the incongruity of delivering such a judgement upon a novel which flickers interdependently between different points of consciousness, Woolf courageously confronts the possibility that what unsettles the reader of *Ulysses* is in fact the sheer force of its novelty: 'Or is it merely that in any effort of such originality it is much easier, for contemporaries especially, to feel what it lacks than to name what it gives?' (Woolf 1925: 191). Significantly, her critical reflection upon Joyce concludes ambiguously poised between praise and blame, unsure exactly how far to endorse the revolutionary method by which he brings us 'closer to what we were prepared to call life itself' (Woolf 1925: 192).

Woolf's honest and self-questioning attempt to think through the implications of *Ulysses* for the novel should be placed in the balance when her more notorious judgements on Joyce and his fiction are considered. By the time the finished novel appeared in 1922 Woolf's views, as her diary records, had hardened considerably: 'An illiterate, underbred book it seems to me; the book of a self-taught working man, and we all know how distressing they are, how egotistical, insistent, raw, striking and ultimately nauseating.' Her final judgement upon laying down the book combines social snobbery and aesthetic revulsion amid a froth of condescension:

I'm reminded all the time of some callow board school boy, full of wits and powers, but so self-conscious and egotistical that he loses his head, becomes extravagant, mannered, uproarious, ill at ease, makes kindly people feel sorry for him and stern ones merely annoyed; and one hopes he'll grow out of it; but as Joyce is 40 this scarcely seems likely. (Woolf 1953: 47, 49–50)

A far more sustained and wide-ranging assault upon Joyce's achievement appeared in Wyndham Lewis' polemical essay 'An Analysis of the Mind of Mr James Joyce' (1927a). Lewis levels three principal criticisms at Joyce's work: it is the product of a gifted craftsman rather than an original artist; it reproduces the static and lifeless world of the new 'time-philosophy' at the expense of the dynamic presentation of concrete social experience; while for all its myriad detail *Ulysses* is, contra Pound, governed by an aesthetic of generalisation that subordinates linguistic and social nuance to cliché and received ideas. Devoid of original ideas himself, Joyce, Lewis argues, simply abandoned himself to an obsession with the denotation of detail and the recreation of sensuous particulars. Yet insofar as Joyce possessed a sensitive intelligence he was vulnerable to being unduly impressed by every new idea that the cultural zeitgeist produced. The unhappy consequence of Joyce's extraordinary receptivity to new ideas and sensations appears in his slavish adherence to the 'great time-school' of 'Bergson-Einstein-Stein-Proust' whose baleful influence, Lewis alleges, resonates throughout *Ulysses* (Lewis 1927a: 106).

By surrendering the historical dimension of his art to merely 'psychological time' and the individual's sense of 'duration', Joyce's writing, Lewis argues, assumes a static and mechanistic form. It is static because it substitutes an immersion in sensation for the development of character and plot; it is mechanistic to the degree that character and moral consciousness are determined by the relentless recapitulation of past experience. In the final instance, Lewis contends, Joyce lacked any real capacity for ideas; as he puts the matter in one of his more pointed asides: '[T]here is not very much reflection going on at any time inside the head of Mr James Joyce' (Lewis 1927a: 106). Moreover, Joyce had no really creative relation to the idea of psychological relation; it simply afforded him a convenient schema within which to unfold the interior life of stock character types over 800 pages. His lack of imagination revealed itself in a susceptibility to verbal clichés and a predisposition towards the 'general label' (Lewis 1927a: 118). The vulgar generality of his 'craftsman-mind' stood revealed in his recourse to the clichés represented by 'a stage Jew (Bloom), a stage Irishman (Mulligan), or a stage Anglo-Saxon (Haines)' (Lewis 1927a: 113). Even Joyce's famous elaboration of stream-of-consciousness had a narrow psychological origin: Joyce never really developed as a person, only as a craftsman; he seized upon the new technique of 'telling from the inside' because it offered a mechanism by which he might discharge a lifetime of disorderly impressions in one continuous narrative stream. In Joyce's hands, Lewis concludes, the momentous new revelation of interior time and expressive duration is transformed into the 'very nightmare of the naturalistic method' (Lewis 1927a: 108).

For all its wit and brio, Lewis' broadside offers an exaggerated and unfocused account of *Ulysses*. Only a very partial critic could judge *Ulysses* to be the expression of an imagination enslaved to cliché and received opinion; it was precisely this failure of linguistic self-consciousness that Joyce composed 'Nausicaa' to satirise. Similarly, Lewis' insistence that the art of *Ulysses* is unbalanced by Joyce's narrow obsession with he inferiority of psychological experience is hard to credit, given Joyce's fascination with the built space of the city and his attention in episodes like 'Cyclops' and 'Oxen of the Sun' to the political, cultural and linguistic contexts of modern Irish life. Lewis was certainly one of the first critics to raise the problem of Stephen's prickly and self-regarding character ('What induced Joyce to place in the centre of his very large canvas this grotesque character, Stephan [sic] Dedalus?'), although his imperviousness to Joycean irony prevented him from thinking through the problem posed by his own question; the issue would not be satisfactorily resolved until Hugh Kenner's radical reassessment of Stephen's character thirty years later (Lewis 1927a: 116).

Although Joyce affected to disdain Lewis' critique, he was undoubtedly discomposed by *Time and Western Man*; his discomposure became in turn the inspiration for the first extended study of *Ulysses*. Joyce had long planned to collaborate with a critic in order to usher his own opinions upon the novel into print. His flank exposed by Lewis' attack, Joyce's eye alighted upon Stuart Gilbert, who had recently translated *Ulysses* into French. With Joyce's encouragement, Gilbert agreed to write an introductory study of the novel based upon the notes he had made for his translation. While Joyce was not Gilbert's collaborator in any formal sense, he took care to make his original structural plan for the novel available to the younger man and kept a watchful eye upon the book's progress, sometimes suggesting contexts for discussion or supplying specific background material (Ellmann 1983: 601n.).

Gilbert's study bears the impress of the historical circumstances in which it was written. It must be remembered that *Ulysses* was still the subject of censorship in the late 1920s and therefore unavailable for easy perusal and discussion; in order for his readers to have any understanding of the claims he was making, Gilbert felt the need to reproduce large slabs of the novel alongside his detailed and sometimes paraphrasing commentary. Part of the historical value of Gilbert's book, then, is that he was both critic and midwife; his work provided many readers with their first acquaintance with Joyce's novel. Finding himself in the singular position of writing the first extended critical introduction to *Ulysses*, Gilbert tackled the problem directly: 'In writing this commentary I have borne in mind the unusual circumstance that, although *Ulysses* is probably the most-discussed literary work that has appeared in our time, the book itself is hardly more than a name to many' (Gilbert 1930: 9). His other critical motivation was more nuanced: aware of Bennett's injunction that more help was required to render *Ulysses* comprehensible to a general readership, he resolved to establish a set of firm expository principles while staunchly defending Joyce from the polemical intervention of detractors such as Lewis. Gilbert underlined the first objective by reproducing the elaborate schema for the novel's eighteen episodes that Joyce had originally supplied to Larbaud. This plan, which correlated information such as the Homeric title, scene, time, bodily organ and 'technic' or narrative form represented by each episode, offered a symbolic shorthand from which Joyce's larger epic framework might be reconstructed. The local intricacies of Gilbert's reading of the novel quickly suggested the critical futility of cleaving too closely to Joyce's symbolic schema, but his introduction of the episode titles Joyce omitted from the finished novel proved widely influential and have been in use almost continuously ever since. In order to give the reader a firm foothold in Joyce's labyrinthine text, meanwhile, Gilbert proceeded quickly to underline some of the novel's key aesthetic principles. Notwithstanding the reputation *Ulysses* has gained amongst certain critics and younger writers, the book has nothing in common with a 'fantasia of the unconscious'; the novel is, in fact, 'a work essentially classical in spirit, composed and executed according to rule of design and discipline of almost scientific precision' (Gilbert 1930: 10). The 'key' to *Ulysses*, to borrow Larbaud's term, lies in its structure of mythic correspondence; these allusions, while never simply parodic, are intended to evoke a comic sense of the divergence between classical and modern standards.

Throughout his study Gilbert takes pains to emphasise Joyce's classical literary heritage. One controversial consequence of this insistence is Gilbert's dismissive attitude to Joyce's *Irishness*. The sensibility of Gilbert's Joyce is European rather than Irish in nature; but he is only able to corroborate this highly partial perception by transforming *fin-de-siècle* Dublin into a 'Hellenic' city-state (Gilbert 1930: 28). This tendency in Gilbert's criticism has had the effect of diminishing the cultural specificity of Joyce's representation of Irish life and has proved vulnerable to national and postcolonial readings of *Ulysses*. In one other area, however, Gilbert has proved a useful point of departure for subsequent readers. Taking issue with those critics who have represented *Ulysses* as a novel which has language as its central presence and supreme value, Gilbert emphasises instead the meticulous *realism* of Joyce's epic. Like Homer's *Odyssey*, he argues, *Ulysses* depicts in highly stylised language a particular form of European civilisation at a particular historical moment. Joyce's genius, like Homer's, was to find a point of synthesis between literary invention and epic verisimilitude in which the contours of a society are disclosed as if for the first time (Gilbert 1930: 87).

Another member of Joyce's inner circle, the painter Frank Budgen, provides an illuminating insight into Joyce's working methods and compositional technique. Partly a record of his friendship with Joyce in post-war Zurich and partly an episode-by-episode guide to *Ulysses*, Budgen's memoir *James Joyce and the Making of Ulysses* reproduces the essential content of voluminous conversations with Joyce concerning the novel's style, form, history, themes and influences. It was in these conversations that Joyce expounded at length upon his reasons for adopting the *Odyssey* as a mythic parallel for his epic of modern Dublin life and his identification of Ulysses as the most 'complete all-round character' in Western literature (Budgen 1934: 15). Amid a welter of contextual detail, Budgen also highlights Joyce's intention to create in *Ulysses* the 'epic of the human body' and his redefinition of the very nature of the epic hero (Budgen 1934: 21).

The Reception of *Finnegans Wake*

Doubtless aware that the bewilderment and hostility *Ulysses* provoked in many critics was likely to be exacerbated by the avant-garde challenge of *Work in Progress*, Joyce prepared the ground for his new work by soliciting the opinions (while defending the novel's style and intentions) of an inner circle of friends and admirers. The initial results were not encouraging: Pound, Robert McAlmon and Joyce's brother Stanislaus remained resolutely unimpressed by his experiment; meanwhile Harriet Shaw Weaver, one of Joyce's greatest champions, finally broke ranks in November 1926 and appealed to him to publish a fully annotated edition in order to elucidate the text's myriad obscurities. Weaver's plaintive appeal for a comprehensive key and glossary would not be answered for another eighteen years, but other members of the Joycean circle quickly took matters into their own hands. In order both to celebrate the revolutionary modernism of *Work in Progress* and explain aspects of its style and intellectual heritage to a wider audience, a group of Joyce's friends and supporters, organised by Eugene Jolas, editor of the Parisian surrealist avant-garde magazine *transition*, published a collection of essays defending the new work. Characteristically Joyce kept a watchful eye upon the preparation of his defence; he even supplied the collection's eccentric title *Our Exagmination Round his Factification for Incamination of 'Work In Progress'*. The tone of the collection was set by Jolas' own essay 'The Revolution of Language and James Joyce' which posits a necessary linguistic division between the work of the genuinely avant-garde artist and the mode of cultural production of modern industrial society. The real 'metaphysical problem' confronting the contemporary artist, Jolas asserts, is the generally degraded condition of modern language. Too much modern literature remains in thrall to 'worn-out verbal patterns' and the denuded sensibility of journalistic prose. In order to liberate literature from the commercial commodification of language, the avant-garde artist must first recognise 'the autonomy of language' and then use this autonomy to create an original 'verbal vision of time and space' (Beckett et al. 1936: 79). The need for this novel and wholly distinctive verbal vision becomes even more pressing following the elucidation of the subconscious by psychoanalysis: the consequent emergence of this 'new field for magical explorations and comprehensions' requires a new 'instrument of language' to chart its myriad possibilities. Precisely such an instrument is fashioned by the revolutionary style of *Work in Progress* which takes to its limit modernist and surrealist experimentation with time and consciousness and thereby wholly reinvents 'the old relationships between words and thought' (Beckett et al. 1936: 84).

A rather more nuanced, although equally celebratory assessment of Joyce's imaginative innovation in *Work in Progress* was provided by Samuel Beckett's essay 'Dante . . . Bruno. Vico . . . Joyce'. Beckett's essay represents the first attempt to examine in any detail Joyce's artistic reconfiguration of Viconian ideas. Beckett condensed Vico's thought into three main points, each of which influences the form, style and thematic organisation of *Work in Progress*: a theory of the development of human society; a treatise on the origin and evolution of language; and the identification of myth as the original ground of historical consciousness. He also advanced two significant claims concerning the style of Joyce's new work. In *Work in Progress*, Beckett argues, linguistic form is not an external adornment designed merely to dazzle or provoke; form and content are, instead, indistinguishable one from another: 'Here form *is* content; content *is* form' (Beckett et al. 1936: 14). Warming to his theme, Beckett

encapsulated his formalist thesis in a statement that had pejorative implications for the reception of the broader historical and cultural dimensions of Joyce's fiction: 'His writing is not *about* something; *it is that*
something itself.' At the same time, Beckett made the important observation that part of the notorious difficulty of *Work in Progress* arises
because Joyce 'desophisticated language' by attempting to return it from
abstraction to its concrete, material and sensuous roots (Beckett et al.
1936: 15). Although intended sincerely as praise, Beckett's insistence
upon the purely formalist nature of Joyce's stylistic experimentation did
a good deal to discredit Joyce's work with a number of critics; conversely,
later criticism has done much to underline the highly political dimension
of Joyce's radical formal innovations.

The efforts of the *transition* essayists were accentuated by Edmund
Wilson's insightful account of Joyce's new vision and style. Despite pos-
sessing only the most fragmentary knowledge of the novel gleaned from
the instalments published in *transition*, Wilson managed to provide a
remarkably prescient, if inevitably flawed, rendition of the novel's basic
plot and structure. Wilson focuses in particular upon Joyce's 'unique
genius for the presentation of psychological states' and his invention of a
post-Freudian dream-language capable of intimating the buried cultural
history of a universal human nature (Wilson 1931: 225). The challenge
Joyce sets himself in *Work in Progress* is to bring the subconscious to life:

> A single one of Joyce's sentences, therefore, will contribute two or three dif-
> ferent meanings – two or three different sets of symbols; a single word may
> combine two or three. Joyce has profited, in inventing his dream-language,
> by Freud's researches into the principles which govern the language contin-
> ually spoken in dreams. (Wilson 1931: 229)

The most controversial aspect of Wilson's analysis is his claim that the
'dream-narrative' that constitutes the entire content of the novel is solely
the imaginative projection of H. C. Earwicker's dreaming consciousness.
In this account, each of the novel's multitudinous elements.

> are all aspects, the dramatic projection of aspects, of Earwicker himself: men
> and women, old and young, stronger and weaker, river and mountain, tree
> and stone – it is the dreamer who speaks or is spoken to, who sees or is seen,
> in all of them. (Wilson 1931: 230)

Wilson's reading of Joyce's dream-structure has proved contentious
amongst subsequent critics, several of whom argue that the novel is the
representation of a dreaming consciousness from a position *outside* – but
which momentarily represents itself *within* – the novel's narrative world
(Hart 1962).

Wilson's exegetical and speculative labours were insufficient to convince F. R. Leavis, who sounded a dissenting note in his article 'Joyce and "The Revolution of the Word" '. Leavis' account, which ranges across the published extracts of *Work in Progress*, *Our Exagmination* and Eugene Jolas' laudatory essay on Joyce, 'The Language of Night', is unequivocal in its initial judgement: the extant sections of Joyce's new novel suggest that it is 'not worth the labour of reading' (Leavis 1933: 193). The tenor of Leavis' argument throughout is that of a former admirer lamenting the squandering of a prodigious talent; to read *Work in Progress* is to 'regret the use to which James Joyce has put his genius since he published *Ulysses*'. Joyce's preoccupation with linguistic style and form has now become his primary concern; consequently his work can establish only a tenuous and contingent relation to the imaginative experience it seeks to express. Joyce's prose, Leavis insists, was not always so quick to surrender imaginative concretion to linguistic self-consciousness; this much is demonstrated by *Ulysses*, where 'the rich complexity [of the aesthetic experience] it offers derives from the intensely imagined experience realised in the words'. But by surrendering his aesthetic sense to what Leavis takes to be the mere suggestiveness of word associations, Joyce is no longer able to sustain a productive synthesis of thought and representation. To justify a verbal medium as challenging and opaque as *Work in Progress*, Leavis concludes, Joyce required a 'commanding theme, animated by some impulsion from the inner life capable of maintaining a high pressure' (Leavis 1933: 196). *Ulysses* discovered such a theme in Joyce's biography and the historical particularity of his portrait of the artist's predicament; the imaginative and emotional pressure exerted by this material found a linguistic correlative in the array of styles Joyce brought to bear upon it. Lacking a similarly unifying structure (save for the obscure Viconian 'idea' of an all-embracing ideal and timeless history), *Work in Progress* abandons formal and thematic coherence for the random generation of stylistic effects.

Leavis' disappointed response was mirrored by a number of Joyce's former admirers. For every approving critic like Padraic Colum, alive to Joyce's formal and stylistic innovations, there was heard the sorrowful objection of previously sympathetic readers like Gerald Gould to the fundamental 'aesthetic dishonesty' of Joyce's new linguistic medium (Deming 1970b: 393). The reviews when the novel was finally published were in turn exultant, bewildered, admiring, appalled, sorrowful and dismissive. Inveighing against the 'philistine exasperation and the intellectual snobbery which have combined to envelop Joyce's reputation',

Harry Levin redirected critical attention from the mass of erudition that already encrusted the novel towards the delights of linguistic invention that bejewel its surface (Deming 1970b: 694). In the teeth of prevailing opinion, Levin advanced other corrective judgements: *Finnegans Wake* is a Rabelaisian comedy, delighting in the coarse, bawdy and sensual aspects of life, not the morbid psychodrama it is sometimes assumed to be; its language is not merely learned and etymologically recondite but immersed in 'Irish life, in the streets and monuments, the sounds and smells, the pubs and stews of Dublin'; while, far from being wholly pre-occupied with arcane patterns of symbolism, the novel is permeated throughout by the theme of original sin (Deming 1970b: 695). Levin's praise for the novel was not unqualified: his tantalising suggestion that the hermetic linguistic self-consciousness of *Finnegans Wake* showed Joyce to be a master of English 'with so much to express and so little to say' has reverberated in later and less admiring responses to the novel (Deming 1970b: 703). That heartfelt acclaim for aspects of Joyce's achievement could co-exist with a profound critical detachment from the novel's aims and aesthetic is indicated by Alfred Kazin's review of the novel; if the triumph of *Ulysses*, to reprise T. S. Eliot's notorious phrase, was to make the world possible for art, the threat of its successor was to dissolve the world into the shimmering kingdom of letters (Deming 1970b: 686–8). Richard Aldington, unlike Kazin, did not hesitate to condemn the work as a bewildering and unbeguiling collocation of 'futile inventions, tedious ingenuities, and verbal freaks' (Deming 1970b: 690). The various positions established by Levin, Kazin and Aldington would each receive amplification in the post-war period; but the debate they helped to initiate was quickly subsumed by the eruption of World War Two a few months later.

The Post-War Critical Scene

The thirty or forty years between the end of World War Two and the explosion of critical interest in Joyce's work in the 1970s and 1980s caused by the emergence of modern literary and cultural 'theory' saw the debate over his achievement and legacy steadily intensify. To the extent that Joyce's corpus became central to the modernist canon in these decades, John Coyle is right to call them 'years of consolidation'; this term is only accurate, however, insofar as it is remembered that the meaning and value of Joyce's writing was vigorously contested throughout this period. A substantial gesture towards the consolidation of Joyce's reputation during this time was made by Harry Levin, who published the first extended critical introduction to his work, having already intervened in earlier debates. Appearing in the year of Joyce's death, Levin's study makes use of a number of new sources and documents, such as Herbert Gorman's biography, in order to clarify the different stages of Joyce's development as an artist. The time for a general introduction to Joyce seemed propitious, Levin suggests, for a number of reasons: the immediate controversies surrounding Joyce's work had abated by 1941; the ban on *Ulysses* had been lifted; while the critical attitude towards Joyce's writing was beginning to move from widespread rejection to a more general acceptance of its literary merits. With the passing of the years and the advent of the war literary sensibility appeared to have emerged sufficiently from the culture of modernism to judge the significance of Joyce's work 'against the broad perspective of literary history'. Levin is careful to locate Joyce within the mainstream traditions of modern European literature in defiance of those critics who regarded him as an eccentric and maverick Irishman. His discussion is littered with references to Thomas Mann, Gustave Flaubert, Emile Zola and the French symbolist poets; like Stuart Gilbert before him, Levin is instrumental in establishing Joyce's reputation as a giant of *European* literature. Joyce's fiction, in Levin's view, reveals both 'striking originality' and a 'deep sense of tradition' (Levin 1944: 5). Both an exemplary innovator and a profoundly transitional figure, Joyce's literary development is marked by a creative antagonism between the principles of 'richness and reality' that Levin identifies with symbolism and naturalism respectively (Levin 1944: 21). The arc of Joyce's imaginative progress describes a transition from naturalism's 'disciplined revision of nineteenth-century realism' to the referential autonomy of symbolist technique. All of Joyce's early work, Levin maintains, led towards *Ulysses*, which combines these two traditions in a rich and productive synthesis. For this reason *Ulysses* occupies a pivotal position in Joyce's own development and in the culture of the twentieth century. Although *Finnegans Wake*, by contrast, must be understood as a 'symbolist experiment', it reprises Joyce's two main themes of the artist and the city while managing to reconfigure the dialectic between naturalism and symbolism in a radically new fashion. The consistency of outlook underlying Joyce's entire series of stylistic modulations becomes clear, Levin asserts, once we recognise that 'the *Portrait of the Artist*, so direct in treatment, should be devoted to the problems of art; while *Finnegans Wake*, where the figure of the artist has disappeared into the complexities of his technique, should be concentrated upon the *minutiae* of city life' (Levin 1944: 21–2).

The strengths and weaknesses of Levin's analysis are particularly evident in his reading of *Portrait*. Thinly conceived by Levin in the first instance as a candid autobiography, his representation of the novel as based on a literal transcript of the first twenty years of Joyce's life yields little sense of its richly comic interplay between narration and protagonist. Where Levin's reading really comes into its own, though, is in its sensitivity to the relationship in Joyce's prose between literary style and modes of perception. 'Joyce's own contribution to English prose,' Levin contends, 'is to provide a more fluid medium for refracting sensations and impressions through the author's mind – to facilitate the transition from photographic realism to esthetic impressionism' (Levin 1944: 42). Furthermore, Joyce's language 'exalts the habit of verbal association into a principle for the management of experience' by sensuously recreating the passage from primary sense-impressions towards verbalisation and the conscious integration of images and affects into a coherent vision of the world. Levin's receptivity to the transfiguring effects wrought by the fluid medium of Joyce's prose also made him suspicious of those moments in *Ulysses* in which the refinement of style threatened to become an end in itself (Levin 1944: 73).

Levin's intuition that Joyce was bringing himself no closer to life by indulging in a series of self-conscious stylistic adventures was shared by the Marxist critic Georg Lukàcs whose discussion of *Ulysses* formed one part of his trenchant critique of the ideology of modernism. Lukàcs wanted to correct what he saw as the prevalent misapprehension that the literature of so-called 'modernism' and the avant-garde is the genuinely modern literature (Lukàcs 1962: 13). This misapprehension is based upon two widely held prejudices concerning the limitations of the classic realist novel: the sense that realist techniques are too superficial to represent the complexity of contemporary social existence; and the belief that the emergence of modern social realism has rendered obsolete the world-view of the traditional realist novel. Against this trend, Lukàcs writes in defence of the contemporary 'bourgeois' realism of writers like Anatole France, Theodore Dreiser and Thomas Mann whose work records the fragmentation of social and imaginative life under modern industrial conditions. It is precisely this capacity to represent the totality of social relations, Lukàcs argues, that has been relinquished by the sterile dogmas of modernist anti-realism with its self-regarding preoccupation with form and style, fascination with streams of perception and flows of sense-data, reckless disintegration of personality and external reality into the formless interior world of the sensualist or neurotic, and its hypersensitivity to abnormal mental states. What is lost in the modernist obsession with the 'abstract potentiality' of sense-experience and subjective perception is any trace of the 'dialectic between the individual's subjectivity and objective reality' that animates classic realism. The loss of the 'concrete potentiality' of social existence glimpsed in the relationship between the subject and the external world in which she lives, Lukàcs concludes, renders invisible the historical contexts of contemporary life (Lukàcs 1962: 24).

It is inadequate, Lukàcs claims, to speak of Joyce as a 'stylist' if such a term implies interior monologue is for him a mere stylistic device; instead it is 'the formative principle guiding the narrative pattern and the presentation of character'. Technique, in Joyce's hands, has become something 'absolute'; it is now entirely synonymous with the 'aesthetic ambition' of the novel. Joyce's immersion of his reader in 'perpetually oscillating patterns of sense-and-memory data' gives rise to 'an epic structure which is *static*, reflecting a belief in the basically static character of events'. In turn the perceiving consciousness is wholly abstracted from complex social relations, bequeathing an 'image of man' which is by nature 'solitary, asocial, unable to enter into relationships with other human beings' (Lukàcs 1962: 20).

Insofar as Lukàcs is correct to perceive in modernist writing a weakening of the relationship between interior life and objective social experience, Joyce would appear to be an unlikely representative of such a practice. Bloom's interior monologues are continually opened to a flood of external stimuli; the pressure of external reality leads him frequently to reflect upon his social and racial marginalisation within the modern Irish metropolis. If it is true, as Lukàcs claims, that modern allegory destroys the 'coherence of the world' by severing the connection between individual and collective experience, this criticism can hardly be made of a novel like *Ulysses* that holds in synthesis the abstract particularity of sensual impressionism with the linguistic, cultural and historical contexts of modern European civilisation (Lukàcs 1962: 43).

At the same time that Lukàcs was pressing a reductive image of Joyce into service to support his contention that 'modernism means not the enrichment, but the negation of art' (Lukàcs 1962: 45), another critic was arguing instead that modernist writing absorbed into itself and revivified the highest traditions of European literary culture, while discovering, in Joyce, its most distinguished practitioner. Hugh Kenner is the doyen of Joyce's critics, a scholar who single-handedly reconfigured Joyce's image in modern letters, and his *Dublin's Joyce* (1955) has some claim to be the greatest work on Joyce ever written. When Kenner came to write a preface to the second edition thirty-two years later, he drew attention to the key chapter, 'The Portrait in Perspective', in which he had first suggested that part of the burden of Joyce's works was 'Stephen's limitations, limitations sufficient to make it implausible that an extrapolated Stephen had managed to write them' (Kenner 1987: xii). What was original in the first instance about Kenner's reading of *Portrait* was the ironic distance it interposed between Joyce's authorial perspective and Stephen's more restricted angle of vision. No longer was *Portrait* discussed as if Stephen's character and attitudes might be identified with Joyce's own, or the novel reconstructed as a thinly veiled autobiography. In Kenner's hands the novel's dominant feature became the sinuous and almost imperceptible mode of irony through which Joyce expressed Stephen's interiority and aesthetic ambitions in a style to which his protagonist might aspire but could never hope to emulate.

Such keen discrimination between the perspectives and qualities of author and character would mean, Kenner ruefully acknowledged, that he 'would one day find myself called the bell-wether of the Stephen-hating school' (Kenner 1987: xii). Certainly he goes to elaborate lengths to distinguish the two figures. Joyce's 'recasting' of Stephen's character is now judged to be one of the principal differences between *Stephen Hero* and *Portrait*:

> In the reconceived *Portrait* Joyce abandoned the original intention of writing the account of his own escape from Dublin. One cannot escape one's Dublin. He recast Stephen Dedalus as a figure who could not even detach himself from Dublin because he had formed himself on a denial of Dublin's values. He is the egocentric rebel become an ultimate. There is no question whatever of his regeneration. (Kenner 1987: 112)

Stephen's failure to detach himself from the Dublin world he condemns accordingly renders absurd any uncritical acceptance of his vainglorious self-liberation at the novel's conclusion: 'And it is quite plain from the final chapter of the *Portrait* that we are not to accept the mode of Stephen's "freedom" as the "message" of the book' (Kenner 1987: 132).

Massively influential as these judgements have been for subsequent Joyce criticism, Kenner also subtly reshaped our understanding of *Portrait* in other ways. His alertness to the 'contrapuntal opening' of the novel in which an 'Aristotelian catalogue of senses, faculties, and mental activities is played against the unfolding of the infant conscience' suggests how its first two pages 'enact the entire action in microcosm' (Kenner 1987: 114). The various ways, moreover, in which language gradually imposes itself, like a physical sensation, on Stephen's mind demonstrates how Joyce 'can cause patterns of words to make up the very moral texture of Stephen's mind' (Kenner 1987: 117). Not only does this hypersensitivity to language afford us insight into Stephen's moral consciousness; it also provides a vital clue to his enthralment to his own gift for rhetoric: 'We cannot read *Finnegans Wake* until we have realized the significance of the way the mind of Stephen Dedalus is bound in by language. He is not only an artist: he is a Dubliner' (Kenner 1987: 119). Leaving to one side the richness and virtuosity of Kenner's close reading of particular passages, part of the originality of his approach consists in the stylistic connections it establishes between different phases of Joyce's writing. Characterising the aesthetic dictum behind the unsettling style of *Dubliners* as '[l]aying hold on the subject, not expressing an attitude to it', Kenner explains how this mode of ironic equivocation and occluded point of view blossomed into the radical narrative experiments of *Portrait* and *Ulysses* (Kenner 1987: 50).

In *Joyce's Voices* (1979) Kenner develops a reading of *Ulysses* as a thoroughgoing subversion of the entire literary art of 'fiction' developed in the seventeenth century which gradually replaced older oral, picaresque and theatrical traditions with a new narrative discipline based upon the orderly and objective presentation of evidence. This evidential or 'realistic' mode reached its apotheosis in the nineteenth-century novel; and it was this style of writing that *Ulysses* exploded:

> As the great age of twentieth-century Modernism recedes, it grows increasingly clear that the decisive English-language book of the century was *Ulysses*, the first pivotal book in English since *Paradise Lost*. Its example underlay *The Waste Land*, which terminated Eliot's first poetic period. And it directed the decisive reordering of the early *Cantos* which Pound undertook early in the 1920's. Pound resisted, and Eliot as we shall see passed over in silence, the fact that *Ulysses* commences in tacit adherence to the canons of naturalism, of Objectivity, and then disorients readers by deserting them, for reasons that have never been satisfactorily explained. Its profusion of styles – what are we to make of *that*? (Kenner 1979: xii–xiii)

Kenner proceeds to make a very great deal of it. The initial sign of Joyce's transition from a tacit adherence to naturalism towards a form of stylistic heteroglossia may be detected, Kenner suggests, in his refashioning of free indirect style into a device that systematically disorders naturalism's scrupulously neutral sequence of narrative presentations (Kenner 1979: 12). Returning to the famous opening sentence of 'The Dead' ('Lily, the caretaker's daughter, was literally run off her feet'), he points out that our difficulty with what Lily's solecism 'literally' might mean represents for us 'the fear of the Word and the beginning of reading' (Kenner 1979: 15). Joyce's radical extension of the interplay of perspectives that free indirect style makes possible, Kenner argues, will lead eventually to the multiple styles of *Ulysses*. One of the remarkable aspects of *Ulysses* is that the novel dissolves the unity of its narrative voice into a number of partial, located and subjective points-of-view (Kenner 1979: 18). What we see at the beginning of *Ulysses*, Kenner maintains, in an analysis that anticipates the much-vaunted insights of post-structuralist criticism, is the dissolution of the 'objective metalanguage' or impersonal narrative voice of realist fiction into a series of idiomatic perspectives (Kenner 1979: 68). Thus in 'Telemachus' the traditional voice of third-person narrative is divided between an objective mode of denotation and a secondary voice which gently brushes up against the idiom of particular characters, subtly displacing the denotative style into a subjective arrangement of images and sensations. Such displacement is fundamental to Joyce's design because it suggests that the commonly shared 'objective' reality which it is the task of realism to represent is produced by a multiplicity of interpretations of a world that we each will into coherence: 'No "objective" style, Joyce is already hinting, can in truth be discovered to exist, no registration of so-many-things-almost-in-an-equal-number-of-words; an attempt to simulate one will itself be a style, a narrator's role' (Kenner 1979: 71).

So thoroughgoing, some critics contend, is Joyce's dissolution of objectivity into the manifold styles of *Ulysses* that it is no longer clear whether 'irony', understood as the interplay between a normative and restricted or partial reading of events, may any longer be judged an adequate term to describe its system of rhetorical effects. This issue is focused most forcibly by Wayne C. Booth who, in a famous discussion of Joyce, suggests that *Portrait* poses almost insuperable problems of ironic distance and narrative perspective. The principal difficulty with which the novel presents us, Booth contends, is that the uncertainty of Joyce's irony and his elision of the point of view of author and protagonist make it impossible absolutely to determine whether Stephen's actions and beliefs are being endorsed or satirised at any particular juncture. How, Booth asks, are we to reconcile the novel's 'implicit demand that we maintain our capacity for ironic judgement' with the 'deep plunges' of interior monologue and stream-of-consciousness that immerse us as readers in its flow of thought and sensation (Booth 1961: 324)? Because Joyce ties our perspective so tightly to the consciousness of an 'ambiguously misguided protagonist', Booth continues, we can no longer discern an absolute, or even qualified but still perceptible, distance between truth and misconception, with ruinous consequences for our understanding of the relationship between irony and sincerity. These problems of perspective become potentially incalculable when we consider Joyce's dependence upon epiphany – a device that requires 'complete identification' with the character who experiences it – for many of the novel's emotional and tonal effects. Indeed, Joyce's decision to place at the heart of the novel 'a figure who experiences epiphanies, an epiphany-producing device' who is 'himself used by the real author as an object ambiguously distant from the norms of the work' renders the novel's complications of distance incapable of resolution (Booth 1961: 332).

The problem of narrative distance and point of view in *Portrait* is evident, Booth suggests, in the episode recounting Stephen's rejection of the priesthood:

> Is his rejection of the priesthood a triumph, a tragedy, or merely a comedy of errors? Most readers, even those who follow the new trend of reading Stephen ironically, seem to have read it as a triumph: the artist has rid himself of the chains that bound him. . . . Well, which *Portrait* do we choose, that of the artistic soul battling through successfully to his necessary freedom, or that of the child of God, choosing, like Lucifer, his own damnation? No two books could be further from each other than the two we envision here. There may be a sufficient core of what is simply interesting to salvage the book as a great work of the sensibility, but unless we are willing to retreat into babbling and incommunicable relativism, we cannot believe that it is *both* a portrait of the prisoner freed and a portrait of the soul placing itself in chains. (Booth 1961: 327–8)

The fact that many critics have felt able to assent to precisely the proposition Booth's final sentence dismisses might lead us to treat his claims with a degree of caution. Joyce's technique, in this scene as elsewhere, is to invest a perception with the authenticating force of subjective emotion while gradually exposing its uncertain relation to the inner reality of a situation. In his rejection of his vocation, Stephen feels himself to have renounced a lower world of spiritual and moral servitude for a higher world of art, and Joyce imbues Stephen's narrative with the degree of passionate sincerity commensurate to this conviction; but the nature of this imaginative liberation must also be judged against Cranly's acidulous observation that in making a new religion out of art Stephen is merely reproducing at another level his submission to externally imposed values. The third position in this contest of counterposed forces is supplied by the reader, who must consider Stephen's revaluation of art in the wake of Cranly's sense of its contradictions before deciding how questions of character and motivation should be interpreted. If we attend to the broader pattern of judgements within which Stephen's self-perception is either challenged by an exterior viewpoint or repeated in a context that casts doubt upon its original integrity, some sense of the aesthetic distance Booth claims to have been lost by Joyce's epiphanic method is restored to the novel. That Stephen is *not* to be viewed with what Booth calls 'the same deadly seriousness with which he views himself' is clear from a number of instances (Booth 1961: 327). As Hugh Kenner has argued, Stephen's austere credo of aesthetic impersonality comes incongruously from a poet whose lyrics reflect a supreme consciousness of his own 'perishing joy' (Kenner 1987: 98). Far from signalling a 'retreat into babbling and incommunicable relativism', the novel's delicate structure of revaluations and repetitions ask us to hold the thought of Stephen's 'liberation' *and* his prospective unfreedom in imaginative synthesis. This juxtaposition of apparently irreconcilable perspectives without an established hierarchy of significance may have ruinous implications for Booth's approach to the novel, but it extends to the reader possibilities of imaginative and ethical discrimination previously denied by author-based readings. It was this new style of reading, which substituted an account of the various interpretative and subject positions opened up by texts for the traditional concern with authorial values and point of view, that was developed by post-structuralist criticism of Joyce in the following decades.

Whilst the debates about the style and epic ambition of *Ulysses* continued to rage, the three of four decades after Joyce's death also saw the first concerted efforts to come to terms with the vast challenge of *Finnegans Wake*. The opening salvo in what was to be an extended critical engagement was fired by Joseph Campbell and Henry Morton Robinson in their *A Skeleton Key to Finnegans Wake* (first publ. 1944). Seeking to overturn the already prevalent view that the *Wake* merely constituted 'a perverse triumph of the unintelligible', Campbell and Robinson argued instead that the novel might prove to be 'the keystone of the creative arch that Joyce had been constructing carefully ever since his youth' (Campbell and Robinson 1947: 7). In an attempt to substantiate this claim, they compiled the first page-by-page guide to the *Wake* which condensed, simplified and paraphrased the novel's heavily freighted text. The *Key*'s economical and lucid introduction to the *Wake*'s narrative form, symbolic structure and its compressions and condensations of meaning provided the first systematic overview of the novel and became an essential point of departure for subsequent critical studies. The valuable critical service performed by Campbell and Robinson was, however, compromised to a degree by the portentous and overblown claims that they made for the novel in the *Key*'s introductory remarks:

> If the present book does nothing else, it should make henceforth impossible the early rejection of Joyce's work as remote from the interests and problems of the modern world. The *Wake*, at its lowest estimate, is a huge time-capsule, a complete and permanent record, of our age. If our society should go smash tomorrow (which, as Joyce implies, it may) one could find all the pieces, together with the forces that broke them, in *Finnegans Wake*. (Campbell and Robinson 1947: 8)

It is uncertain if any novel could live up to hyperbole like this or how seductive the image of the *Wake* as a 'terminal moraine' full of 'theological bric-a-brac' might prove to the uncommitted reader. These caveats notwithstanding, the *Key*'s insistence that the *Wake*'s myriad difficulties began to resolve themselves 'as soon as the well-disposed reader picks up a few compass clues and gets his bearings' offered an important challenge to the novel's reputation as an unreadable avant-garde curiosity (Campbell and Robinson 1947: 13).

Help for the reader of a much more specialised kind was also forthcoming in the form of Adaline Glasheen's *A Census of Finnegans Wake* (1956). Glasheen's *Census* undertook the preliminary, but exhausting, labour of naming and identifying the vast constellation of characters who populate the *Wake*'s pages. Drawing upon a distinction between 'proper tropes' or 'an allusion that illuminates thought, mood and act' and 'the names of the archetypes and historical characters that serve as *leitmotivs*', she compiled an elaborate system of cross-references that brings as close to the surface as is practicable Joyce's subterranean network of themes, references and symbols (Glasheen 1956: xiv). Attentive throughout to the *Wake*'s comic cacophony of voices, Glasheen's 'Preface' argued that Joyce's playful art should also be understood as a defiantly revisionist history:

> Joyce, of course, meant to be confusing. He is out to get history by patiently demonstrating the chaos of the past and our pitiful inability to know anything about it at all. Three whole sections of *Finnegans Wake* (Book 1, ii, iii, iv) go to prove that Carlyle was right when he called 'Foolish History' the synopsis of rumour; and then Joyce goes on to demonstrate that rumor is as valid a source of information as contemporary records, scholarly learning, literature, art, mathematics, psychoanalysis, or table turning. Misunderstanding, malice, sympathy, space, time, wit, learning, art, language, shifts in sensibility – all combine to distort the past out of recognition. (Glasheen 1956: x)

Two other features of the *Census* develop the critical apparatus with which the *Wake* was to be read. Glasheen's brief 'Synopsis' of the novel's plot clarifies essential details of narrative development without implying, like Campbell and Robinson, that the *Wake* was the dreaming expression of what Harry Levin called 'the sodden brain of a snoring publican' (Levin 1944: 124). Meanwhile her graphic table of 'Who Is Who When Everybody Is Somebody Else' charts the mutations of time, place and symbol that are played out in the novel's complex naming strategies.

A great advance in our understanding of the literary, scriptural and mythological contexts of *Finnegans Wake* was made by James S. Atherton's *The Books at the Wake* (1959). In an effort to place interpretation of the *Wake* on a more solid footing, Atherton suggested that the meaning of the novel should first be sought in the details of Joyce's life and reading. The difficulties *Finnegans Wake* presents are, he argued, threefold: Joyce writes simultaneously upon several narrative planes; he draws extensively upon private autobiographical experience; and he imbues the novel with his antiquarian knowledge of a vast number of other books. Setting himself the enormous task of tracing the *Wake*'s literary sources and allusions, Atherton explores first the 'Structural Books' (works such as Vico's *New Science*) which help confer a narrative and conceptual logic upon the novel; he then elucidates a compendium of particular texts, including works by Homer, Dante, Swift, Pascal and a succession of Irish writers and historians, that Joyce makes use of within individual sections of the novel; and, lastly, he examines a number of 'Sacred Books', such as the Old and New Testaments and *The Book of the Dead*, that inform the *Wake*'s scriptural and mythological framework. Never before had the intricate intertextuality of the novel been so systematically discussed; Atherton's pioneering work helped redefine the terms on which the literary evaluation of the *Wake* might henceforth proceed. Unfortunately the necessarily eclectic and piecemeal character of Atherton's study led him occasionally to privilege the discrete narrative fragment over the broader narrative structure that lent it its meaning and significance. Echoing Stanislaus Joyce's dismissive assessment of the *Wake* as a crossword puzzler's bible, Atherton's claim that the novel is 'intended as something between a bible and a crossword puzzle' to which 'the keys are provided' had the baleful effect of transforming it into a cryptogram to be decoded rather than read, thereby deflecting attention from the very literary qualities he had worked so hard to elaborate (Atherton 1959: 20).

Two critical works published in the early 1960s developed *Wake* studies in different, but complementary, directions. In 1962 Clive Hart's *A Concordance to Finnegans Wake* appeared which traced the symbolic and thematic development of the verbal motifs from which Joyce composed the novel. Deliberately restricting himself to the 50 per cent of the

novel constructed from English language materials, Hart presented a
primary index and concordance of almost every word that forms the
Wake's vocabulary, an alphabetically arranged list of the 'syllabifications'
or the inner parts of compound and portmanteau-words, and a collection of 'overtones' or words indicated by, but not orthographically
present within, Joyce's compound linguistic formations. A number of
studies in the following twenty years would be indebted to Hart's lexical,
morphological and semantic research. Charting a course backward from
the finished text to the embryonic material from which it developed,
David Hayman returned to the 9,000 pages of typescript, holograph and
revised proof presented by Harriet Weaver to the British Museum in
order to discover 'a guide to the runes of the creative process' implicit in
Joyce's compositional method (Hayman 1963: 4). In Hayman's hands
this voluminous manuscript material yields a rich harvest; in the history
of Joyce's textual revisions, he argues, the *Wake*'s basic plan, germinal
ideas and primary symbolic patterns are revealed with unrivalled clarity.
Unquestionably the most important insight Hayman provides into
Joyce's compositional techniques is that he progressed always from the
denotation of image and motif to the complication of its textual components. Returning to an earlier version, Joyce would often double or triple
the length of a narrative section, refocusing its elements, broadening its
original context, simultaneously heightening and diffusing the range of
its symbolic resonance (Hart 1962b: 9).

William York Tindall's *A Reader's Guide to Finnegans Wake* (1969)
reconstituted many of the lexical, archetypal and symbolic elements identified by Atherton and Hart into a detailed page-by-page narrative paraphrase of the novel. By far the most accessible of the various guides to
the *Wake*, Tindall's book astutely foregrounds the narrative frame Joyce
reconfigured from Vico and Bruno and the 'dialectical process within a
closed system of moving and changing parts, each of which interpene-
trates its opposites' that structures the novel's pattern of discordant and
opposed energies (Tindall 1969: 11). Alive to Joyce's sophisticated narrative arrangement of dream materials for 'feelings aslip', Tindall also
highlights the often parodic use Joyce makes of the representational
strategies of the dream-work. Taken together with Joyce's reworking of
the montage principle of early cinema, the narrative principles of condensation, displacement and substitution lend the *Wake* the decentred
structure 'of parts placed side by side without transition, parts in a
variety of rhythms, shapes, and tones' characteristic of a modernist long
poem like *The Waste Land* (Tindall 1969: 17–18). Unwilling to follow
Edmund Wilson in attributing the novel's multiplying narratives to the

dreaming mind of Earwicker alone, Tindall's solution is to reconceive *Finnegans Wake* as the expression of the collective cultural unconscious of humanity in general:

> Problem: if the *Wake* is a dream, who is the dreamer? Our first guess is H.C.E., but are Sanskrit and Finnish within his linguistic capacity; does his learning include Vico, Stephen's nightmare of history, and the *Annals of the Four Masters*? But if Earwicker, more than a simple publican of Dublin, is everybody everywhere at all times, he could be the great 'Sommboddy' we are after. The *Wake*, then, would be the dream of Everyman or, since Joyce saw himself in this capacity, of James Joyce, a collective consciousness drawing upon the collective unconscious. (Tindall 1969: 19)

'For some time,' Clive Hart observes in the introduction to his *Concordance*, 'there have been suggestions about the possible appearance one day of a much more ambitious work – a complete dictionary of *Finnegans Wake*' (Hart 1962b: i). Whilst the notion of a 'complete' account of any aspect of the novel is doubtless an impossible dream, two studies by Roland McHugh significantly advanced our understanding of its lexical and contextual possibilities. Noting that 'much published exegesis' of the *Wake* exhibits 'a depressing indifference to context and continuity', McHugh argues that the cohesion of the novel's different parts will be appreciated 'only when the reader has formulated canons for distinguishing them' (McHugh 1976: 2). By focusing upon Joyce's 'sigla' or the manuscript markings he used to denote 'certain characters and conceptual patterns underlying the book's fabric', McHugh sets out to demonstrate the *Wake*'s implicit unity of theme, symbol and idea, and to 'establish a series of pathways between the chapters which should facilitate their penetration' (McHugh 1976: 3). One virtue of this approach is that McHugh's emphasis upon Joyce's configuration of textual abbreviations and markings redirects critical attention to the structural and contextual, rather than 'human', elements of the story; the 'personages' and 'characters' denoted by Joyce's sigla, McHugh suggests, should be read as 'fluid composites, involving an unconfined blur of historical, mythical and fictitious characters, as well as non-human elements' (McHugh 1976: 10). Four years later, McHugh developed the insights of his earlier work into his magisterial and indispensable *Annotations to Finnegans Wake*. Drawing widely upon the entire received history of *Wake* research, McHugh's *Annotations* provided a page-by-page gloss to individual words, isolated phrases, allusions and historical personages; its publication refined knowledge of Joyce's linguistic complexities to a new standard and brought the primary phase of *Wake* studies to a form of completion.

Post-Structuralist Joyce

A profound relationship between Joyce's modernism and post-structuralism criticism has existed almost since the inception of Jacques Derrida's deconstructive intervention in the late 1960s. Certainly a continuing attention to Joyce's writing has been one of the axes around which post-structuralist literary thought has organised itself over the last forty years. In his early work Derrida used Joyce to challenge what he saw as the constitutive principle of Western metaphysics: the centrality of the thinking subject capable of unifying all difference within a single voice. In contrast to the drive towards univocity expressed by this metaphysics, Joyce's writing, Derrida argued, was characterised by a radical equivocity: the proliferation of subject and speaking positions that cannot be totalised by any singular voice or consciousness. This emphasis upon the equivocity of our very semantic origin inflected post-structuralism criticism in general within which Joyce was often hailed as one of the few writers to resist the metaphysical drive to presence that characterised key stages of Western thought. In his *Introduction to Edmund Husserl's Origin of Geometry*, Derrida argues that Husserl's phenomenology realises the desire of metaphysics for the single origin (in consciousness) of diverse systems. Joyce's work, by contrast, presents incommensurable voices unified, if at all, by only the provisional rhetorical structures of the modernist book. The intellectual congruity between Joyce's modernism and post-structuralism is underscored by Attridge and Ferrer (1984). Explaining that their collection is intended both for those with an interest in Joyce and those with an interest in literary theory, they maintain that the combination of these two concerns is not something fabricated for their book:

> but is a matter of history, a history which the essays themselves exemplify: between the late 1960s and the early 1980s Joyce's writing was a stimulus, a focus, and a proving-ground for new modes of theoretical and critical activity in France, whose widespread impact has been one of the most striking features of the intellectual climate of recent years. (Attridge and Ferrer 1984: ix)

Although what they call the 'affinity between Joyce and the theory of the Text and the Subject being elaborated in Paris' continues to be of signal importance, the point, Attridge and Ferrer caution, is not to read Joyce's work as an illustration of a particular theory or orthodoxy; the writing practice of both Joyce and his post-structuralist readers suggests, in fact, the opposite: that there is no 'metalanguage' within which a theory can read a text without *itself* being read in turn by the text under discussion:

> This is particularly true of Joyce: any reader cannot but feel that the text constantly overreaches the landmarks established by the best critical constructions. It is impossible to exert any mastery over it, its *shifts* are such that you can never pin it down in any definite place – it always turns up again, laughing, behind your back. (Attridge and Ferrer 1984: 10)

The problem of interpretative 'mastery' and the mechanisms of a text's 'infinite productivity' are at the heart of Derrida's essay upon *Finnegans Wake*, 'Two Words for Joyce'. Here Derrida confronts once again the importance of Joyce to his own philosophy: '[E]very time I write, and even in the most academic pieces of work, Joyce's ghost is always coming on board' (Derrida 1984: 149). And yet the *event* of Joyce's writing – an event that far exceeds the local determination of meaning by motifs like plot, character or the fragile unity of the 'book' itself – is of such power and scope that one is 'not only overcome by him, whether you know it or not, but obliged by him, and constrained to measure yourself against this overcoming' (Derrida 1984: 147). This profound sense of ambivalence is, Derrida muses, perhaps the inevitable entailment of encountering a corpus like this, which, continually impressing upon us a sense of our inevitable failure to master its complexity, reminds us that every reading of Joyce is a reading still about to begin:

> With this admiring resentment, you stay on the edge of reading Joyce – for me this has been going on for twenty-five or thirty years – and the endless plunge throws you back onto the river-bank, on the brink of another possible immersion, *ad infinitum*. Is this true to the same extent of all works? In any case, I have the feeling that I haven't yet begun to read Joyce, and this 'not having begun to read' is sometimes the most singular and active relationship I have with this work. (Derrida 1984: 148)

One reason for Derrida's attitude of 'admiring resentment' is that every critical commentary upon *Finnegans Wake*, including his own, seems already outflanked by a text that appears to encompass and reinvent the history of Western culture in its generalised textual equivocity:

> *Finnegans Wake* is a little, a little what?, a little son, a little grandson of Western culture in its circular, encyclopedic, Ulyssean and more than Ulyssean totality. And then it is, simultaneously, much bigger than even this odyssey, it comprehends it and this prevents it, dragging it outside itself in an entirely singular adventure, from closing in on itself and on this event. The future is reserved in it. (Derrida 1984: 149)

Derrida is not just arguing that Joyce's work is difficult or open to *several* readings; his point is that in using the very vehicle of meaning – the literary signifier or inscribed word – Joyce's text exposes the limit of meaning. On the one hand, words are *words* or signifiers only if they intend or refer beyond themselves to sense (this is the necessary condition of meaning). On the other hand, there can be no final *arrival* at this meaning, and this impossibility is celebrated in a Joycean text that ceaselessly *multiplies* the opening of signification. For what does a work like *Finnegans Wake* suggest, with its 'babelizing' narrative logic and its ceaseless working and unworking of the logic of sense, but the necessary impossibility of an ultimate reading or a univocal narrative (Derrida 1984: 145)?

Derrida's playful subversion of the 'great anterior text' of *Finnegans Wake* – a subversion that is also in its style and method an act of the utmost fidelity – focuses upon Joyce's use of the two words 'He War' (Joyce 1975: 258). How many words, he asks, can Joyce lodge in just these two words by dint of his continuous 'babelizing' of language:

> I spell them out: HE WAR and sketch a first translation: HE WARS – he wages war, he declares or makes war, he is war, which can also be pronounced by babelizing a bit (it is in a particularly Babelian scene of the book that these words rise up), by Germanising them, then, in Anglo-Saxon, He war: he was – he who was ('I am he who is or who am',' says YAHWE). Where it was, he was, declaring war, and it is *true*. Pushing things a bit, taking the time to draw on the vowel and to lend an ear, it will have been true, *wahr* ['true' in German], that's what can be kept [*garder*] or looked at [*regarder*] in truth. (Derrida 1984: 145)

Because the 'truth of Babel' that Joyce inscribes at the core of *Finnegans Wake* links writing, truth (*wahr*), identity ('I am'), vision (the play between 'I' and 'eye'), authorship and God ('Yahweh'), no 'first translation' is able to totalise the range of supplementary significations generated by Joyce's prose. By repeating and mobilising the play of equivocity across the intelligible threshold of language, Joyce releases 'the greatest power of the meanings buried in each syllabic fragment, subjecting each atom of writing to fission in order to overload the unconscious with the whole memory of man: mythologies, religion, philosophies, sciences, psychoanalysis, literatures' (Derrida 1984: 149). Derrida emphasises the general equivocity of Joyce's style by highlighting the undecideable play it institutes between ear and eye or spoken and written text. Reproducing an extended section from the novel, he inspects the neologism 'phonemanon' because it typifies 'the whole Babelian adventure of the book, or rather its Babelian underside' (Derrida 1984: 153). Listening to the passage Derrida quotes, we hear 'phenomenon', signifier of the event, chance or happenstance; *reading* the passage, we see 'phoneme', the mark of writing that inaugurates and divides sense from itself, and also, we might add, 'phoneme – anon', the economy of spacing and deferral that precedes and exceeds the self-presence of identity and meaning. This play *between* speech and writing in *Finnegans Wake*, Derrida argues, passes *through* writing itself, opening each word up to the 'multiplicity of languages in it', deconstructing, as it does so, the 'hegemony of a single language' (Derrida 1984: 156).

Stephen Heath's reading of *Finnegans Wake* precedes Derrida's mature account by a decade, but it is marked throughout by an engagement with deconstructive thought. Beginning from the premise that the very act of reading Joyce continues to present a considerable problem for criticism, Heath argues that *Finnegans Wake* has created two rigorously complementary poles of critical reaction:

> [T]he first, faced with the specific practice of writing in Joyce's text and thus with the impossibility of converting that text into a critical object, rejects it as 'aberration'; the second, seeking to preserve Joyce's text for criticism, finds itself obliged to that end to 'reduce' its writing to the simple carrier of a message (a meaning) that it will be the critic's task to 'extract from its enigmatic envelope'. (Heath 1984: 31)

The problem with the first approach is that it compounds the novel's reputation as 'aberrant' and unreadable; the problem with the second is that it imposes ideas of continuity and unity upon a mode of writing that opens out 'onto a multiplicity of fragments of sense, of possibilities, which are traced and retraced, colliding and breaking ceaselessly in the play of this text that resists any homogenisation' (Heath 1984: 31–2). One reason *Finnegans Wake* resists homogenisation is that it is a profoundly 'ambiviolent' text: both its dissolution of stylistic unity into a 'network of specific practices' and its discontinuous and ambivalent narrative structure do violence to a model of criticism based upon 'continuity and identity' where meaning is conceived as 'the construction of the Author-source' (Heath 1984: 33). Where traditional criticism of Joyce '*ex*plicates, opening out the folds of the writing in order to arrive at the meaning', *Finnegans Wake* should be read instead as a 'permanent *inter*plication, a work of folding and unfolding in which every element becomes always the fold of another in a series that knows no point of rest' (Heath 1984: 32). Each part of *Finnegans Wake* reads, reconfigures and complicates what had preceded it, simultaneously extending and suspending its chain of reference, within a potentially inexhaustible series of textual relays where no one narrative level can exhaust or account for any of the others. Insofar as the novel may be said to 'develop', it develops according to this continual 'hesitation of sense' with the 'final revelation of meaning' being 'always for "later"' (Heath 1984: 31).

One of the first book-length, and certainly one of the most controversial, post-structuralist readings of Joyce was advanced by Colin MacCabe (1978). Concerned with both an analysis of Joyce and a reassessment of the entire practice of literary criticism, MacCabe set himself the task of establishing a new understanding of 'both the politics of reading and the reading of politics' (MacCabe 1978: 1). Central to his thesis is the proposition that Joyce's writing transforms the relations between reader and text in ways that have profound revolutionary implications. MacCabe claims that Joyce's work is concerned pre-eminently with 'the material effects of language and with the possibilities of transformation' (MacCabe 1978: 2). Sketching throughout his discussion a homology between the circulation of discourses within a literary text and the configuration of social and political discourses constitutive of the world within which that text functions, MacCabe contends that Joyce's stylistic radicalism forces us to rethink the relations between these discourses in ways that transform both them and ourselves. This transformation, which no longer guarantees the assumed distinction between the pre-textual subjectivity of the literary critic and the discourses of literary fiction, has considerable implications for the possibility and practice of literary studies:

> This metamorphosis and displacement presents literary criticism with its own impossibility. Interpretation as the search for meaning must cease when both meaning and interpreter become functions of the traverse of the material of language. In its place we might begin the study of the positions offered to the subject within language and of how literature confirms and subverts those possibilities. (MacCabe 1978: 2)

The challenge MacCabe poses to Joyce studies and literary studies more generally is indicated by his critique of what he calls the classic realist text. In order to carry out its task of interpretation, he argues, 'literary criticism must be able to identify what is represented, independently of the form of the representation'. Such identification is only possible:

> if the discourse of the critic is in a position to transform the text into content, and, to undertake this transformation, the relation between the language of the text and the language of the critic must be that which obtains between an object – and a meta-language. A meta-language 'talks

about' an object-language and transforms it into content by naming the object-language (accomplished through the use of inverted commas) and thus being able to identify both the object-language and its area of application. It is from the position of the meta-language that correspondence between word and world can be established. (MacCabe 1978: 13)

The hierarchical relation outlined here between the various 'object-languages' of a text and an encompassing 'meta-language' that orders them into sense by imposing a set of universal norms, values and truths that interpret and explain them for the reader defines for MacCabe the structural principle of classic literary fiction. It is precisely this relationship between meta- and object-language, in which the former presents itself as a 'window on reality' while viewing every object-language as material for reinterpretation, that Joyce's writing places into jeopardy:

> A text is made of many languages, or discourses, and the critic's ability to homogenise these articulations is related to their prior organisation within the text. Joyce's texts refuse the very category of meta-language and a critical discourse is thus unable to obtain any purchase on the text. None of the discourses which circulate in *Finnegans Wake* or *Ulysses* can master or make sense of the others and there is, therefore, no possibility of the critic articulating his or her reading as an elaboration of a dominant position within the text. (MacCabe 1978: 13–14)

By constantly threatening the dissolution of every interpretative position into the play of language, Joyce's writing compels us self-consciously to rely upon our own critical discourses to order his novels into coherence and, in so doing, to become aware of the stereotypes, presuppositions and desires that these interpretative discourses embody. His work is able to generate this extreme critical self-consciousness because it progressively abolishes the distance between the language of the text and the language of the reader upon which the very possibility of an omniscient and impersonal meta-language depends. Crucial to this journey is the *signifier*, the material token (written or aural word) through which we supposedly arrive at meaning, the concept or the signified. For MacCabe, Joyce's revolution overturns the traditional hierarchy of the signified, which subordinates the signifier to mere vehicle or medium interpreted by a superior critical discourse. MacCabe's account retraces the steps Joyce took to abolish this critical distance: his radical development in *Dubliners* and *Portrait* of a free indirect style which resists the reduction of the text's multiplicity of discourses to a common discourse shared by writer and reader; his adumbration in *Ulysses* of a montage-principle or radical separation of the novel's discursive elements in order to liberate the signifier from the signified so that unconscious and repressed desires may enter the domain of utterance; and the relentless exhibition of the polyvalent possibilities of the signifying chain in *Finnegans Wake* that exposes us to the material fact of sexual difference along with the 'constitutive processes that render us sexed and civil subjects' (MacCabe 1978: 133).

Maud Ellmann (1981) also developed another influential, if rather more inscrutable, post-structuralist critique of Joyce. Drawing like MacCabe upon Freudian and Lacanian psychoanalytic theory, her analysis of *Portrait* sets itself defiantly at odds with those traditional critics – such as Lewis and Kenner – who discussed the novel in terms of the relationship of sympathy or disaffection between author and protagonist. Where these critics scrutinised the ways in which Joyce's fiction rendered an already constituted world or subjectivity, Ellmann explores how different subject positions are continually opened up and reconfigured – or, to use her rather more arcane vocabulary, 'membered' and 'disremembered' – by the material flows of language, desire and corporeality. In common with much post-structuralist criticism, Ellmann eschews a comprehensive account of the text under discussion, seeking instead to identify 'the circulation of textual and sexual economies' by which identity constitutes and reconstitutes itself (Ellmann 1981: 192). Her essay pursues 'the notion of identity as process' by attending to those moments where the illusion of autonomous and self-identical subjectivity is rent and torn asunder. This cleavage of the subject is revealed by the tissue of 'scars' that punctuate the narrative surface of the novel, those 'blank spots' and 'temporary pauses' in which meaning is suddenly evacuated from the text, confronting us instead with the chain of significations that bring both subjectivity and representation into being.

Joyce and Feminism

One of the most striking feminist approaches to Joyce was taken by the French psychoanalyst Julia Kristeva. According to Kristeva there is a psychic position *between* the coherent, meaningful and systemic position of language (the symbolic) and the undifferentiated, unconscious position of infant plenitude (the pre-Oedipal moment when the child is *not yet* fully separated from the mother). Kristeva terms this position the 'semiotic' and accords it two features: it is a bodily, mobile and fluid process of differentiation (such as the sounds of gurgling or cries made by an infant); and, in its difference from the fully formed social system of language, the semiotic is disruptive of paternal law (for the father, in being other than material plenitude, is the image of law and culture). She argues further that modernist literature, in its disruption of stable positions of meaning and judgement and its revolutionary deployment of sound, rhythm, and the materiality of language, embodies a semiotic force capable of bringing the paternal law of culture into crisis (Kristeva 1981). Because women within Western culture are not accorded the position of lawful speaking subject, Kristeva suggests that it is male authors such as Joyce who have the power to revolutionise language by a destruction of meaningful system which is, nevertheless, not a fall into precultural chaos. 'Poetic language', such as Molly's monologue at the end of *Ulysses*, with its refusal of meaningful punctuation, judgement, logic and sequence, in fact recalls the sounds and rhythms of the semiotic position. In so doing, it abrogates the subject's blithe separation of itself from maternal indifference. All poetic language, in Kristeva's view, is therefore revolutionary *and* incestuous, with Joyce's modernism exemplifying a mode of writing that is *neither* the lawful position of the father nor the Oedipal chaos associated with the mother.

In her study of feminist responses to Joyce, Karen Lawrence notes the uneasy and frequently rebarbative relationship between Joyce and feminism:

> Joyce and feminism – a difficult conjunction, a seemingly forced connection between a man who is quoted as saying, 'I hate women who know anything' and a movement that applauds women's intellect and rights. Perhaps the 'and' conjoins opposites, such as black and white. (Lawrence 1990: 237)

Such would be the view, Lawrence concedes, of critics who regard 'Woman' in Joyce as 'confined to her body, excluded from the productions of culture'. It is certainly a view shared by Gilbert and Gubar, who see Molly's entire character as 'a choice of matter over mind' (Gilbert and Gubar 1985: 518). Significantly, the perceived antagonism between Joyce's work and feminism is anticipated by Joyce's work itself: both *Ulysses* and *Finnegans Wake*, Lawrence reminds us, 'contain numerous examples of women accusing men of misleading and misrepresenting them' (Lawrence 1990: 237). These examples include Martha Clifford's reproach of Bloom in 'Circe' and Molly's denunciation of her husband's meddling in female affairs throughout her monologue. Moreover, as Bonnie Scott points out, Anna Livia laments the circumscription of her own and Molly Bloom's identity by an authoritarian male pen (Scott 1987: 127). Lawrence acknowledges that the complaint of feminist readers that women in Joyce are condemned to a 'merely material existence' is frequently supported by textual evidence and reinforced by the sometimes essentialist judgements of critics like Tindall, Ellmann and Kenner (Lawrence 1990: 239). This charge receives additional support from elements of Joyce's biography, especially his dream of Molly Bloom 'reproaching him for his prurient interest in women's business' and for his 'presumptuous attempt to lend voice to female desire' (Lawrence 1990: 238). But what this particular feminist reading ignores, Lawrence maintains, is the way in which 'Joyce's texts partly deconstruct the symbolic encoded forms of their own representations and expose the workings of male desire' (Lawrence 1990: 239). Observing that Joyce's work 'implicitly acknowledges' that a male writer's representation of female experience 'is never objective, but rather involves a combination of *hubris*, assault, fascination, even envy', Lawrence argues that Joyce's ambivalent relationship to the female 'other' enables him simultaneously to depict and unmask male anxieties about female power. Indeed, the profound sense in Joyce's later works that 'woman in writing' is always 'beyond his control' is one effect of Joyce's deconstruction of monolithic cultural constructions of 'man' and 'woman' (Lawrence 1990: 240–1).

In a finely nuanced review of aspects of Joyce's gender politics in *Portrait*, Suzette Henke notes that females are 'present everywhere and nowhere' in the novel; they 'pervade' it, 'yet remain elusive' (Henke 1982: 82). Because these women are 'portrayed almost exclusively from Stephen's point of view', she explains, they often appear as 'one-dimensional projections' of his 'narcissistic imagination', only subsequently to emerge as the 'psychological "other"', forceful antagonists in the novel's dialectical structure'. Ultimately, Henke declares, women appear in the novel as 'emblems of the flesh – frightening reminders of sex, generation and death'. Her analysis of the novel seeks initially to establish the basis of what she sees as Stephen's misogyny in the binary structures of infantile experience. In the child's perception of gender difference, she points out, 'the mother seems to be in touch with the overwhelming chaos of nature. The father, in contrast, offers a model of logocentric control' in which actions are governed by reason and emotional distance (Henke 1982: 82). Tracing Stephen's subsequent psychological and emotional development, Henke describes his gradual rejection of female 'nature' and his acceptance of 'an ethic of male stoicism' in order to adjust himself to the 'code of masculine loyalty' (Henke 1982: 84). This course demands that he 'cast off his allegiance to maternal figures'; in the ensuing battle between the male and female principles 'Mother Church emerges as a bastion of sexual repression defended by hysterical women' (Henke 1982: 85–6). Stephen's fundamental fear of what he perceives as emotional entrapment by women leads him to reconfigure a number of misogynist stereotypes: the virgin and the whore, 'the Catholic Virgin' and the 'bird-girl' or 'aesthetic muse'. He either idealises or fears women; but his idealisation of the feminine is really a means to express an aspect of his own personality: 'In his return to ritualistic devotion, Stephen has actually become involved in an aesthetic love affair with his own soul. The anima, the feminine aspect of his own psyche, has won his passion and holds him enthralled' (Henke 1982: 93). However, the crucial factor in Joyce's representation of gender, Henke reminds us, lies in the *distinction* between his authorial perspective and Stephen's misogynistic attitudes. The 'pervasive irony' that tinges Stephen's reflections suggests that his misogyny is an 'example of his youthful priggishness', one of the 'adolescent traits he has to outgrow on his path to artistic maturity'. 'Not until *Ulysses*,' Henke concludes, 'will a new model begin to emerge – one that recognizes the need for the intellectual artist to "make his peace" with woman and to incorporate into his work the vital, semiotic flow of female life' (Henke 1982: 102).

Elaine Unkeless takes a more critical view of Joyce's gender politics in her discussion of his representation of Molly as a 'conventional' and stereotypical housewife. She begins from the premise that although 'many readers' have found Molly an 'elusive and multifaceted character', the 'traits' with which Joyce endows her 'stem from conventional notions of the way a woman thinks and acts' (Unkeless 1982: 150). Joyce's characterisation of Molly returns obsessively to her corporeal and sexual nature: 'Most of Molly's actions are associated directly and indirectly with sex, and non-sexual activities are scarcely mentioned.' Joyce, she continues, does not encourage his reader to observe the Molly who 'runs a household'; instead he describes Molly as 'a middle-class housewife who would like to be a queen' (Unkeless 1982: 150). Molly's 'one significant act' on 16 June is to conduct an affair with Boylan; by delineating Molly 'mainly as a sexual being', Joyce 'confines her character to a conventional mold' (Unkeless 1982: 153). Unsurprisingly, given Joyce's stereotypical portrait of Molly, critics like Stanley Sultan and Darcy O'Brien condemn Molly for begrudging 'what "little housework" she has to do' and imply that she is 'not fulfilling her feminine role' (Unkeless 1982: 150). These views are licensed, Unkeless maintains, by Joyce allowing Bloom to supplant Molly as the 'feminine warmth of the hearth' even though she actually 'performs most of the drudgery' (Unkeless 1982: 150–1). But although Unkeless insists that Joyce's thinking about women remains inflected by stereotypical thinking, she also detects an ambivalence in his novelistic position: Joyce's 'derision' of Molly, it must be accepted, 'is not predominantly bitter'; but his 'comedy is based on a

supposition that a woman's method of thinking is irrational and discon-
nected' (Unkeless 1982: 155). Joyce's pejorative vision of Molly
expresses itself in 'Penelope', Unkeless concludes, where, in an episode
'which consists only of thoughts', Molly 'belittles the importance of
words' (Unkeless 1982: 162). Here Molly's 'poor use of language' and
'lack of intellect' gradually reduce her to 'a stereotype of the simple-
minded woman' (Unkeless 1982: 162). 'As Joyce himself says in his
letters,' Unkeless reminds us, 'Molly is limited, and she is so in large part
because she is confined to preconceived ideas of the way a woman thinks
and behaves' (Unkeless 1982: 165).

Unkeless' view of Molly accords in broad measure with Marilyn
French's assessment that 'Molly is the mythic, the archetypal other. Not
only for Bloom but for the rest of Dublin, she is the woman as the object
of desire' (French 1982: 259). Similarly, Kate Millett condemns Joyce for
presenting women as 'nature', as a body of 'unspoiled primeval understanding' and a vision of the 'eternal feminine' (1970: 285). Conversely,
Christine van Boheemen (1989) contends that the *écriture feminine* of
Molly's language challenges, without ultimately overthrowing, patriar-
chal 'logocentrism' and its exclusive emphasis upon the centrality of masculine 'reason'. In a similar spirit, Colin MacCabe claims that Molly's
refusal to 'conform to the wishes of men' renders her 'fatal to a fetishism
predicated on a denial of female desire' (1978: 132). Bonnie Scott's judgement upon Molly brings both of these strains of criticism into a productive synthesis:

> Molly should be seen as more than a principle of fertility, or desire. She is
> desired, but not just as a mother; she is sought out as an alternative to struc-
> tures that have been granted undue sovereignty. Molly's language answers
> Robert Graves' quest for the lost, magical language of myth in *The White
> Goddess* . . . Although Molly is not a common individual woman, a femi-
> nist woman, or a goddess, she serves all three. Although still an overcon-
> centrated, male-projected entity, Joyce's female voice has changed literature
> and aroused criticism . . . 'Penelope' is certainly not the last word on female
> consciousness, nor are its extensions in *Finnegans Wake*. However, both
> works tentatively reorder a male-centered, rational world, and make a
> female 'other' an immediate presence. (Scott 1984: 183)

Psychoanalytic Criticism

Joyce's work has a long and involved relationship with psychoanalytic
criticism. This statement might well have irritated Joyce himself.
Acknowledging that in *Ulysses* he had recorded 'what you Freudians call

the subconscious', he qualified this admission by adding 'but as for psy-choanalysis it's nothing more nor less than blackmail' (Ellmann 1983: 524). Despite Joyce's protestations, early readers were quick to perceive a Freudian subtext to his work. Thus in 1922 Edmund Wilson claimed that *Ulysses* was the 'most faithful x-ray ever taken of the ordinary human consciousness' (Deming 1970a: 228). In the same year P. B. Mais in the *Daily Express* sounded the cautionary note that *Ulysses* displayed 'all our most secret and most unsavoury private thoughts' (Deming 1970a: 191). In this context, as Christopher Butler points out, 'the judge-ment of Holbrook Jackson, that "every action and reaction of his [Bloom's] psychology is laid bare with Freudian nastiness", and of Ford Madox Ford that [*Ulysses*] was "a volume of dream-interpretations by a writer called Freud" might have struck the contemporary literate reader as authoritative' (Butler 1990: 272).

Beginning from the premise that 'it is the mother who is the central figure motivating the small boy towards his earliest investigations into the two great sexual problems' – the 'problems' of 'birth' and 'the dif-ference between the sexes' – Jean Kimball's Freudian reading of *Portrait* concentrates upon the relationship between the infant Stephen and Mrs Dedalus (Kimball 1980: 171). This relationship is gradually revealed to have a latent sexual and Oedipal dimension. When Stephen's mother first appears, Kimball points out, 'she is putting on the oilsheet after Stephen has wet the bed, and Joyce is quite certainly aware of the sexual conno-tations of this typical happening' (Kimball 1980: 170). In Jung's essay on the significance of the father, which Joyce bought in Trieste, he could have read Jung's remark that 'from the Freudian standpoint . . . bedwet-ting must be read as an infantile sexual substitute'; when Stephen's con-sciousness shifts from the 'queer smell' of the oilsheet to the observation that 'his mother had a nicer smell than his father', Kimball continues, Joyce is 'carefully setting up an associational progression that is also sex-ually tinged' (Kimball 1980: 170). Joyce's representation of Stephen's mother 'playing the sailor's hornpipe for him to dance' subtly continues this 'chain of sexual association' because ' "horn" is one of the battery of phallic synonyms which Joyce uses in his notorious pornographic letters written to Nora in 1909'. Kimball argues further that the two threats to blind Stephen in *Portrait* – Dante's claim that the eagles will pull out his eyes and the cracking of his glasses at Clongowes – should be understood as a reworking of aspects of the Oedipus myth:

The link between blindness and punishment is, of course, involved in Stephen's first questioning of the authority of the Church, after his unjust punishment at Clongowes, and the punishment of the pandybat echoes throughout *Ulysses* until, in 'Circe,' it attaches again to Oedipus. For Stephen's reference to breaking his glasses 'sixteen years ago' is juxtaposed to the final terms of a complicated allusion to Oedipus, as Stephen adds to the riddle of the Sphinx, solved by Oedipus, a sexual component of his own: 'The beast that has two backs at midnight' (*U*: 560), through which he links Oedipus to Hamlet and to Stephen. (Kimball 1980: 172)

Sheldon Brivic develops aspects of Kimball's critique in an analysis of Stephen's emerging adolescent sexuality. In his reading of Stephen's curiously over-determined reaction to the rushing of dirty water down the hole of a lavatory basin, Brivic conjectures that Stephen's repetitive use of words like 'suck', 'queer' and 'cock' to represent this experience hints at a latently 'homosexual' aspect of his developing personality (Brivic 1980: 24). He then extends the psychological resonance of this scene by claiming to uncover its Oedipal subtext: Stephen's disgust at the dirty water swirling down the basin hole is provoked by his 'disgust at his mother's genitals, represented quite vividly by the swirling hole'. Brivic claims further that the image Stephen relays of his father pulling at the basin stopper 'may be a screen for the primal scene, the earliest vision of intercourse between parents'. 'Through the dream technique of distortion by reversal,' he continues, 'pulling the plunger may stand for pushing it, but it also represents injury of mother by father.' Stephen's memory tacitly links sex to violence and castration; the scene's broader verbal patterning suggests an implicit sexual ambivalence at the core of Stephen's personality:

> Emphasis on hot and cold suggests ambivalence in Stephen's reaction to the scene. *Ulysses* blows 'hot and cold' to describe Bloom as bisexual. Stephen's washbasin scene is given a dense homosexual atmosphere by the lavatory setting and repetition of the words queer, suck and cock . . . In this bathroom vision of anxious mystery Joyce shows consciousness of Stephen's unconscious. (Brivic 1980: 24)

Joyce's attempt to capture in language the associative logic of Molly Bloom's unconscious has also received a degree of critical attention. Julia Kristeva has contributed one of the most influential psychoanalytic readings of this episode. Kristeva's main contribution to psychoanalysis was her resistance to Jacques Lacan's post-structuralism. Whereas Lacan insisted that we speak as subjects only insofar as we are subjected to the symbolic order, and that what is beyond the symbolic can only be fantasised as absent, Kristeva argued for experiences which are *neither* the coherent, lawful structures of the symbolic *nor* the undifferentiated abyss of the pre-linguistic. She concentrated on marginal and disruptive positions where the subject's borders are abrogated. One of her most influential concepts was that of the abject: those bodily productions which are neither willed, nor personal, but contaminate the division between subject and object. The appearance of abjection, she argues, is directly tied to certain *styles* of language. In her discussion of abjection, Kristeva considers Joyce's *Ulysses* not merely because Joyce writes about abject themes, although he does that as well (Molly's menstruation or Leopold's defecation), but because Joyce's way of writing is bodily or hysterical. Words have a sensuous and physical immediacy for Joyce; his writing immerses the reader in the affective materiality of language, thereby disrupting the judging position of the subject (the 'I think') and returning us to the series of bodily drives from which subjectivity is constituted. In the abject Joycean text, the word as sound and as signifier is *between* the radically pre-linguistic point of indifference and the fully formed subject of judgement. In her reading of the Molly monologue, Kristeva highlights the abject quality of this 'hysterical' mode of writing:

> How dazzling, unending, eternal – and so weak, so insignificant, so sickly – is the rhetoric of Joycean language. Far from preserving us from the abject, Joyce causes it to break out in what he sees as prototype of literary utterance: Molly's monologue. If that monologue spreads out the abject, it is not because there is a woman speaking. But because, *from afar*, the writer approaches the hysterical body so that it might speak, so that he might speak, using it as springboard, of what eludes speech and turns out to be the hand to hand struggle of one woman with another, her mother of course, the absolute because primeval seat of the impossible – of the excluded, the outside-of-meaning, the abject. (Kristeva 1982: 22)

Elsewhere John Bishop offers a subtle and original repositioning of Joyce's work in general – and *Finnegans Wake* in particular – in relation to psychoanalytic theory (1986). Momentarily putting to one side Joyce's famous quip concerning all those 'Jung and easily Freudened', Bishop claims that it is 'impossible' for any reader seriously interested in coming to terms with *Finnegans Wake* to ignore *The Interpretation of Dreams* (Bishop 1986: 16). Freud's work, at one level, 'broke the ground that Joyce would reconstruct; in so doing, he 'arguably made *Finnegans Wake* possible'. Bishop's purpose, however, is to 'offer a Joycean reading of Freud, and not a Freudian reading of Joyce' (Bishop 1986: 18). Joyce, he maintains, may well have been influenced by Freudian insights, but these insights were reworked and revaluated by Joyce's deeper intuition of aesthetic form. Accordingly, it is fruitless to transcribe the syntax and structure of *Finnegans Wake* back into the terms of a Freudian typology because Joyce's dream-work sedulously develops its own internal logic: 'Joyce thought about psychic interiors throughout his literary career and about "nightlife" daily for almost twenty years' (Bishop 1986: 17). Furthermore Bishop contends, in an acute observation suggesting the extent to which psychoanalytic criticism of Joyce will always need to be supplemented by a poetics of history, language and culture, that Joyce's 'real authority' in the study of the unconscious was Vico and not Freud (Bishop 1986: 17–18). Comparing the privilege psychoanalysis accords the irrational and occluded aspects of mental life with Vico's insistence on the centrality of rationality to human existence, Bishop declares:

> Twentieth century psychoanalysis proposes to isolate and cure the irrationally disturbed components of personality by analyzing the fears and fixations inherited from parents in an impressionable, irrational infantile past. Vico's axiomatic observation that rationality is a man-made structure historically evolved out of animal unreason will suggest why Joyce would have regarded Freudian theory as a diminution of Vico's insights. (Bishop 1986: 183–4)

Political Joyce

One of the first systematic attempts to analyse the character and content of Joyce's politics was made by Dominic Manganiello (1980). Beginning from the observation that the 'tenor of innumerable critical statements about Joyce is that he was indifferent to politics', Manganiello ranges across the breadth of Joyce's fiction, lectures and articles to demonstrate the centrality of a particular conception of the political to Joyce's work (Manganiello 1980: 1). This conception of politics had nothing in common with direct intervention into current public debates; Joyce, Manganiello argues, hated didacticism of any kind and maintained a profound distrust of the traditions of Church and state that regulated mainstream Irish political opinion (Manganiello 1980: 2). Joyce's refusal to commit himself to a particular tradition or party should not, however, be interpreted as a sign of indifference to politics; the function of a political art for Joyce was to create a new aesthetic vision of modern culture wherein political divisions could be transcended in the name of ideal political principles. 'For Joyce the great question in literature is not allegiance to any particular party or platform,' Manganiello contends. 'The writer must marshal the feelings and events of the time, political in their implication, into a possible order, and interpret day-to-day issues in the light of the loftier struggles of ideals, and the puncturing of illusions' (Manganiello 1980: 3).

Joyce's 'general awareness of Irish politics' expressed itself in a number of lasting commitments. From an early age he resented the depredations of English imperial policy in Ireland: 'Like his fellow countrymen, Joyce considered this long-sustained English presence in Ireland an occupation' (Manganiello 1980: 8). This conviction emerged forcefully in the lecture 'Ireland, Isle of Saints and Sages' he delivered in Trieste in 1907. 'Ireland is poor,' Joyce maintained, 'because English laws ruined the country's industries' (Manganiello 1980: 14). Rebellion against imperial authority was therefore the moral and political right of a tyrannised country. Yet Joyce was keenly aware that 'Irishmen were also capable of misguided gestures of political extremism' (Manganiello 1980: 8). Indeed, Manganiello claims, the memory of one such act, the Phoenix Park Murders of 1882, 'forced Joyce to take a stand against physical violence and against the physical force tradition in Irish history.' Joyce maintained, moreover, a life-long suspicion of the indigenous tradition of treachery and self-betrayal that had so often brought low Ireland's best hopes of independence. This tradition stretched, according to Joyce's sweeping historical gaze, from Dermot MacMurrough, King of Leinster, who colluded with Henry II in the invasion of Ireland in 1169 to the clerical campaign that brought down Parnell during Joyce's own childhood. 'For Joyce,' Manganiello concludes, 'averting betrayal had become the key political factor in revolutionary Irish history' (Manganiello 1980: 13).

These commitments, when combined with Joyce's profound anticlericalism, underscored the centrality of Parnell to Joyce's politics. 'The Parnell crisis,' Manganiello declares, 'was the pivot from which Joyce viewed the rest of Irish history. The central theme of "betrayal" in his work takes its origin from *the* political event of his youth' (Manganiello 1980: 8). Conflating Joyce's position with the perspective of Stephen Dedalus throughout *Portrait*, Manganiello suggests that Joyce's reading of Irish history led him gradually to assert the limits of political nationalism. Both Stephen's response to the Christmas Day dispute between his father and Dante Riordan and his exchange with his student friend Davin 'clearly indicate that Stephen, like Joyce, interpreted the lesson of Irish history to be that any man attempting to solve the national question risks betrayal' (Manganiello 1980: 16). This perception eventually achieved the status of a fixed position: 'Nationalism, for Joyce, exemplified political delusion in the secular sphere.'

Although Manganiello devotes considerable space to an examination of Joyce's engagement in exile with socialism, anarchism and syndicalism, he contends that Joyce consistently conceived of politics in aesthetic terms. Recalling Joyce's reaction in 1904 to the rejection of his first draft version of *Portrait* by the 'socialist and freethinker' editor of *Dana* Fred Ryan, Manganiello suggests that it was at this point that Joyce began seriously to rethink the very nature of political and intellectual freedom:

> For Joyce, then, the emancipation made possible through literature transcended those notions of freedom embraced by nationalists and socialists. Literature operated as an instrument for altering men's minds. The transformation of institutions does not depend on force, lobbying for peace, or pleading for social justice, but can only follow upon this unsuspected process of changing basic attitudes and prejudices. (Manganiello 1980: 38–9)

This humanist assertion of the ethical transcendence of art inflected each of Joyce's subsequent political positions. These positions were characterised, in Manganiello's view, by Joyce's refusal to commit himself to the tenets of a particular doxa or orthodoxy. Thus Joyce separated himself from the 'purely national movement' of Celtic revivalism by calling himself a 'socialist', but his understanding of socialism was inchoate and ill-formed (Manganiello 1980: 42). He supported the newly-constituted Sinn Féin party and endorsed its policy of parliamentary abstentionism, but later condemned the party for the 'avoidance of the social question' revealed in its critique of Irish affairs (Manganiello 1980: 127). Joyce also recoiled from the Easter 1916 rebellion and the ideal of blood-sacrifice it represented: 'Joyce dismissed the violent sacrifice of self for country, seeing it as a destructive impulse' (Manganiello 1980: 163). The tendency that came to characterise Sinn Féin after 1916 'was the one the Citizen in "Cyclops" represented'; the stake Joyce placed in the party's future diminished accordingly (Manganiello 1980: 170). Eventually Joyce turned his back upon both Sinn Féin politics and the nascent Irish Free State; his final rupture with the latter was precipitated by an incident in which Nora and his children were fired upon by Free State soldiers during a visit home to Galway in 1922 (Manganiello 1980: 166).

Manganiello's humanist image of a Joyce fundamentally opposed to the politics of Irish nationalism has proved controversial with other critics. In a study setting itself the ambitious task of rethinking the relationship between Joycean modernism and the complexities of nationalist politics, Emer Nolan fiercely disputes Manganiello's interpretation of Joyce's vision of art as 'an arena of perfect disinterestedness, individuality and freedom' (Nolan 1995: 46). Observing that such critical constructions of Joycean aesthetics are 'typically organised around the presumed certainty of his unsympathetic representation of Irish separatist nationalism',

Nolan undertakes to analyse Joyce's response to modernity without first presuming a fixed opposition between his version of aesthetic modernism and the discourses of Irish nationalism (Nolan 1995: xi–xii). To read Joyce in these terms, however, means to challenge an entire tradition of Joyce criticism that insistently assimilates his work to both an anti-national and a transnational modernity. Nolan's subaltern reading of Joyce proceeds by pointing out that Ireland underwent an 'abrupt and dis-astrous accession to modernity' (Nolan 1995: xii). This factor merits con-sideration because in circumstances like these modernisation is 'explicitly associated with the culture of the colonial power'. This association made untenable for the colonial Irish a simple choice between the acceptance and rejection of modernity: they wished naturally to accrue the benefits of modernisation, but do so on their own terms. Thus although much metropolitan literary theory – and a good deal of Joyce criticism – con-flates nationalism with a pre- or anti-modern sense of tradition, Nolan suggests that both modernism and nationalism might more precisely be defined in the Irish context by their 'ambivalence towards modernisation, sharing as they do a crucial interest in the issues of cultural change and regeneration, language and popular culture, the realm of the aesthetic and the role of the artist' (Nolan 1995: xii). Far from being implacably opposed to one another, Nolan concludes, Joycean modernism and Irish nationalism can be understood instead as 'significantly analogous dis-courses', and the common perception of them as 'unrelated and antago-nistic' begins to break down (Nolan 1995: xii).

Nolan's critique of Joyce's complicated and complicating relationship with nationalist discourse aims to reintroduce into the reception of Joyce's fiction a sense of both the 'particularity of Irish experience' and the 'full complexity of nationalism in the political culture of modernity' (Nolan 1995: xii–xiii). In a similar spirit, Declan Kiberd's reading of Joyce seeks to establish Joyce's status as a 'post-colonial' writer while subtly reworking the political and aesthetic implications of the term. Kiberd's account begins with the colonial context of Joyce's work:

Joyce's *Ulysses* is often treated as a definitive account of the mind of modern Europe in 1922, the year of its publication: but, for that reason, it is also a recognition that Europe of itself was nothing without its colonial holdings. *Ulysses* is one of the first major literary utterances of the modern period by an artist who spoke for a newly-liberated people. (Kiberd 1996: 327)

Returning like Manganiello to the political essays Joyce wrote in the first decade of the last century, Kiberd underscores Joyce's conviction that Irish 'disloyalty' to the British monarchy was the inevitable consequence of imperial misrule. Joyce's hostility to British imperial policy and his suspicion of the 'good intentions of enlightened British liberals' is worth reviewing, Kiberd suggests, because 'Joyce has too often been portrayed as a cosmopolitan humanist with an aversion to militant Irish nationalism' (Kiberd 1996: 335). Scathing about the economic and cultural effects of British rule, and contemptuous of a national 'revival' that threatened merely to reproduce the 'old imperial mechanisms' at another level, Joyce attempted, from a position of post-colonial exile, to create a vision of his home space that was neither the projection of imperial fantasy nor a revivalist image of a 'pristine' post-imperial Ireland that remained wholly assimilable to the mode of nationalist and imperialist consciousness it sought to denounce (Kiberd 1996: 337). The problem of developing a literary form expressive of the ambivalence, fluidity and instability of Irish experience preoccupied Joyce from the earliest stages of his career:

> There were so many different levels of national consciousness to comprehend: and yet there was available to Joyce no overarching central image, no single explanatory category, no internal source of authority. Too mobile, too adaptable, the Irish were everywhere and nowhere, scattered across the earth and yet feeling like strangers in their own land . . . He began *Ulysses* in the hope of discovering through it a form adequate to this strange experience, one which might allow him eventually to proclaim the tables of a new law in the language of the outlaw, to burrow down into his own 'Third World' of the mind. For an audience in the made world, he wished to evoke a world still in the making. (Kiberd 1996: 328)

Whether or not Joyce, in writing *Ulysses*, felt the imaginative need to burrow down into a 'Third World' of the mind, we should be careful not to envisage the novel as an antithetical repudiation of the 'First World' nature of European Enlightenment culture. For Ireland, Kiberd reminds us, also had its share in the creation of empire; and if the 'meaning' of modern Europe is in part created by the tension between colonial violence and the suffering of native peoples, then 'Ireland affords a field of force in which the relation between the two is enacted within the community' (Kiberd 1996: 343). Taking its impetus from Joyce's sense of the reciprocal relation that bound these experiences one to another, Joycean modernism is defined in one of its principal modes by the development of a novelistic form capable of expressing the dialectical relationship between the opposed forces that constitute modern Irish experience: the tensions between imperialism and subaltern resistance, modernity and undevelopment, oral and print culture, and between 'ancient superstition' and 'the European enlightenment's notions of time and linear progress' (Kiberd 1996: 339–40). Lacking a form to hand to express the enigmatic and self-divided experience of Irishness, Joyce's response, Kiberd claims, was to create an embryonic version of magic realism. The literary form that Salman Rushdie would later famously describe as one that would 'allow the miraculous and the mundane to coexist at the same level – as the same order of event' finds one of its unlikely points of origin in the ironically doubled narratives of *Ulysses*, which continuously juxtapose 'Odyssean marvels against the Irish quotidian' (Kiberd 1996: 338). Magic realism foregrounds the dynamic interpenetration of different orders of cultural experience; the surreal juxtapositions and counterposed narrative structures of this revolutionary new form opened a space within which a radical European modernism might tender a critical accounting of modern colonialism's depredations by simultaneously reinscribing and ironising the stereotypes, rhetorical structures and binary antagonisms that underpinned its grim authority. Such, Kiberd speculates, was the radical dimension of Joycean modernism; it relentlessly reinscribed cultural and political differences and divisions in order to transcend them in the name of a genuinely multicultural vision of Ireland (Kiberd 1996: 339).

If, for Kiberd, *Ulysses* offers a genuinely multicultural text that refuses to respect the ultimate dominance of a single cultural authority, Vincent Cheng focuses upon the way Joyce's fiction examines and subverts contemporary imperial discourses of race and empire. Cheng is fascinated by the manner in which Joyce's work reconfigures the relationship between the imperial centre and the colonial margin, and the attention it pays to the production of images of cultural difference within hegemonic constructions of imperial identity. Drawing throughout his study upon modern versions of 'race theory', and informed by postcolonial critiques of nationalism and colonial dynamics, Cheng's critique explores the ways in which Joyce's work is 'centrally concerned with the relation of race/ethnicity to an imperial power' and 'the relationship between race, ethnicity, imperialism, colonialism, nationalism' inscribed in the 'structures of power' that subtends a broader imperial politics (Cheng 1995: 7). By examining such issues as nineteenth-century English discursive constructions of the Irish 'race', the representation and role of Irish nationalism within discourses of imperial subjugation and colonial resistance, and the conjoined dynamics of imperial and sexual colonisation, Cheng reads Joyce's fiction as a sustained commentary upon the ideologies of racial and imperial politics in early twentieth-century Ireland.

Derek Attridge and Marjorie Howe's edited collection of essays *Semicolonial Joyce* (2000) also examines the importance of Ireland's colonial context to a reading of Joyce's work. Joyce's writings may be termed 'semicolonial', they suggest, because:

> in their dealings with questions of nationalism and imperialism they evince a complex and ambivalent set of attitudes, not reducible to a simple anti-colonialism but very far from expressing approval of the colonial organisations and methods under which Ireland had suffered during a long history of oppression. (Attridge and Howes 2000: 3)

In this spirit, Seamus Deane suggests that for Joyce it is possible to be modern without being colonial; but not to be colonial without being modern. 'Ireland exemplified this latter condition,' in Joyce's fiction, 'and presents it in such a manner that the "traditional" and the "modern" elements seem to be in competition with one another, like two competing chronologies' (Attridge and Howes 2000: 26). Writing on the politics of space in *Ulysses*, Enda Duffy argues that the novel's 'utopia of the elided spaces of official and impoverished Dublin' challenges us to 'imagine a national community that could exist without land as the basis of its right to existence' (Attridge and Howes 2000: 56). Developing a different kind of spatial thematic, Marjorie Howes contends that Joyce responded to the problem of narrating the nation in non-imperial terms by foregrounding spatial scales like the 'local, regional, international', which presented 'alternatives to the category and/or ideology of the nation' so frequently mobilised by colonial discourse (Attridge and Howes 2000: 59). Elsewhere Emer Nolan deconstructs the received critical history of reading 'Cyclops' – and by extension *Ulysses* itself – as simply a clash between nationalism and internationalism by pointing out how both positions are conditioned by the system of modern capitalism they seek to contest (Attridge and Howes 2000: 91). Joseph Valente examines Joyce's interrogation of the:

> dominant late Victorian/Edwardian construct of *manhood*, its supportive – even constitutive – role in the delineation of ethnic differences between colonizing and colonised peoples, and the disabling ambivalence it tapped, almost by design, in the semicolonial space of Ireland, where nationalist resistance grounded itself in many of the gender and racial attitudes of imperialist rule. (Attridge and Howes 2000: 96)

Focusing upon the 'transformation of bodily practices in the modernization of Ireland and on the survival of "nonmodern" forms of cultural difference', David Lloyd explores the forms in which Irish masculinity was being reconstituted by Irish nationalist movements at the turn of the century as well as the 'recalcitrance which the performance of masculinity in popular culture presented to such projects' (Attridge and Howes 2000: 129). Returning to Joyce's earlier writing, Luke Gibbons inspects the 'politics of paralysis' at work in *Dubliners*, discerning the roots of this torpid state in the enervating effects of the Great Famine and the deracination of folk culture by the 'disciplinary regimes' of bourgeois modernity (Attridge and Howes 2000: 156). Kathleen Mullin suggests that by writing in 'Eveline' a 'particularly intricate and politically loaded perversion' of the anti-emigration narratives published in *The Irish Homestead*, Joyce signals his 'estrangement from the kind of nationalism *The Irish Homestead* expected its stories to dictate' (Attridge and Howes 2000: 172). Tracing the 'ghostly imprint' upon Joyce's work of Ireland's 'semicolonial neighbour nation' Scotland, Willy Maley argues that Joyce's writing offers 'a nuanced view of what historians of the early modern period are now calling the "British Problem," that process of conquest, plantation and union that brought a multi-nation state into being' (Attridge and Howes 2000: 201).

The significance of Joyce's work has also been explored by a number of Marxist critics. In an influential analysis, Terry Eagleton suggests that the internal tensions of Joyce's work are a '*production*, not a reflection, of the ideological formation into which Joyce as historical subject was ambivalently inserted – a production which, by putting that ideology to work, exposed its framing limits' (Eagleton 1976: 155). Eagleton points initially to Joyce's position of internal exile from both the Protestant Ascendency and the Romantic Anglo-Irish tradition before teasing out the implications of his necessarily marginal status for his emerging vision of art:

> Born into the Catholic petty bourgeoisie, Joyce rejected the Romantic Anglo-Irish tradition as bankrupt (he thought Yeats 'a tiresome idiot . . . quite out of touch with the Irish people'), and its mystificatory aesthetic of inspirational spontaneity; art instead was a productive *labour*, a massive, life-consuming substitute for the social identity denied by a stagnant, clericist, culturally parochial Ireland. (Eagleton 1976: 154)

Despite writing from a different class standpoint, Joyce was 'as ambiguously related to Irish nationalism as Yeats'; his abandonment of Ireland was in part 'a protest against the bourgeois limitations of nationalism, a decisive rupture with its sentimental patriotism, superstitious religiosity and cultural philistinism'. But where Yeats was historically isolated from nationalism by his cultural identification with 'Ascendency reaction', Joyce's dissociation from nationalism, clericalism and imperialism had to be achieved 'materially and spiritually' through his art (Eagleton 1976: 154). Joyce's work seeks to achieve a state of artistic and moral independence by first exposing the limits of the ideological formation that determines Joyce's cultural and political subjectivity:

Joyce was born into an ideological sub-ensemble of petty-bourgeois
Catholic nationalism – a sub-ensemble which formed a contradictory unity
with the dominant ideology. That relation was then overdetermined by his
expatriatism, which reproduced that initial contradictory unity in quite different terms. The complexity of this formation is 'produced' at the level of
Joyce's aesthetic ideology. For if his espousal of literary naturalism is in one
sense a fidelity to the 'realities' of petty-bourgeois Dublin, it is also a commitment to a cosmopolitan perspective within which those 'realities' could
be critically distanced. (Eagleton 1976: 155)

Europe may have provided Joyce with the opportunity to transcend
'Irish cultural provincialism', but the discourse of European *naturalism*
unhappily reinforced the 'obsessive petty-bourgeois' preoccupations of
Joyce's Irish class standpoint. Self-consciously attentive to the paradoxical position in which his relation to literary naturalism placed him, Joyce
realised that whilst the genre signified for him 'petty-bourgeois paralysis'
(the world depicted so minutely in *Dubliners*), it was also 'contradicto-
rily unified with the serene realism of classical epic and the "realist"
scholasticism of the hegemonic Irish order'. Joyce's response was to
produce a vision of Irish life ironically distanced from the discursive contradictions of naturalism and classic realism while simultaneously laying
bare the *material* divisions that constituted their particular world-view.
Ultimately this characteristic Joycean manoeuvre, in which contradictory
forces are 'resolved' by the factitious unity of art only to be deconstructed
once more into the conditions of their production, becomes one of the
key structural principles of *Ulysses*:

Ulysses 'resolves' the contradiction between 'alienated' artistic consciousness (Stephen Dedalus) and material existence (Leopold Bloom) in its *formal*
tressing of naturalist and mythological codes, just as Joyce himself sur-
mounts this duality in his 'author–as-producer' aesthetic. He rejects the
Romantic subjectivism of Stephen, while preserving (unlike Bloom) the
essentially Romantic creed of total self-dedication to art. But this formal
interpenetration in *Ulysses* is an immense, self-flaunting structural irony, so
elaborately and exhaustively achieved that it draws attention to its fla-
grantly synthetic basis in Homeric myth . . . The unity of material life and
self-exiled artistic self-consciousness which Joyce seeks is achieved not *in* the
work but *by* it: *Ulysses* is a novel about the conditions of its own production, subsisting in its ironic identity with and dissonance from the Homeric
myth which provides its 'raw materials'. (Eagleton 1976: 156)

Another major Marxist critic, Fredric Jameson, sought to unsettle 'traditional interpretations' of *Ulysses* (which he categorised variously as
'mythical', 'psychoanalytic' and 'ethical'), believing that all worked to

defuse the radical political agency of Joyce's work (Jameson 1982: 126). Jameson calls for a way of reading Joyce that involves the 'radical historisation' of his work and which makes us try and account for the 'historical necessity' of its rhetorical and textual structures (Jameson 1982: 128). One way of beginning the 'radical historisation' of Joyce's work, he argues, is to evoke the 'philosophical concept' and 'existential experience' of *contingency* (Jameson 1982: 128). Jameson works here at some distance from theorists of the modern like Roland Barthes for whom the 'radical contingency and meaninglessness of our object world' is simply the consequence of the 'increasing lucidity and self-consciousness of human beings in a post-religious, secular, scientific age' (Jameson 1982: 129). Instead, he elaborates upon a shattering existential insight intrinsic to *Ulysses* itself: the perception that the modern city may be seen to be 'meaningless'. This perception, and the burgeoning sense of alienation it engenders, is born, Jameson argues, of a historical paradox. In earlier, pre-modern societies:

> it was Nature that was meaningless or anti-human. What is paradoxical about the historical experience of modernism is that it designates very precisely that period in which Nature – or the in- or anti-human – is everywhere in the process of being displaced or destroyed, expunged, eliminated, by the achievements of human praxis and human production. The great modernist literature – from Baudelaire and Flaubert to 'Ulysses' and beyond – is a city literature: its object is therefore the anti-natural, the humanised, par excellence, a landscape which is everywhere the result of human labour, in which everything – including the formerly natural, grass, trees, our own bodies – is finally produced by human beings. This is then the historical paradox with which the experience of contingency confronts us . . . how can the city be meaningless? How can human production be felt to be absurd or contingent, when in another sense one would think it was only human labour which created genuine meaning in the first place. (Jameson 1982: 129–30)

The source of these contradictions, Jameson maintains, is to be found in the reconfiguration of the work process and of subjectivity itself under modern industrial conditions. This process is apparent in the alienation of the consciousness of the worker from his own labour, the consequent deconstitution of the psyche of the psychological subject into a collection of incommensurable functions and dispositions, and the dissolution of 'older hierarchical communities, neighbourhoods, and organic groups' into an array of atomised economic individuals by the 'penetration of the money and market system'. Much of the political fascination of *Ulysses* lies in its hypersensitivity to these simultaneously decomposing and reifying processes; the extraordinary social and psychological pressure placed upon Joyce's characters, and the imaginative and sensuous resistance they sometimes manage to oppose to it, constitute a crucial element of the novel's drama. Jameson does not just offer another interpretation of *Ulysses*; he argues that the attempt to unify and give order to the text is itself a response to the alienation of urban capitalism. Joyce's unsettling representations of the broader 'symbolic order', Jameson claims, is rendered most vividly in his reinvention of the spatial and linguistic experience of the modern city. One of the collective tragedies of modernity is the dissolution of the imaginative unity of the 'classical city' into the alienating and reified spaces of 'the suburb or megalopolis or the private car' (Jameson 1982: 135). However, the triumph of *Ulysses* is to create new unities or 'points of totalisation' that permit a 'synthesis of the object (place) and the subject (population)' and make 'shared experience' possible once again (Jameson 1982: 133). Joyce achieves this 'dereification' of modern life by offering a recompense for our civic and social isolation through the shared linguistic medium of gossip:

> [a] kind of speech which is neither uniquely private nor forbiddingly standardised in an impersonal public form, a type of discourse in which the same, in which repetition, is transmitted again and again through a host of eventful repetitions, each of which has its own value. (Jameson 1982: 135)

The dereifying function of gossip is to act as the 'element in which reference – or, if you prefer, the "referent" itself – expands and contracts, ceaselessly transformed from a mere token, a notation, a short-hand object, back into a full-dress narrative' (Jameson 1982: 135). Observing that this process is 'more tangible and more dramatic when we see it at work on physical things', Jameson illustrates its reconfiguring effects upon:

> the statues, the commodities in the shopwindows, the clanking trolleylines that link Dublin to its suburbs (which dissolve, by way of Mr Deasy's anxieties about foot-and-mouth disease, into Mr Bloom's fantasy projects for tramlimes to move cattle to the docks); or the three-master whose silent grace and respectability as an image is at length dissolved into the disreputable reality of its garrulous and yarn-spinning crewman . . . (Jameson 1982: 135)

The power of such exercises in dereification, Jameson concludes, is that by reinscribing the impress of social relations back within the commodity form, they open up 'a perspective in which, at some ideal outside limit, everything seemingly material and solid in Dublin itself can presumably be dissolved into the underlying reality of human relations and human praxis' (Jameson 1982: 136).

But whilst Jameson's critique celebrates the effects of Joyce's dereification of human relations and social spaces, he also sounds a warning about one aspect of his narrative method. There is, he insists, a price *Ulysses* must pay for the seemingly limitless power of its play of reification and dereification. That price is the 'radical depersonalisation' of the artwork caused by Joyce's decision to remove the author from the text, a decision that, in Jameson's words, also 'removes the reader, and finally that unifying and organising mirage or aftermirage of both author and reader which is the "character", or better still, "point of view" ' (Jameson 1982: 136). These imaginative categories formerly served as the 'supports' for the unity of the work of art; but, since their withdrawal, 'only a form of material unity is left, namely the printed book itself, and its material unity as a bound set of pages' within which its cross references are contained. The replacement of 'character' and 'point of view' by the novel's internal play of languages and levels of rhetoric, Jameson continues, threatens to transform the book itself into one more reified product. What saves it from this fate is that its newly depersonalised narrative ('in which the book begins to elaborate its own text, under its own momentum, with no further need for characters, point of view, author or perhaps even reader') itself enacts a *parody* of the schism between subjective and objective experience enforced upon us by the process of reification (Jameson 1982: 138). Nowhere is this parody more apparent than in the extreme tedium visited upon the reader by the 'Ithaca' episode, where the enveloping sense of boredom is generated by 'the infinite subdivision of the objective contents of narrative, breaking "events" into their smallest material components and asking whether, in that form, they still have any interest whatsoever' (Jameson 1982: 140). In this way we are compelled to confront everything that is intolerable about the reification of modern life and its relentless commodification of human experience.

Jameson's generous intuition of the subaltern political potency of Joyce's fiction has not been unanimously shared by other contemporary critics. Indeed for some commentators Joyce's mature fiction is symptomatic of the damaging divide within literary modernism between the interests of a self-selecting cultural élite and the tastes and opinions of a mass audience. Judged according to these perspectives, the 'politics' of Joyce's literary style is indissociable from a broader cultural realignment that aimed to distinguish élite values from the competing claims voiced by the emergent mass literary readership created by late nineteenth-century educational reforms. An influential version of this argument was expounded by John Carey (1992). Carey's thesis, which issues a ringing denunciation of the reaction against 'mass values' implicit in the work of modernist writers such as W. B. Yeats, T. S. Eliot, Virginia Woolf and

D. H. Lawrence, is, in fact, notably ambivalent in its response to Joyce's work (Carey 1992: 18). Carey is compelled initially to concede that 'the early twentieth-century fictional character' who most stands out from the 'dismal representatives of mass man and mass woman' found in other modernist fiction 'is Leopold Bloom in James Joyce's *Ulysses*'. Carey discovers an analogue for his ambivalent response to Joyce in what he takes to be Joyce's own ambivalent representation of Bloom: Joyce empathised with Bloom to a significant degree, Carey claims, whilst employing him nonetheless to emphasise the distinction between the impoverished values of 'mass man' and those of the modernist artist. This ambivalence expresses itself in a variety of ways: thus Bloom is 'not wholly uncultured', but is 'distinctly not a literary intellectual'; while his continual curiosity about the world does not preclude him from exhibiting a profound lack of imagination: 'The only book we see him buy is called *Sweets of Sin*' (Carey 1992: 19). While it is doubtless true that by the novel's conclusion we know Bloom 'more thoroughly than any other character in fiction has ever been known before', such knowledge, Carey insists, does not necessarily breed empathy with his situation: through his role as an advertising-canvasser, Joyce 'pointedly encoils Bloom in newsprint and advertising, which were, for intellectuals, among the most odious features of mass culture' (Carey 1992: 20). Moreover, Joyce's decision to represent Bloom in an avant-garde literary style that shares no organic affinity with his own sensibility or mode of speech renders him a mere object of curiosity within his own story and makes Joyce complicit with literary modernism's rejection of popular and mass culture:

> Can we say, then, that in *Ulysses* mass man is redeemed? Is Joyce the one intellectual who atones for Nietzschean contempt of the masses, and raises mass man, or a representation of mass man, to the status of epic hero? To a degree, yes. One effect of *Ulysses* is to show that mass man matters, that he has an inner life as complex as an intellectual's, that it is worthwhile to record his personal details on a prodigious scale. And yet it is also true that Bloom himself would never and could never have read *Ulysses* or a book like *Ulysses*. The complexity of the novel, its avant-garde technique, its obscurity, rigorously excludes people like Bloom from its readership. More than almost any other twentieth-century novel, it is for intellectuals only. (Carey 1992: 20)

A similarly ambivalent, although considerably more sophisticated, critique of Joyce's aesthetics is presented by Leo Bersani (1990). Bersani's chapter on Joyce, provocatively entitled 'Against *Ulysses*', seeks to expose the cultural and political limitations of Joyce's work by challenging its assumption that the transcendence of art imaginatively resolves and redeems the diremptions of historical experience. Bersani begins by locating *Ulysses* as a central artefact within what he calls the 'culture of redemption'. 'A crucial assumption of the culture of redemption,' he declares, 'is that a certain type of repetition of experience in art repairs inherently damaged or valueless experience' (Bersani 1990: 1). Art, according to this view, gives value, shape and coherence to the fractured body of individual and social experience. However, one frequently unconsidered danger of a belief in the redemptive function of art is that it depends upon 'a devaluation of historical experience and of art' itself (Bersani 1990: 2). This danger ultimately expresses itself in a fundamentally contradictory aesthetic position: the catastrophes of history somehow matter less if they are compensated for by art; yet art, meanwhile, is reduced to a merely 'patching function', and becomes 'enslaved to those very materials to which it presumably imparts value' (Bersani 1990: 1). If art can transcend the force and flux of life, that is, it must also *negate* something in life; and if art negates life it must also negate a crucial moral dimension of its own (Bersani 1990: 2).

Bersani develops his critique of Joyce by focusing upon the absence of a personal style in his work – an absence filled in part by Joyce's strategic use of citation, quotation, intertextuality and a 'nonperspectival point of view' (Bersani 1990: 161). The significance of Joyce's refusal to develop a signature personal style is that it calls into question 'the authority of literature over the materials it incorporates' (Bersani 1990: 163). The diffuse flow of materials and discourses generated by *Ulysses* is, in fact, ultimately transcended and redeemed by the function of Joyce's own art. Joyce's writing performs this function, Bersani explains, by isolating the deracinated cultural discourses of a lost classical tradition and 'reconstitut[ing] them as cultural artifacts within the intertextual designs woven by *Ulysses*' (Bersani 1990: 169). *Ulysses* refigures and recombines cultural fragments into a new aesthetic totality; it becomes in the process both the 'center and the belated origin' of an entire cultural inheritance. The truly fascinating and audacious aspect of Joyce's stylistic impersonality is not, Bersani suggests, that he fuses incommensurable fragments of cultural memory into a single 'Joycean' discourse. Instead, the sheer variety of stylistic devices kept alive and at play in *Ulysses* reveals Joyce's sweeping designs on culture:

> Far from transmuting all his cultural referents into a single, recognizably Joycean discourse, Joyce scrupulously maintains the distinctness of innumerable other styles *in order to legitmize misquoting them*. The accuracy is not merely a referential scruple, just as the inaccuracies are far from being mere sloppiness. We have to recognise the sources of *Ulysses* if we are to

acknowledge its superiority to them. *Ulysses* indulges massively in quotation – quotation of individual characters, social groups, myths, other writers – but quoting in Joyce is the opposite of self-effacement. It is an act of appropriation, which can be performed without Joyce's voice ever being heard . . . Far from contesting the authority of culture, *Ulysses* reinvents our relation to Western culture in terms of exegetical devotion, that is, as the exegesis of *Ulysses* itself. (Bersani 1990: 170)

By appropriating, parodying and misquoting a collection of totemic Western texts, Joyce simultaneously reinvents our relation to the forms of memory they encode and reconstitutes a new cultural narrative from the shards of cultural division. Those forms of continuity and cultural tradition that have steadily been eroded in the process of their historical transmission are now reborn in the very act of explicating the aesthetic totality of *Ulysses* – an act that demands the reconstruction of cultural memory as its imaginative precondition. However, Bersani suggests that the ideal of aesthetic transcendence implicit in Joyce's redemptive labours has potentially perilous consequences for the modes of historical and cultural relation it wishes to preserve. The problem with Joyce's belief in the cultural redemptiveness of the artwork lies in its 'nihilistic indifference to any relation between our experience of reading it and the concealed structures it signifies' (Bersani 1990: 178). But it is in precisely this relation that the cultural resonance and political possibilities of aesthetic experience resides. Joyce's real interest, Bersani maintains, lay not in the fate of 'Western culture' as such, but rather in 'the coherence of a particular broken version of it'. Committed as he was to a culturally redemptive vision of art, Joyce eventually discovered that this coherence was only to be found in the readers' painstaking reconstruction of the 'structurally coherent fragments of Joyce's own cultural consciousness' (Bersani 1990: 178). To be 'against *Ulysses*' does not mean, Bersani finally judges, to be against Joyce's art per se; it signifies an opposition to its mystifying redemptive operation. The nuanced tone of Bersani's last words might bring any book on Joyce to a fitting conclusion: 'Even in writing "against *Ulysses*", we can only feel a great sadness in leaving it – to stop working on *Ulysses* is like a fall from grace' (Bersani 1990: 178).

Further Reading

The primary critical collection of early Joyce materials is to be found in Deming (1970a and b). A number of collections and anthologies of essays on Joyce provide productive points of departure; these include Garrett (1968), Hart and Hayman (1974), MacCabe (1982), Epstein

(1982), Attridge and Ferrer (1984), Scott (1984), Attridge (1990), and Norris (1998). Good introductory studies of aspects of Joyce's work are available in Levin (1944), Kain (1947), Goldberg (1961), Adams (1962), Gottfried (1980), Lawrence (1981), Blamires (1988), and Bernard Benstock (1991; 1994). The readings in the second half of this section have drawn upon several different methodological approaches; readers keen to familiarise themselves with these styles of interpretation might usefully begin by consulting Barry (1995). More generally, Eagleton (1976) offers a synoptic guide to the intersection between Marxist theory and literature. Moi (1985) and Colebrook (2004) provide helpful introductions to feminist literary theory and gender studies. Wright (1984) contains a clear guide to psychoanalytic theory, while Kevin Hart (1989) offers a lucid introduction to deconstruction. Hayman (1963), Kain and Scholes (1965), MacNicholas (1979) and Connolly (1997) contribute important archival and textual research. Staley (1989) has compiled a valuable critical bibliography of Joyce.

Bibliography

Biographical Works

Banta, Melissa and Oscar A. Silverman (eds) (1987), *James Joyce's Letters to Sylvia Beach 1921–40* (Bloomington: University of Indiana Press).

Beach, Sylvia (1959), *Shakespeare and Company* (London: Faber and Faber).

Ellmann, Richard [1959] (1983), *James Joyce* (Oxford: Oxford University Press).

Gorman, Herbert (1941), *James Joyce: A Definitive Biography* (London: Bodley Head).

Joyce, James (1957), *Letters of James Joyce*, ed. Stuart Gilbert (London: Faber and Faber).

— (1966), *Letters of James Joyce*, ed. Richard Ellmann (London: Faber and Faber).

— (1975), *Selected Letters of James Joyce*, ed. Richard Ellmann (London: Faber and Faber).

Joyce, Stanislaus (1958), *My Brother's Keeper: James Joyce's Early Years*, ed. Richard Ellmann (London: Faber and Faber).

— (1971), *The Complete Dublin Diary*, ed. George H. Healey (Ithaca: Cornell University Press).

Lidderdale, Jane and Mary Nicholson (1970), *Dear Miss Weaver: Harriet Shaw Weaver 1876–1961* (London: Faber and Faber).

Maddox, Brenda (1988), *Nora: A Biography of Nora Joyce* (London: Hamish Hamilton).

Potts, Willard (ed.) (1979), *Portraits of the Artist in Exile: Recollections of James Joyce by Europeans* (Seattle: University of Washington Press).

Pound, Ezra (1968), *Pound/Joyce: The Letters of Ezra Pound to James Joyce with Pound's Essays on Joyce*, ed. Forrest Read (London: Faber and Faber).

Power, Arthur (1974), *Conversations with James Joyce*, ed. Clive Hart (London: Millington).

Early Critical Responses and Articles

Aldington, Richard (1939), 'Review', *Atlantic Monthly* (June clxiii: n.p.); reprinted in Robert H. Deming (1970b), *James Joyce: The Critical Heritage Volume Two: 1928–41* (London: Routledge), p. 690.

Angeli, Diego (1918), 'An Italian Comment on *A Portrait*', *Egoist* 5 (2): 30; reprinted in Robert H. Deming (1970a), 114–16.

Bennett, Arnold (1922), 'James Joyce's *Ulysses*', *Outlook* (29 April): 337–9; reprinted in Deming (1970a), pp. 219–22.

Eliot, T. S. (1923), 'Ulysses, Order, and Myth', *The Dial* lxxv: 480–3; reprinted in Frank Kermode (ed.) (1975), *The Selected Prose of T. S. Eliot* (London: Faber and Faber), pp. 175–8.

Garnett, Edward (1959), 'Reader's Report on *A Portrait of the Artist as a Young Man*', in Richard Ellmann, *James Joyce* (Oxford: Oxford University Press), pp. 416–17; reprinted in Deming (1970a), pp. 81–2.

Gould, Gerald (1914), 'Dubliners', *New Statesman* 3 (374–5); reprinted in Deming (1970a), pp. 62–3.

— (1928), 'Comment', *Observer* (9 December 1928); reprinted in Deming (1970b), pp. 392–3.

Kazin, Alfed (1939), 'Review', *New York Herald Tribune* (21 May 1939); reprinted in Deming (1970b), pp. 685–8.

Kettle, Thomas (1907), 'Review', *Freeman's Journal* (June): n.p.; reprinted in Deming (1970a), p. 37.

Larbaud, Valéry (1922), 'The *Ulysses* of James Joyce', *Criterion* 1 (1): 94–103; reprinted in Deming (1970a), pp. 252–62.

Leavis, F. R. (1933), 'James Joyce and the Revolution of the Word', *Scrutiny* 2 (2) (September): 193–201.

Levin, Harry (1939), 'On First Looking into *Finnegans Wake*', *New Directions in Prose and Poetry*: 253–87; reprinted in Deming (1970b), pp. 693–703.

Mais, S. P. B. (1922), 'An Irish Revel: and some Flappers', *Daily Express* (25 March 1922); reprinted in Deming (1970a), p. 191.

Murray, John Middleton (1922), 'Review', *Nation & Athenaeum* 31: 124–5; reprinted in Deming (1970a), pp. 195–8.

Pound, Ezra (1914), 'Dubliners and Mr James Joyce', *Egoist* 1 (14): 267; reprinted in Deming (1970a), pp. 66–8.

— (1922), 'James Joyce et Pécuchet', *Mercure de France* clvi: 307–20; reprinted in Deming (1970a), trans. Fred Bornhauser, pp. 263–7.

Symons, Arthur (1907), 'A Book of Songs', *Nation* 1 (17) (June): 639; reprinted in Deming (1970a), pp. 38–9.

Wells, H. G. (1917), 'James Joyce', *Nation* 20: 710–12; reprinted in Deming (1970a), pp. 86–8.

Zabel, Morton (1930), 'The Lyrics of James Joyce', *Poetry* 36 (July): 206–13; reprinted in Deming (1970a), pp. 45–8.

Criticism of James Joyce in Books

Adams, Robert M. (1962), *Surface and Symbol: The Consistency of James Joyce's Ulysses* (London: Oxford University Press).

Atherton, James S. (1959), *The Books at the Wake: A Study of Literary Allusions in James Joyce's Finnegans Wake* (London: Faber and Faber).

— (1966), 'The Joyce of Dubliners', in Thomas F. Staley (ed.), *James Joyce Today: Essays on the Major Works* (Bloomington: Indiana University Press), pp. 28–53.

Attridge, Derek (ed.) (1990), *The Cambridge Companion to James Joyce* (Cambridge: Cambridge University Press).

— (2000), *Joyce Effects: On Language, Theory and History* (Cambridge: Cambridge University Press).

— (ed.) (2004), *James Joyce's Ulysses: A Casebook* (Oxford: Oxford University Press).

Attridge, Derek and Daniel Ferrer (eds) (1984), *Post-Structuralist Joyce: Essays from the French* (Cambridge: Cambridge University Press).

Attridge, Derek and Marjorie Howes (eds) (2000), *Semicolonial Joyce* (Cambridge: Cambridge University Press).

Barry, Peter (1995), *Beginning Theory* (Manchester: Manchester University Press).

Beckett, Samuel, et al. (1936), *Our Exagmination Round his Factification for Incamination of Work in Progress* (Paris: Shakespeare and Company).

Begnal, Michael and Fritz Senn (eds) (1974), *A Conceptual Guide to Finnegans Wake* (University Park: Pennsylvania State University Press).

Benstock, Bernard (1988a), 'The Gnomonics of Dubliners', *Modern Fiction Studies* 34 (4): 519–39.

— (ed.) (1988b), *James Joyce: The Augmented Ninth* (Syracuse: Syracuse University Press).

— (1991), *Narrative Con/texts in Ulysses* (Basingstoke: Macmillan).

— (1994), *Narrative Con/Texts in Dubliners* (Basingstoke: Macmillan).

Benstock, Shari (1980), 'Who Killed Cock Robin? The Sources of Free Indirect Style in *Ulysses*', *Style* 14 (3): 259–73.

Bersani, Leo (1990), *The Culture of Redemption* (Cambridge: Harvard University Press).

Bishop, John (1986), *Joyce's Book of the Dark: Finnegans Wake* (Madison: University of Wisconsin Press).

Blamires, Harry [1966] (1983), *The Bloomsday Book: A Guide through Joyce's Ulysses* (London: Methuen and Co).

Booth, Wayne C. (1961), *The Rhetoric of Fiction* (Chicago: Chicago University Press).

Brivic, Sheldon (1980), *Joyce between Freud and Jung* (New York: London National University Publications Kennikat).

Brown, Richard (1985), *Joyce and Sexuality* (Cambridge: Cambridge University Press).

Budgen, Frank (1934), *James Joyce and the Making of Ulysses* (London: Grayson and Grayson).

Bulson, Eric (2006), *The Cambridge Introduction to James Joyce* (Cambridge: Cambridge University Press).

Burgess, Anthony (1965), *Here Comes, Everybody: An Introduction to Joyce for the Ordinary Reader* (London: Faber).

Bushri, Suheil Badi and Bernard Benstock (eds) (1982), *James Joyce: An International Perspective: Centenary Essays in Honour of the late Sir Desmond Cochrane* (Gerrards Cross: Smythe).

Butler, Christopher (1990), 'Joyce, Modernism, and Post-Modernism', in Derek Attridge (ed.), *The Cambridge Joyce Companion* (Cambridge: Cambridge University Press), pp. 259–82.

Campbell, Joseph and Henry Morton Robinson [1944] (1947), *A Skeleton Key to Finnegans Wake* (London: Faber and Faber).

Carey, John (1992), *The Intellectuals and the Masses: Pride and Prejudice among the Literary Intelligentsia 1880–1939* (London: Faber and Faber).

Cheng, Vincent (1995), *Joyce, Race and Empire* (Cambridge: Cambridge University Press).

Cixous, Hélène (1972), *The Exile of James Joyce*, trans. Sally A. J. Purcell (New York: David Martin).

— (1984), 'Joyce: The (R)use of Writing', in Derek Attridge and Daniel Ferrer (eds), *Post-Structuralist Joyce: Essays from the French* (Cambridge: Cambridge University Press), pp. 15–30.

Colebrook, Claire (2004), *Gender* (Basingstoke: Palgrave Macmillan).

Connolly, Thomas E. (1997), *James Joyce's Books, Portraits, Manuscripts, Notebooks, Typescripts, Page Proofs: Together with Critical Essays about some of his Works* (New York: Edward Mellen).

Coyle, John (ed.) [1997] (2000), *James Joyce: Ulysses, A Portrait of The Artist as a Young Man* (Duxford: Icon).

Dalton, Jack P. (1972), 'The Text of "Ulysses" ', in Fritz Senn (ed.) (1972), *New Light on Joyce from the Dublin Symposium*, Bloomington: Indiana University Press, pp. 99–119.

Deming, Robert H. (1970a), *James Joyce: The Critical Heritage Volume One: 1902–27* (London: Routledge).

— (1970b), *James Joyce: The Critical Heritage Volume Two: 1928–41* (London: Routledge).

Derrida, Jacques (1984), 'Two Words for Joyce', in Derek Atridge and Daniel Ferrer (eds) (1984), *Post-Structuralist Joyce: Essays from the French* (Cambridge: Cambridge University Press), pp. 145–60.

— (1988), 'Ulysses Gramophone: Hear say yes in Joyce', trans. Tina Kendall, in Bernard Benstock (ed.), *James Joyce: The Augmented Ninth* (Syracuse: Syracuse University Press), pp. 27–75.

Eagleton, Terry (1970), *Exiles and Emigrés: Studies in Modern Literature* (London: Chatto and Windus).

— (1976), *Criticism and Ideology: A Study in Marxist Literary Theory* (London: NLB).

Ellmann, Maud (1981), 'Disremembering Dedalus: *A Portrait of the Artist as a Young Man*', in Robert Young (ed.), *Untying the Text: A Post-Structuralist Reader* (London: Routledge), pp. 189–206.

— (1982), 'Polytropic Man: Paternity, Identity and Naming in *The Odyssey* and *A Portrait of the Artist as a Young Man*', in Colin MacCabe (ed.), MacCabe (1982), pp. 73–104.

Ellmann, Richard (1954), *The Identity of Yeats* (London: Macmillan).

— [1972] (1974), *Ulysses on the Liffey* (London: Faber and Faber).

— (1977), *The Consciousness of Joyce* (London: Faber and Faber).

Epstein, Edmund L. (1982), *A Starchamber Quiry: A James Joyce Centennial Volume 1882–1982* (London: Methuen).

Fairhall, James (1993), *James Joyce and the Question of History* (Cambridge: Cambridge University Press).

French, Marilyn (1982), *James Joyce's Ulysses: The Book as World* (London: Sphere).

Froula, Christine (1996), *Modernism's Body: Sex, Culture and Joyce* (New York: Columbia University Press).

Garrett, Peter K. (ed.) (1968), *Twentieth Century Interpretations of 'Dubliners': A Collection of Critical Essays* (New Jersey: Prentice-Hall).

Gibson, Andrew (2002), *History, Politics and Aesthetics in Ulysses* (Oxford: Oxford University Press).

Gilbert, Sandra M. and Susan Gubar (1985), 'Sexual Linguistics: Gender, Language, Sexuality', *New Literary History* 16: 513–43.

Gilbert, Stuart (1930), *James Joyce's Ulysses: A Study* (London: Faber and Faber).

Glasheen, Adaline (1956), *A Census of Finnegans Wake: An Index of the Characters and Their Roles* (Evanston: Northwestern University Press).

Goldberg, Samuel Louis (1961), *The Classical Temper: A Study of James Joyce's Ulysses* (London: Chatto and Windus).

Gottfried, Roy K. (1980), *The Art of Joyce's Syntax in Ulysses* (London: Macmillan).

Groden, Michael (1977), *Ulysses in Progress* (Princeton: Princeton University Press).

Grose, Kenneth (1975), *James Joyce* (London: Evans Bros).

Harkness, Marguerite (1984), *The Aesthetics of Dedalus and Bloom* (Lewisburg: Bucknell University Press).

Hart, Clive (1962a), *Structure and Motif in Finnegans Wake* (London: Faber and Faber).

— (1962b), *A Concordance to Finnegans Wake* (Minneapolis: University of Minnesota Press).

Hart, Clive (ed.) (1969), *James Joyce's 'Dubliners': Critical Essays* (London: Faber and Faber).

Hart, Clive and Fritz Senn (eds) (1968), *A Wake Digest* (Sydney: Sydney University Press).

Hart, Clive and David Hayman (eds) (1974), *James Joyce's Ulysses: Critical Essays* (Berkeley: University of California Press).

Hart, Kevin (1989), *The Trespass of the Sign: Deconstruction, Theology and Philosophy* (Cambridge: Cambridge University Press).

Hayman, David (ed.) (1963), *A First Draft Version of Finnegans Wake* (London: Faber and Faber).

— (1970), *Ulysses: The Mechanics of Meaning* (New Jersey: Prentice-Hall).

Heath, Stephen (1984), 'Ambiviolences: Notes for reading Joyce', in Derck Attridge and Daniel Ferrer (eds), *Post-Structuralist Joyce: Essays from the French* (Cambridge: Cambridge University Press) pp. 31–68.

Henke, Suzette (1982), 'Stephen Dedalus and Women: A Portrait of the Artist as a Young Misogynist', in Suzette Henke and Elaine Unkeless (eds), *Women in Joyce* (Urbana: University of Illinois Press) pp. 82–107.

— (1990), *James Joyce and the Politics of Desire* (London: Routledge).

Henke, Suzette and Elaine Unkeless (eds) (1982), *Women in Joyce* (Urbana: University of Illinois Press).

Herr, Cheryl (1986), *Joyce's Anatomy of Culture* (Urbana and Chicago: University of Illinois Press).

Hofheinz, Thomas C. (1995), *James Joyce and the Invention of Irish History: Finnegans Wake in Context* (Cambridge: Cambridge University Press).

Jameson, Fredric (1982), ' "Ulysses" in History', in W. J. McCormack and Alistair Stead (eds), *James Joyce and Modern Literature* (London: Routledge and Kegan Paul), pp. 126–41.

Johnson, Jeri (1989), ' "Beyond the Veil": Ulysses, Feminism, and the Figure of Woman', in Christine van Boheemen (ed.), *Joyce, Modernity, and its Mediation* (Amsterdam: Rodopi), pp. 201–28.

Kain, Richard (1947), *Fabulous Voyager: James Joyce's Ulysses* (Chicago: The University of Chicago Press).

Kain, Richard and Robert E. Scholes (eds) (1965), *The Workshop of Daedalus: James Joyce and the Raw Materials for A Portrait of the Artist as a Young Man* (Evanston: Northwestern University Press).

Kenner, Hugh (1965), 'Joyce's Portrait: A Reconsideration', *University of Windsor Review* 1: 1–15.

— (1978), *Joyce's Voices* (Berkeley: University of California Press).

— (1980), *Ulysses* (London: George Allen and Unwin).

— [1955] (1987), *Dublin's Joyce* (New York: Columbia Press).

Kiberd, Declan (1996), *Inventing Ireland: The Literature of the Modern Nation* (London: Vintage).

Kimball, Jean (1980), 'Freud, Leonardo and Joyce: The Dimensions of a Childhood Memory', *James Joyce Quarterly* 17 (2): 165–82.

Kristeva, Julia (1981), *Desire in Language: A Semiotic Approach to Literature and Art*, ed. Leon S. Roudiez, trans. Thomas Gora, Alice Jardine and Leon S. Roudiez (Oxford: Blackwell).

— (1982), *Powers of Horror: An Essay on Abjection*, trans. Leon S. Roudiez (New York: Columbia Press).

Lawrence, Karen (1981), *The Odyssey of Style in Ulysses* (Princeton: Princeton University Press).

— (1990), 'Joyce and Feminism', in Derek Attridge (ed.), *The Cambridge Joyce Companion* (Cambridge: Cambridge University Press) pp. 237–58.

Leavis, F. R. (1933), 'James Joyce and the Revolution of the Word', *Scrutiny* 2 (2): 193–201.

Levin, Harry [1941] (1944), *James Joyce: A Critical Introduction* (London: Faber and Faber).

Lewis, Wyndham (1927a), 'An Analysis of the Mind of the Joyce', in Wyndham Lewis, *Time and Western Man* (London: Chatto and Windus), pp. 91–130.

Lewis, Wyndham (1927b), *Time and Western Man* (London: Chatto and Windus).

Lewis, Wyndham (1937), *Blasting and Bombadiering* (London: Eyre and Spottiswoode).

Litz, A. Walton (1961), *The Art of James Joyce* (Oxford: Oxford University Press).

Lukàcs, Georg (1962), *The Meaning of Contemporary Realism*, trans. John and Necke Mander (London: Merlin).

MacCabe, Colin (1978), *James Joyce and the Revolution of the Word* (Basingstoke: Macmillan).

— (ed.) (1982), *James Joyce: New Perspectives* (Brighton: Harvester).

MacNicholas, John (1979), *James Joyce's Exiles: A Textual Companion* (New York: Garland Publishing).

McHugh, Roland (1976), *The Sigla of Finnegans Wake* (London: Edward Arnold).

— (1980), *Annotations to Finnegans Wake* (London: Routledge).

Maddox, James H. (1978), *James Joyce's Ulysses and the Assault upon Character* (Brighton: Harvester).

Magalaner, Marvin and Richard M. Kain (1957), *Joyce: The Man, The Work, The Reputation* (London: John Calder).

Magee, Patrick (1988), *Paperspace: Style and Ideology in Joyce* (Lincoln and London: University of Nebraska Press).

Mahaffey, Vicki (1988), *Reauthorizing Joyce* (Cambridge: Cambridge University Press).

Mahaffey, Vicki (1990), 'Joyce's Shorter Works', in Derek Attridge (ed.), *The Cambridge Companion to James Joyce* (Cambridge: Cambridge University Press), pp. 185–211.

Mangianello, Dominic (1980), *Joyce's Politics* (London: Routledge).

Mason, Ellsworth and Richard Ellmann (eds) (1959), *Critical Writings of James Joyce* (London: Faber and Faber).

Millett, Kate (1970), *Sexual Politics* (London: Hart Davis).

Moi, Toril (1985), *Sexual/Textual Politics: Feminist Literary Theory* (London: Metheuen).

Morris, Beja (ed.) (1973), *James Joyce – Dubliners and A Portrait of the Artist as a Young Man: A Casebook* (London: Macmillan).

Nolan, Emer (1995), *Joyce and Nationalism* (London: Routledge).

Norris, Margot [1974] (1976), *The Decentered Universe of Finnegans Wake* (Baltimore: Johns Hopkins University Press).

— (1992), *Joyce's Web: The Social Unraveling of Modernism* (Austin: University of Texas Press).

— (ed.) (1998), *A Companion to James Joyce's Ulysses: Biographical and Historical Contexts, Critical History, and Essays from Five Contemporary Critical Perspectives* (Boston: Bedford Books).

Parrinder, Patrick (1984), *James Joyce* (Cambridge: Cambridge University Press).

Peake, C. H. (1977), *James Joyce: The Citizen and the Artist* (London: Edward Arnold).

Piette, Adam (1996), *Remembering and the Sound of Words: Mallarmé, Proust, Joyce, Beckett* (Oxford: Clarendon Press).

Rabaté, Jean-Michel (1991), *Joyce upon the Void: The Genesis of Doubt* (New York: St Martin's Press).

— (2001), *James Joyce and the Politics of Egoism* (Cambridge: Cambridge University Press).

Reizbaum, Marilyn (1999), *Joyce's Judaic Other* (Stanford: Stanford University Press).

Restuccia, Frances (1989), *Joyce and the Law of the Father* (New Haven: Yale University Press).

Riquelme, John Paul (1981), 'Pretexts for Reading and for Writing: Title, Epigraph, and Journal in *A Portrait of the Artist as a Young Man*', *James Joyce Quarterly* 18 (3): 301–21.

— (1983), *Teller and Tale in Joyce's Fiction: Oscillating Perspectives* (Baltimore: Johns Hopkins University Press).

Riquelme, John Paul (1990), '*Stephen Hero, Dubliners* and *A Portrait of the Artist as a Young Man*: Styles of Realism and Fantasy', in Derek Attridge (ed.), *The Cambridge Companion to James Joyce* (Cambridge: Cambridge University Press), pp. 103–30.

Roughley, Alan (1991), *James Joyce and Critical Theory: An Introduction* (London: Harvester).

Scholes, Robert E. (1979), 'Semiotic Approaches to a Fictional Text: Joyce's Eveline', *James Joyce Quarterly* 16 (1): 65–80.

Scholes, Robert E. and Richard M. Kain (1965), *The Workshop of Daedalus: James Joyce and the Raw Materials for A Portrait of the Artist as a Young Man* (Evanston: Northwestern University Press).

Scott, Bonnie Kime (ed.) (1984), *Joyce and Feminism* (London: Harvester).

— (1987), *James Joyce* (London: Harvester).

Seed, David (1992), *James Joyce's Portrait of the Artist as a Young Man* (London: Harvester).

Segall, Jeffrey (1993), *Joyce in America: Cultural Politics and the Trials of Ulysses* (Berkeley: University of California).

Seidell, Michael (2002), *James Joyce: A Short Introduction* (Oxford: Blackwell).

Senn Fritz (ed.) (1972), *New Light on Joyce from the Dublin Symposium* (Bloomington: Indiana University Press).

— (1980), 'Bloom among the Orators: The Why and the Wherefore and All the Codology', *Irish Renaissance Annual* 1 (1): 168–90.

— (1984), *Joyce's Dislocutions: Essays on Reading as Translation*, ed. Jean-Paul Riquelme (Baltimore: Johns Hopkins University Press).

— (1995), *Inductive Scrutinies: Focus on Joyce*, ed. Christine O'Neill (Dublin: Lilliput Press).

Spoo, Robert (1994), *James Joyce and the Language of History: Dedalus's Nightmare* (London: Oxford University Press).

Staley, Thomas F. (1989), *An Annotated Critical Bibliography of James Joyce* (London: Harvester).

Steinberg, Erwin R. (ed.) (1979), *The Stream of Consciousness Technique in the Modern Novel* (Port Washington: Kennikat Press).

Thornton, Weldon (1961), *Allusions in 'Ulysses': An Annotated List* (Chapel Hill: University of North Carolina Press).

— (1994), *The Antimodernism of Joyce's 'Portrait of the Artist as a Young Man'* (Syracuse: Syracuse University Press).

Tindall, William York, (1959), *A Reader's Guide to James Joyce* (London: Thames and Hudson).

— (1969), *A Reader's Guide to Finnegans Wake* (London: Thames and Hudson).

Torchiana, Donald T. (1986), *Backgrounds for Joyce's Dubliners* (London: Allen and Unwin).

Unkeless, Elaine (1982), 'The Conventional Molly Bloom', in Suzette Henke and Elaine Unkeless (eds), *Women in Joyce* (Urbana: University of Illinois Press), pp. 150–68.

Valente, Joseph (1995), *James Joyce and the Problem of Justice: Negotiating Sexual and Colonial Difference* (Cambridge: Cambridge University Press).

van Boheemen, Christine (1987), *The Novel as Family Romance: Language, Gender and Authority from Fielding to Joyce* (Ithaca: Cornell University Press).

— (ed.) (1989), *Joyce, Modernity, and its Mediation* (Amsterdam: Rodopi).

Vanderham, Paul (1998), *James Joyce and Censorship: The Trials of Ulysses* (Basingstoke: Macmillan).

Walzl, Florence L. (1982), 'Dubliners: Women in Irish Society', in Suzette Henke and Elaine Unkeless (eds), *Women in Joyce* (Urbana: University of Illinois Press), pp. 31–56.

Warner, Francis (1982), 'The Poetry of James Joyce', in Suheil Badi Bushri and Bernard Benstock (eds), *James Joyce: An International Perspective: Centenary Essays in Honour of the Late Sir Desmond Cochrane* (Gerrards Cross: Smythe), pp. 115–27.

Williams, Raymond (1968), *Drama from Ibsen to Brecht* (London: Chatto and Windus).

Wilson, Edmund (1931), *Axel's Castle: A Study in the Imaginative Literature of 1870–1930* (New York: C. Scribner and Sons).

Wright, Elizabeth (1984), *Psychoanalytic Criticism: Theory in Practice* (London: Routledge).

Woolf, Virginia (1925), *The Common Reader* (London: Hogarth Press).

— (1953), *A Writer's Diary: Being Extracts from the Diary of Virginia Woolf*, ed. Leonard Woolf (London: Hogarth Press).

Young, Robert (ed.) (1981), *Untying the Text: A Post-Structuralist Reader* (London: Routledge).

Index